Palgrave Macmillan Studies in Banking and Financial Institutions

Series Editor

Philip Molyneux
Bangor University
United Kingdom

Aim of the series

The Palgrave Macmillan Studies in Banking and Financial Institutions series is international in orientation and includes studies of banking systems in particular countries or regions as well as contemporary themes such as Islamic Banking, Financial Exclusion, Mergers and Acquisitions, Risk Management, and IT in Banking. The books focus on research and practice and include up to date and innovative studies that cover issues which impact banking systems globally.

More information about this series at
http://www.springer.com/series/14678

Stefania Patrizia Sonia Rossi
Editor

Access to Bank Credit and SME Financing

palgrave
macmillan

Editor
Stefania Patrizia Sonia Rossi
Department of Economics and Business
University of Cagliari
Italy

Palgrave Macmillan Studies in Banking and Financial Institutions
ISBN 978-3-319-82333-1 ISBN 978-3-319-41363-1 (eBook)
DOI 10.1007/978-3-319-41363-1

Printed on acid-free paper

This Palgrave Macmillan imprint is published by Springer Nature
The registered company is Springer International Publishing AG
The registered company address is Gewerbestrasse 11, 6330 Cham, Switzerland

For my mother, brilliant mind, source of strength and inspiration.

Stefania

Foreword

Following the global financial and European sovereign debt crises, liquidity shortage and heavy restrictions on bank financing have worsened conditions in credit markets for non-financial firms in Europe. Given their importance as drivers of employment, growth, and innovation in the European economy, easy access to credit becomes crucial especially for small- and medium-sized enterprises (SMEs), which dominate the business landscape in Europe and rely heavily on bank financing. The difficulties in accessing and obtaining a bank loan appear even more severe in the stressed countries that are struggling with the negative consequences of the financial crisis due to their macroeconomic weaknesses and financial fragility. Such distress increases the likelihood of credit crunch phenomena—as banks tend to transfer the stress to the borrowers—which, in turn, affect access and cost of funding for enterprises.

These issues were discussed by leading scholars in the field at the international workshop 'Access to Bank Credit and SME Financing', held in Pula, Sardinia, on 10 October 2015. This book collects some of the papers presented at the workshop and is organised into two parts.

The first part, *Credit Market Environment and SME Finance in Europe*, focuses on the issue of viability in credit access and on the financing difficulties encountered by SMEs. It is widely accepted in the literature that SMEs pay more for bank financing than larger firms because of the SME's peculiarities, such as higher observed default rates and more exposure to idiosyncratic risk, stronger reliance on the domestic economy, a narrower set of available financing options, intrinsic lack of ability to produce high-quality collateral, and lack of transparency related to their creditworthiness.

In addition to these features, the structure of the credit market, the fragility of the banking system, the sovereign debt crisis, and the social, institutional, and legal framework all seem to play a role, widely recognized in the literature, in affecting SME access to credit.

The chapters collected in this part investigate the abovementioned issues using different perspectives and methodological strategies and provide state-of-the-art insight into SME financing in Europe.

It is worth noting that several studies included in this part of the book rely on unique data provided by the ECB Survey on the Access to Finance of Enterprises (SAFE), which, since 2009, collects comparable, timely, and frequent financial information about access to credit and financing constraints experienced by firms as well as a series of firm characteristics related to SMEs in the European Union.

The first chapter by Ferrando and Mavrakis examines the external financing channels of non-financial firms, comparing SMEs and mid-caps with large enterprises over the period 2009–2015. In particular, the chapter offers an analysis of the non-bank funding available to SMEs (i.e. grants/subsidized loans, trade credit, other loans, leasing, debt securities, mezzanine financing, equity) and uses the SAFE data to assess whether these alternative sources of funding are accessible to SMEs and how their use differs across firms and countries. After demonstrating that trade credit as an alternative to bank loans is the most common source of funding for 'credit constrained firms', the authors highlight the different pattern between constrained firms in *stressed* versus *non-stressed* countries. The evidence shows that it is more difficult for constrained firms in stressed countries to switch between sources of financing. Further, the results show that large firms access various sources of financing more easily, while the market-based funding is rarely accessible to SMEs.

In the second chapter, Moro, Maresch, Ferrando, and Barbar investigate how the ability of banks to recover loans from borrowers in financial distress affects the propensity of banks to supply credit as well as the propensity of SMEs to apply for bank loans. Combining the

SAFE data with data from the World Bank Doing Business dataset, the evidence shows that while banks' recovery rates seem to negatively affect the firms' decision to apply for credit, surprisingly, it does not affect the banks' decision to provide credit. Additionally, the study shows that banks' recovery rates play a different role depending on the country-level macroeconomic context. The authors compare the economically weak countries with the strong ones and find that high recovery rates affect loan applications in the economically strong countries, and the banks' decision to provide a loan in the weak countries.

In Chap. 3, Galli, Mascia, and Rossi combine two strands of the literature: one that looks at the effects of legal-institutional factors and one that focuses on the impact of social capital in the credit markets. They shed light on the determinants of the cost of funding for SMEs in the euro area. In particular, the authors' goal is to verify whether features such as the institutional and legal framework and the level of social capital significantly affect the cost of funding for SMEs in the euro area. The authors perform an empirical analysis based on a large sample of 22,295 firm-level observations from 2009 to 2013 for a sample of 11 euro area countries, taken from the SAFE. Their findings show that a less efficient judicial system as well as a higher degree of concentration in the banking industry increases the cost of funding for SMEs. The cost of funding for SMEs is, instead, reduced when the market share of cooperative banks and the social capital are higher. Overall, the study supports the view that a better institutional environment and a wider presence of social capital produce positive externalities in the credit market.

The analysis carried out in Chap. 4 by Stefani and Vacca is rooted in the literature on gender discrimination in the credit market. The authors investigate whether the gender of the firm's manager/owner affects the access of small firms to credit. The credit constraint of non-financial firms may, in general, be either due to rejection by the bank (lender), or due to self-restraint from the borrower who decides not to apply for a loan, fearing the lender's rejection. Relying on a large sample of SMEs (SAFE data) pertaining to the main euro area countries, the evidence shows that firms with female leadership use smaller amounts and less heterogeneous sources of external finance than their male counterparts. In addition, as they anticipate a rejection by the lender, they self-restrain in applying to bank loans more than male-led firms and experience a higher rejection rate. However, the econometric analysis does not provide evidence that banks are biased against female-led firms. Rather, the different patterns for female- and male-led firms are largely explained by some endogenous characteristics of female-led firms that structurally affect their credit constraint.

Chapter 5 focuses on the evolution of the cost of financing for SMEs across banks and countries in the euro area over the period 2007–2015. Using the interest rate differential on loans—the small firm financing premium (SFFP)—Holton and McCann test whether smaller firms pay an interest rate premium compared with larger firms when borrowing from banks. Their findings show that there has been a divergence in financing conditions across firm types; SMEs, compared with larger firms, have experienced a disproportionate increase in borrowing costs and a decline in access to credit. This deterioration has been particularly acute in stressed economies: a clear bifurcation in the SFFP between stressed and non-stressed economies in late 2010 emerges from the analysis. The authors are also able to show that the increase in banks' non-performing loan and credit default swap (CDS) spreads is associated with the increased cost of borrowing for SMEs as measured by the increase in the SFFP.

In Chap. 6, Mascia, Mattana, Rossi, and D'Aietti investigate the causal relation between sovereign and bank credit risk in order to understand whether increases in sovereign risk (measured via sovereign CDS spreads) have an impact on the market perception of bank credit risk (measured via banks' CDS quotes). The contagion effect between stressed sovereigns and the banking industry may be due to the exposure of domestic banks to their own country's public debt. Based on daily quotes from 24 banks, pertaining to 7 euro-zone countries, for the period between 1 January 2010 and 27 May 2014, the chapter provides empirical evidence that sovereign CDSs have played a relevant role during the sovereign debt crisis in Europe, that is, the market perception about a country's credit risk significantly affected the evolution of banks' CDSs. These findings support the view that distressed banks, in response to the developments in sovereign debt turmoil, reduce lending to the private sector and increase the cost of funding for enterprises. This, in turn, penalises especially the SMEs, which, as often shown in the literature, heavily rely on bank financing.

Finally, Chap. 7 by Brogi and Lagasio contributes to the debate about the determinants of bank lending by investigating whether the financing constraints in accessing bank credit for SMEs stem from their creditworthiness and fragility in the financial structure. The evidence provided in the chapter is based on a large sample of 500,000 annual financial statements of SMEs from the 4 largest euro area countries (France, Germany, Italy, and Spain) in the period 2006–2014. The authors show that credit rationing suffered by SMEs depends mainly on their excessive leverage. They also suggest that SMEs need more equity rather than more debt in order to grow. The chapter provides insights for policy makers as well. In addition to promoting expansionary monetary policies, policy makers should support SMEs access to equity financing. The issue is particularly relevant for the European economic policy agenda.

The second part of the book, *SME funding and the role of alternative non-bank finance in Italy*, is a collection of microeconomic essays, which analyse the effects of the global financial crisis on the financial structure of SMEs, with a particular focus on the Italian market. In particular, the contributions here discuss the effects on enterprises induced by the Basel regulations as well as the differences among Italian regions in terms of cost of funding for SMEs. Further, some studies discuss the importance of diversification in funding for SMEs, and analyse how regulators may facilitate access to the array of financing instruments available to businesses (*inter alia*, minibonds, ELTIFs) as an alternative to the traditional bank lending channel.

In Chap. 8, Vozzella and Gabbi present an empirical investigation based on a large sample of Italian SMEs in the period 1997–2013. They aim to assess whether these companies' credit portfolios are diversified and how regulation (i.e., Basel) may affect lending choices. In particular, the study examines how the relationships between asset correlation and size as well as asset correlation and risk affect the access to credit for non-financial companies. The evidence indicates that Basel requirements considerably overestimate the fair capital absorption for SMEs and underestimate the need for capital of firms with the highest probability of default. This leads to a potential adverse selection problem; the paper advocates the revision of the regulatory framework to calibrate the asset correlation coefficients and address the issue of procyclicality.

Chapter 9 by Malavasi and Aliano aims at explaining the reasons for the differences in interest rates charged on loans to SMEs (denoted as 'spread') in the Italian regions for the period 2010–2014. The authors use data from several sources (Bank of Italy, ISTAT, Prometeia). They take into consideration the characteristics of both the demand and the supply of loans, employing two indexes for the demand side (one that captures the industrial specialization in each region and another that measures the degree of concentration in bank lending by borrower size, and one index of the bank lending specialisation for the supply side). They provide evidence that, compared with the northern regions, SMEs in southern Italy pay higher interest on loans. Further, an unfavourable relation between interest spreads and credit quality is detected.

Chapter 10 by Malavasi, Riccio, and Aliano provides an analysis of the market for the so-called *minibonds* that started to operate in Italy for SMEs in 2013. This market offers a way of funding for enterprises, alternative to the most traditional banking channel. The study, based on balance sheet data from Aida (Bureau van Dijk) as well as on specific data taken from company reports (available online) offers an analysis of the characteristics of the issuer companies in the period 2013–2015. The evidence shows that issuers' characteristics vary according to the type of main organisational structure and according to the motivation declared when approaching this instrument. The chapter also offers some policy implications aimed at improving this instrument's ability to satisfy the financial needs of an increasing portion of SMEs.

An analysis of ELTIFs (European long-term investment funds)—a new vehicle specifically created to stimulate SMEs financing—concludes this book. In Chap. 11, Crespi analyses the Italian asset management sector (which has seen an increase of 95% during the period 2011–2015) and examines the actual (and potential) amount of financial resources used by mutual funds to finance SMEs. Addressed through a quantitative analysis of the investments made by open-end mutual funds managed by domestic investment houses, the topic is of great interest to both researchers and authorities. The findings show that there are funds available and they may be potentially dedicated to SME financing if adequate commercial strategies and the right investment instruments (ELTIFs and other funds specialized in SMEs financing) were used.

Acknowledgements

The papers in this book have been discussed in several seminars and presented at the international workshop 'Access to bank credit and SME financing', a satellite session of the CLADAG Annual Meeting, held in Pula, Sardinia, on 10 October 2015 (http://convegni.unica.it/cladag2015/satellite-meeting/).

The Workshop, hosted by the Department of Economics and Business of the University of Cagliari, was organized as a deliverable at the end of the second year of the research project, 'The global financial crisis and the credit crunch—Policy implications'. As scientific coordinator of the project, I gratefully acknowledge the research grant from the Autonomous Region of Sardinia, *Legge Regionale 2007, N. 7* [Grant Number CRP-59890, year 2012]. Additionally, as conference organiser, I would like to thank all the conference participants for their active discussions during the presentations.

As editor of this book, I would like to thank all the authors for their contributions as well as the referees who acted as reviewers for the chapters published in this volume.

Furthermore, I am thankful to Philip Molyneux, series editor for Studies in Banking and Financial Institutions, for the opportunity to edit this volume, and to the staff at Palgrave Macmillan, especially Aimee Dibbens and Alexandra Morton, for helpful guidance.

Finally, a special thanks goes to Danilo Mascia for the precious assistance in the preparation of this volume as well as for the support in organising the international workshop.

Stefania P.S. Rossi
Cagliari, April 2016

Contents

Notes on Contributors

Mauro Aliano is an Assistant Professor of Banking and Finance at the University of Cagliari, Faculty of Economics, Law and Political Sciences. He is a specialist in applying statistics techniques for analysing financial markets, in methods for analysing financial instruments, and in portfolio models. In 2012, he was a Research Fellow at the University of Rome Tor Vergata.

Julia Barbar holds a BSc in Accounting and Finance (Lebanese American University) and an MSc Finance (Cranfield University). She was Financial and Managerial Teacher's Assistant at the Lebanese American University. Her research interest is the ownership structure of SMEs and family-owned businesses.

Marina Brogi is Full Professor of International Banking and Capital Markets and Corporate Governance at Sapienza University, where she also serves as Deputy Dean of the Faculty of Economics. She teaches in graduate, MBA, PhD and executive courses at Sapienza University, SDA Bocconi and Luiss Business School. Since January 2014 she has been one of the five top-ranking independent academics appointed among the 30 members that make up the Securities and Markets Stakeholder Group of the European Securities and Markets Authority. She is author of many international publications, and her research interests are bank management, capital markets and corporate governance.

Fabrizio Crespi is a Researcher at the University of Cagliari and a Contract Professor at ALTIS (the Postgraduate School Business & Society of the Catholic University of the Sacred Heart of Milan). After completing a PhD in "The economics of institutions and business systems", he has focused his academic career on financial innovation. His main research concerns asset-backed securitization, asset management products, asset allocation and financial planning, and innovative portfolio strategies.

Roberto D'Aietti has been a Research Assistant in Financial Economics at the Department of Economics and Business of the University of Cagliari, where he also received his Master's in Economics.

Annalisa Ferrando is Principal Economist at the Capital Markets/Financial Structure Division of the European Central Bank. Previously, she worked at the Bank of Italy and at the European Commission. Her current research interests lie in corporate finance, firms' financial decisions, and financing constraints. In these fields she has published numerous journal articles and working papers.

Giampaolo Gabbi is Professor of Financial Investments and Risk Management at the University of Siena and Professor at SDA Bocconi Milan. He holds a PhD in Financial Economics from Bocconi University and acts as a researcher in many international research projects, such as Forecasting Financial Crises, Measurements, Models and Predictions (FOC) and Financialisation, Economy, Society and Sustainable Development (FESSUD). He has published articles in refereed journals, including the Journal of Economic Dynamics and Control, Nature Scientific Report, European Financial Management, Journal of International Financial Markets, Institutions & Money, and The European Journal of Finance.

Emma Galli is Professor of Public Finance at the Department of Social and Economic Sciences of Sapienza University of Rome . She has recently been a visiting scholar at the University of the Witwatersrand in Johannesburg and at the University of Rennes 1. Her research in fiscal policies, decentralization, economics of institutions, and economics of corruption has led to several articles published in national and international journals, as well as monographs and edited books.

Sarah Holton is an Economist in the Monetary Analysis Division of the European Central Bank. She holds a PhD from University College Dublin and her research interests are in the areas of small and medium enterprise financing constraints and the transmission of monetary policy through the banking system.

Valentina Lagasio is a PhD student in Management, Banking and Commodity science, specialising in Banking and Finance at La Sapienza University of Rome, where she graduated in Finance with honours in 2014. Her current research interests mainly concern banking and financial intermediation, banking supervision, monetary policy transmission mechanisms and corporate governance.

Roberto Malavasi is Chair of Financial Markets and Institutions at the Department of Economics and Business of the University of Cagliari. He has taught banking and finance for more than 40 years. His publications comprise various articles as well as textbooks in finance and international finance.

Daniela Maresch is Assistant Professor and Vice Head of the Institute for Innovation Management (IFI) at Johannes Kepler University Linz. She gained practical experience in financial reporting and in corporate law before moving to academia in 2014. Her research focuses on the roles of the legal environment and trust in bank lending, the social impact of disruptive technologies, and protection of intellectual property rights in entrepreneurial firms. Her research has been published in entrepreneurship and financial journals.

Danilo V. Mascia is a Research Fellow at the University of Cagliari (Italy) and a Visiting Academic Research Fellow at Leeds University Business School (UK). After gaining his BSc and MSc in Economics in Sardinia, he moved to the University of Amsterdam, where he was awarded the title of MSc in Business Economics. He later received his PhD in Business Economics from the University of Cagliari, together with the title of Doctor Europaeus. His research interests are in the areas of banking, regulation, and financing of small and medium firms.

Paolo Mattana is Professor of Economics and Head of the Department of Economics and Business of the University of Cagliari (Italy). He currently conducts courses in Financial Econometrics and Macroeconomics. His research activity mainly focuses on growth theory (indeterminacy issues and chaotic solutions) and on time series analysis in the context of regional and financial economics, and it comprises publications in international journals.

Emmanouil Mavrakis is Senior Economist at the Capital Markets/Financial Structure Division of the European Central Bank, seconded from the Bank of Greece. He has previously held several positions in the financial sector and has a lengthy academic experience. He has taught financial economics and banking for many years, and his research interests include banking, financial markets, investments, monetary economics, and NFCs' financing conditions.

Fergal McCann is Senior Economist in the Financial Stability Division of the Central Bank of Ireland. He holds a PhD from University College Dublin and his research interests are in the areas of small and medium enterprise financing, mortgage default, and macroprudential policy.

Andrea Moro (Laurea, MBA, PhD) is Reader at Cranfield University, where he is director of MSc Finance programmes and lectures Corporate Finance (MBA) and Entrepreneurial Finance (MSc). He spent fifteen years in the consultancy sector as financial advisor for SMEs before moving to academia in 2008. He originally joined The Open University and then University of Leicester. His area of interest is small business finance and lending relationships. He has published in both entrepreneurial and finance journals. He is currently non-executive board member of two schools.

Giuseppe Riccio is an Associate Professor of Business Administration at the University of Cagliari, Faculty of Economics, Law and Political Sciences. He previously worked in the banking supervision division of the Bank of Italy. His books cover topics related to the financial statements of banks.

Stefania P.S. Rossi is Professor of Economics at the Department of Economics and Business of the University of Cagliari (Italy). Since obtaining her PhD in Economics from the University of Rome Tor Vergata, she has been a Postdoctoral Visiting Scholar at Stanford University. She has been appointed as Economist at the World Bank and as Professor at the University of Vienna as well as at the International Diplomatic Academy of Vienna. Her publications comprise many articles in the field of international monetary economics, financial markets and banking, published in international academic journals as well as in edited books.

Maria Lucia Stefani is currently the head of the Library Division at the Bank of Italy. She started her work at the Bank of Italy, dealing with studies in economic history, and then regional economic research. Her main academic interests are banking and gender economics, on which she has authored various articles and book chapters. She obtained her PhD in Economics from the European University Institute in Florence (Italy).

Valerio Vacca is Senior Economist in the Bank of Italy's Financial Stability Directorate. He is currently a member of an international study group on the ex-ante appraisal of macroprudential instruments. Previously, he dealt with regional economic research and monetary policy implementation. His main research interests are financial stability, banking, finance, and non-bank finance for firms. He has authored articles and book chapters in these areas. He graduated from the Bocconi University in Milan.

Pietro Vozzella is currently a Research Fellow at the Department of Management and Law of the University of Siena. His current and past research fields include banking and financial systems, financial regulation and economics, and access to bank credit and SME financing. He also worked for two years in an Italian banking institution in the Credit Risk Management unit. He has published in The European Journal of Finance, Intereconomics: Review of European Economic Policy and PLoS ONE.

List of Figures

List of Tables

Part I

Credit Market Environment and SME Finance in Europe

1

Non-Bank Financing for Euro Area Companies During the Crisis

Annalisa Ferrando and Emmanouil Mavrakis

1.1 Introduction

The financial crisis has raised concerns about the potential overreliance of euro area non-financial corporations on banks for external financing. This is particularly true for small- and medium-sized enterprises (SMEs) and mid-caps, which usually have little direct access to capital markets and depend on effective bank financing in addition to equity finance. The strong dependency of SMEs and mid-caps on bank financing has left them more exposed to the post-crisis weaknesses and deleveraging needs of the EU banking sector. This article focuses on the financing of non-financial corporations, comparing SMEs and mid-caps with large enter-

JEL Classification: D22, E22, G32, L25

A. Ferrando (✉) • E. Mavrakis
Capital Markets/Financial Structure Division of the European Central Bank, European Central Bank, Frankfurt, Germany
e-mail: annalisa.ferrando@ecb.int

S.P.S. Rossi (ed.), *Access to Bank Credit and SME Financing*, Palgrave Macmillan Studies in Banking and Financial Institutions, DOI 10.1007/978-3-319-41363-1_1

prises in the period from 2009 to mid-2015, using firm-level information derived from the European Central Bank/European Commission (ECB/EC) survey on the access to finance of enterprises (SAFE).

In particular, this chapter examines the extent to which the available external funding sources, except bank loans and overdrafts—grants/subsidized loans, trade credit, other loans, leasing, debt securities, mezzanine and equity—are accessible to companies and how their use differs across firms and countries. As a first outcome, it is illustrated that trade credit is the most common source of finance once bank loans and bank overdrafts are excluded. Furthermore, other bank-related instruments, like grants/subsidized loans and leasing, are used much more frequently than the market-based instruments of debt securities, mezzanine and equity. Furthermore, for most of the instruments there is a clear pattern that the frequency of use increases with size of firm. This confirms that large firms typically have better and more diversified access to the various sources of finance.

Econometric analysis provides some novel evidence on the use of non-bank external sources of finance during the crisis. We consider as a dependent variable the direct replies of surveyed firms reporting whether they have made use of a specific non-bank financing source. As determinants we include a set of firms' specific factors related to their demographics and financial situation and factors related to bank financing, like bank lending costs and credit standards, and an indicator of bank credit constraints. These variables are particularly useful for detecting possible substitution relationships between bank and non-bank sources. In addition, we control for country-level variables related to real activity (GDP growth and unemployment rate), and we distinguish between euro area countries that were less affected by the crisis and those that were more severely affected.

Our empirical results signal that, during the crisis period, 'credit constrained firms'—i.e., those firms which, in the survey, reported that they were constrained in their access to bank loans—tended to switch more often than firms without credit constraints to non-bank financing (trade credit, leasing). It appears, though, that firms in countries most affected by the crisis faced more difficulties in carrying out this switch in financing. Moreover, informal constraints, which relates to firms that do not apply for bank loans because of fear of rejection, seem to restrict much more the availability of non-bank sources of finance. Generally, the findings in our analysis confirm that market-based financing sources are used less frequently by non-financial corporations and, to an even lesser extent, by SMEs than is trade credit or other forms of loans. Although, capital markets represent an important alternative source of financing for non-financial corporations, they are accessible mainly to larger firms with high credit ratings and those which are generally located in larger countries with more developed financial markets.

What follows is a short literature review of the capital structure of firms, a presentation of the empirical evidence on the use of non-bank sources of finance, and econometric analysis with robustness checks on the determinants of the usage of non-bank financing instruments. Finally, some preliminary policy conclusions complete the chapter, in particular, taking into consideration the recent debate on the development of a genuine European Capital Markets Union and its impact on access to finance for SMEs.

1.2 Capital Structure of Euro Area Enterprises

SMEs have a central role in the European economy, accounting for more than 99.8% of all euro area non-financial corporations, employing 86.8 million people (two-thirds of euro area workforce) and generating about 57.7% of value added (European Investment Fund 2014). In past years there has been increasing research interest in the capital structure and access to finance by SMEs (Beck et al. 2008; Berger and Udell 1998; Cassar 2004; Chavis et al. 2011; Cosh et al. 2009; Huyghebaert and Van de Gucht 2007). SME business activity and growth bear heavily the impact of imperfections in bank credit markets (Zecchini and Ventura 2009). In fact, their financial structure is more dependent on bank loans than larger firms, due to an asymmetric information problem (lack of credit information), a shorter operating track record (European Central Bank 2014a) and to the difficulty of accessing alternative sources of financing (Berger and Udell 2006; Jaffee and Russell 1976; Stiglitz and Weiss 1981). The European sovereign debt crisis in particular had a large adverse effect on European banks and resulted in a tightening of financing channels for many European firms (Ferrando and Mulier 2015a). As pointed out by Gambacorta and Marques-Ibanez (2011), increased risk-taking by banks prior to the crisis caused a decrease in banks' ability to lend during the crisis.

European non-financial corporations finance their investments largely through bank loans. During the crisis many banks started to deleverage in order to adjust to funding pressures. This process has been reinforced by changes in regulation (higher capital requirements, introduction of liquidity requirements). As a consequence, credit has become less available and more costly for companies. Berger and Udell (2006) suggest that issues may occur with regulation changes in lending and findings by Popov (2016) reveal that banks decrease lending when faced with tighter regulation.

Moreover, Ferrando et al. (2013) note that the smaller amount of credit coming from the banking sector has likely resulted in a funding gap. This bank-based gap could be filled by alternative types of financing (Wehinger 2012). However, market imperfections might result in a general funding gap for SMEs (Mason 2009). Michaelas et al. (1999) provide empirical evidence about information and agency problems for SMEs when accessing finance.

The main objective of this paper is to broaden the analysis of firm funding apart from bank lending in order to examine the extent to which firms diversify across different financing instruments. Replacing bank credit with equity financing would reduce the debt burden of the euro area non-financial corporate sector and the potentially negative impact of bank deleveraging on the economy. However, access to equity financing for SMEs, and in particular for those in the earlier stages of the business life-cycle, is difficult owing to their smaller size, less detailed financial statements and shorter track records. According to Van Auken (2001), equity investments are generally more costly. Moreover, Berggren et al. (2000) point out that not all SME owners/managers are willing to grow at the cost of losing control and find a relation between increasing firm size and diminishing aversion to outside control.

Since the onset of the crisis, euro area companies have tried to increase access to market-based financing, including different financing instruments, such as equity and debt securities. However, SMEs in particular can simply not afford the fixed costs of either bond issuance or going public with issuing stocks. This means that bank loans remain for them practically the only available financing source.

However, many studies demonstrate that small firms have more difficulties to access credit if compared to large firms (Berger and Udell 2006). There is widespread evidence (European Central Bank 2014a, b) that bank-related financing conditions deteriorated most for euro area SMEs compared to larger firms. Especially, bank lending constraints have been found to affect SMEs more severely in comparison to larger firms (Artola and Genre 2011; Ferrando and Griesshaber 2011; Holton et al. 2013). Access to finance for SMEs has always been challenging, but due to the financial market crisis, such access in Europe deteriorated (Drakos 2012; Ferrando and Mulier 2015a). The difficulty of accessing bank credit increases in crisis periods when the risk aversion of banks is higher.

Prior empirical studies investigate the impact on SMEs' demand for financing instruments by factors such as size, age, growth, profitability, ownership and industry (Chittenden and Hutchinson 1996; Ferrando and Griesshaber 2011; Michaelas et al. 1999). According to empirical evidence, these effects change over the business cycle and in particular in times of financial crises (Carbo-Valverde et al. 2016; Casey and O'Toole 2014; Psillaki and Eleftheriou 2015; Taketa and Udell 2007). Empirical evidence suggests that access to finance is positively correlated with firm size (Popov 2016; Hadlock and Pierce 2010; Ferrando et al. 2007). Furthermore as suggested by Ferrando et al. (2013), age and ownership structures have an impact on how the financing gap affects firm financing.

1.3 Empirical Evidence on the Use of Non-Bank Sources of Finance

The empirical analysis carried out in this chapter uses a sample of euro area companies that participated in the SAFE survey. This is a survey compiled in a joint activity by the European Central Bank and the European Commission. It is performed through a questionnaire filled out by non-financial corporations via phone interviews, wherein most of the surveyed firms are SMEs (around 90%). The SAFE survey contains information on the use of alternative sources of finance (trade credit, informal or other company loans, market financing and grants) and on the financial situation of the surveyed firms. The data used in this chapter refers to first ten waves for the period 2009 and 2014, relating to Austria, Belgium, Germany, Spain, Finland, France, Greece, Ireland, Italy, Netherlands and Portugal. Table 1.1 shows the number of observations in our sample for different countries, the total number being 68,796.

On the basis of the SAFE sample it is possible to calculate the frequency with which euro area non-financial corporations, in different countries and of different sizes or age, have recourse to various financing instruments. Firms surveyed in the SAFE are asked whether or not they had used a set of financing instruments in the preceding six-month period.[1] These instruments range from internal sources (retained earnings), leasing, grants/subsidized bank loans, and bank financing (credit lines, overdrafts, credit cards and loans) to various sources of non-bank external finance such as trade credit, other loans (informal or from a related company), issued debt, mezzanine financing and equity. For the purpose of this chapter, Table 1.2 shows the percentage of companies that

Table 1.1 Number of observations in the sample

Country	Observations
AT	4136
BE	4152
DE	10018
ES	10022
FI	3814
FR	10025
GR	4120
IE	3813
IT	10015
NL	4337
PT	4344
Total	68796

Source: ECB (SAFE) and authors' calculations

[1] For a similar analysis using information derived from the SAFE, see Casey and O'Toole (2014).

Table 1.2 Use of non-bank financing instruments across countries (weighted averages)

	Trade credit	Other loans	Leasing	Issued debt[a]	Equity	Mezzanine	Grants
AT	54	40	65	10	26	18	35
BE	45	39	51	11	17	13	32
DE	53	48	71	7	34	21	34
ES	63	37	42	12	13	14	36
FI	70	34	70	22	19	16	26
FR	33	28	51	6	15	4	22
GR	69	20	40	-	21	7	31
IE	86	40	51	14	20	12	29
IT	72	30	42	11	20	7	30
NL	67	47	71	5	11	33	24
PT	59	29	44	12	10	8	40
Total	57	38	56	9	21	14	31

Note: [a]Issued debt statistics are calculated without Greece, due to unavailability of data

made use of non-bank sources of finance across these countries. Bank-based instruments such as grants/subsidized loans and leasing are used much more frequently than market-based instruments such as debt securities, mezzanine financing and equity. Trade credit is the widest used source of finance across the surveyed countries.

Across firm size, grants/subsidized loans and leasing are also used frequently, especially by medium-sized and large firms (see Table 1.3). While leasing appears as the most used instrument, at least for medium-sized and large firms, it is not necessarily the most important in terms of volume or in terms of financing new investment. For most of the instruments, there is a clear pattern: the percentage of use increases with the size of the firm. This confirms that large firms typically have better and more diversified access to the various sources of finance. It is also interesting to note that micro and small firms used mostly trade credit followed by leasing and other loans, whereas medium-sized and large firms have more frequent recourse to leasing, followed by trade credit and other loans. Across all sizes of firms, issued debt is the least used instrument, followed by mezzanine, equity and grants.

The share of companies making use of more than one non-bank external source of finance increases with the size of the firm (see Table 1.4). Out of all firms using non-bank external sources of finance, 60% made

Table 1.3 Use of non-bank financing instruments by firm size (weighted averages)

	Trade credit	Other loans	Leasing	Issued debt[a]	Equity	Mezzanine	Grants
Micro	52	26	34	6	16	7	24
Small	55	30	53	6	20	10	29
Medium	60	38	63	6	24	15	34
Large	62	48	68	13	24	20	37
Total	57	38	56	9	21	14	31

Note: [a]Issued debt statistics are calculated without Greece, due to unavailability of data

use of just one financing source and the rest of the enterprises used at least two sources. Micro (71%), small (62%) and medium-sized (53%) firms mainly used one non-bank instrument of finance, while the majority (57%) of large firms used two or more of these financing sources.

Nevertheless, the age of firms does not seem to have any significant impact on the simultaneous use of financing sources (Table 1.5).

However, when we look at intensive use of each individual non-bank financial instrument, our data signal a clearly increasing pattern with age of firm, and this is valid for most of the instruments (Table 1.6). For older firms (5 years or more), trade credit is the most used instrument, followed by leasing and other loans, whereas younger firms (less than 5 years) use mostly leasing, followed by trade credit and other loans. Across all ages of firms, issued debt is the least used instrument followed by mezzanine, equity, and grants. Overall, considering the two instruments that appear to have the higher percentages, younger and larger enterprises use mostly leasing followed by trade credit while, older and smaller firms prefer mostly trade credit followed by leasing.

Among industrial, construction and trade firms, trade credit is the most used instrument followed by leasing and other loans, while enterprises operating in the services sector use mostly leasing, followed by trade credit and other loans. Across all sectors, issued debt is the least used instrument, followed by mezzanine, equity and grants (Table 1.7).

As our dataset covers only the crisis period when banks restricted their supply of credit, one natural step in the analysis is to focus on the behaviour

Table 1.4 Simultaneous use of non-bank financing instruments by firm size (weighted averages)

	1 instrument	2 instruments	3 or more instruments
Micro	71	23	6
Small	62	29	10
Medium	53	34	13
Large	44	37	20
Total	60	30	11

Table 1.5 Simultaneous use of non-bank financing instruments by firm age (weighted averages)

	1 instrument	2 instruments	3 or more instruments
Less than 2 years	59	30	11
Between 2 and 5 years	61	29	10
Between 5 and 10 years	63	27	10
10 years or more	62	28	10
Total	60	30	11

Table 1.6 Use of non-bank financing instruments by firm age (weighted averages)

	Trade credit	Other loans	Leasing	Issued debt[a]	Equity	Mezzanine	Grants
Less than 2 years	38	31	47	2	17	6	29
Between 2 and 5 years	46	31	49	5	15	10	26
Between 5 and 10 years	54	34	54	7	18	13	30
10 years or more	59	39	56	10	23	15	32
Total	57	38	56	9	21	14	31

Note: [a]Issued debt statistics are calculated without Greece, due to unavailability of data

Table 1.7 Use of non-bank financing instruments by sector (weighted averages)

	Trade credit	Other loans	Leasing	Issued debt[a]	Equity	Mezzanine	Grants
Industry	62	43	58	9	23	16	34
Construction	57	32	53	8	18	12	30
Trade	61	37	50	8	22	15	27
Services	52	36	57	9	21	13	31
Total	57	38	56	9	21	14	31

Note: [a]Issued debt statistics are calculated without Greece, due to unavailability of data

of credit constrained firms in choosing non-bank finance. Several papers use direct survey replies to create indicators of financial constraints (European Central Bank 2015; Beck et al. 2014; Bircan and De Haas 2015; Casey and O'Toole 2014; Ferrando and Griesshaber 2011; Ferrando et al. 2015; Popov 2016). Following this line of the literature, we use an indicator that considers not only firms that applied for a bank loan and saw a rejection in their application, or decided not to accept the loan proposal because of too high interest rates or too limited amount offered, but also firms that were discouraged in their loan application due to possible rejection. Chart 1.1 reports the percentage of firms which are affected by credit constraints in each country over the sample period. In the chart the indicator is split in its components. It can be seen that percentages of credit constrained firms are higher in countries most affected by the financial and sovereign debt crises in the euro area between 2009 and 2014. In particular, focusing on the last survey round in our sample, the highest percentages of credit constrained firms are seen in Greece (30%), Ireland and the Netherlands (20% each), followed by Italy (19%). In the lowest range, only a small percentage of Austrian, German and Finnish firms are signalling credit constraints (5%). Although there is some variability over time, the country ranking has not changed much, indicating some persistency in the difficulty to access credit at country level.

A further step in our empirical investigation is to quantify how the use of the different financing instruments changes for credit constrained and non-constrained firms. We report the statistics in Table 1.8. Credit constrained firms signal more often that they use trade credit [6 percentage points (pp) more than non-constrained firms (fourth row in Table 1.8), other loans (5 pp) and mezzanine finance (1 pp)], and they issued more debt securities (1pp). At the same time they use less leasing (–6 pp), equity (–1 pp) and grants (–3 pp). To test whether these differences are significant from a statistical point of view, we performed a t-test on the equality of the weighted means, and the last row reports the statistical significance at 5%. All the differences among the two groups of firms are significant except in the case of equity.

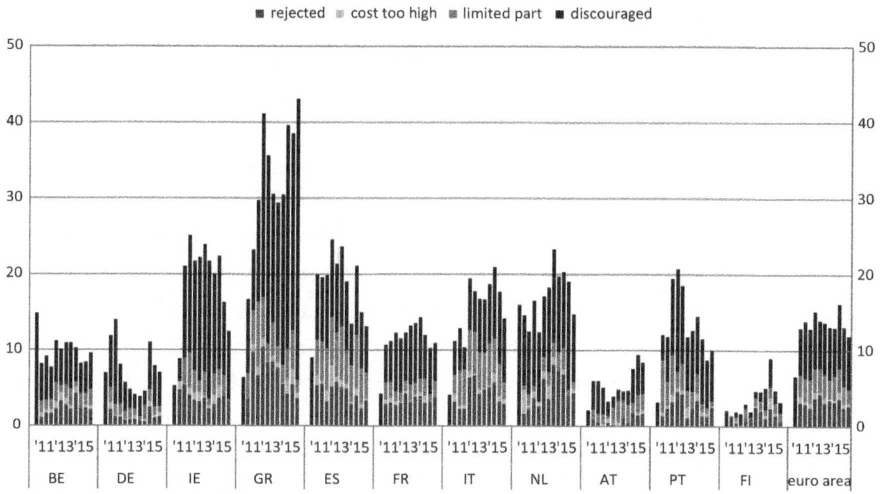

Chart 1.1 Credit constrained firms in the sample period (weighted averages) (Note: see Table 1.12 for a detailed explanation of the indicator)

Table 1.8 Use of non-bank financing instruments by credit constrained firms (weighted averages)

CC index	Trade credit	Other loans	Leasing	Issued debt[a]	Equity	Mezzanine	Grants
No	56.0	36.3	55.8	8.4	21.1	13.3	30.8
Yes	61.8	41.7	50.2	9.7	19.7	14.6	27.5
Total sample	57	38	56	9	21	14	31
Diff CC-NCC	5.8	5.4	−5.7	1.3	−1.4	1.3	−3.3
Stat diff	Yes	Yes	Yes	Yes	No	Yes	Yes

Note: [a]Issued debt statistics are calculated without Greece, due to unavailability of reliable data. Statistical difference based on a t-test on the equality of the weighted means

1.4 Econometric Analysis on the Determinants of the Usage of Non-Bank Financing Instruments

To deepen further our analysis, we perform an econometric analysis to provide additional information on the use of non-bank external sources of finance during the crisis, taking into consideration several factors that could influence the choice of firms from their characteristics to the economic situation in the countries where they are located. More specifically, our dependent variable is a dummy variable, which takes value 1 if the firm had used a specific external source of non-bank finance in the preceding six months and 0 otherwise. The variable is regressed on two different sets of factors (see Box 1 for details). The first set comprises firm-specific variables related to the company's demographics and financial situation and our firm-level indicator of bank credit constraints. The second set includes variables related to bank financing, such as bank lending costs and credit standards. These variables are particularly useful for detecting possible substitution relationships between bank and non-bank sources. Furthermore, country-level variables related to real activity (GDP growth and the unemployment rate) are taken into account in the analysis. We also make a distinction between countries that were less affected by the crisis (Belgium, Germany, France, Netherlands, Austria and Finland) and those that were more severely affected (Ireland, Greece, Spain, Italy and Portugal).

From Table 1.9 we can see that most of the sources of finance are positively correlated with the indicator of credit constraints except in the case of leasing and grants.

Table 1.10 reports econometric results of the factors affecting the probability of firms to use a specific non-bank financing in each column. Starting from the first row and focusing on those firms that reported to be constrained in their access to bank loans, the results show that they were more likely to rely on non-bank financing (trade credit and leasing and other loans) than firms that did not report constraints. The coefficient on the use of equity is also statistically significant, and there is evidence that constrained firms made less use of grants, indicating that firms that had already been denied bank loans found it difficult to benefit from public schemes aimed at obtaining guaranteed bank loans. Furthermore, credit constrained firms in countries more severely affected by the crisis (in the third row) found it more difficult to switch from bank loans to other sources of finance than did firms with the same kind of constraints in other countries. Looking at more specific firm-level characteristics, micro and small firms have more difficulty switching to non-bank finance than do medium-sized ones. As for age, our estimates are in most cases posi-

Table 1.9 Correlation between different sources of finance and the indicator of credit constraints

	Trade credit	Other loans	Leasing	Equity	Issued debt	Grants	Mezzanine	CC index
Trade credit	1							
Other loans	0.3292*	1						
Leasing	0.2425*	0.2425*	1					
Equity	0.2623*	0.3125*	0.2197*	1				
Issued debt	0.2353*	0.2251*	0.1737*	0.3162*	1			
Grants	0.2010*	0.1817*	0.2025*	0.1549*	0.1607*	1		
Mezzanine	0.2763*	0.4235*	0.2523*	0.3212*	0.3434*	0.2212*	1	
CC index	0.0406*	0.0834*	–0.0224*	–0.0012	0.0330*	–0.0154*	0.0448*	1

Sig.: *p<0.05

Table 1.10 Alternative sources of firm financing—estimated results

	1	2	3	4	5	6	7
Variables	Trade credit	Other loans	Leasing	Issued debt	Equity	Mezzanine	Grants
Borrower and country risks							
Bank constraints	0.084***	0.090***	0.054***	−0.011	0.037*	−0.004	−0.039**
Stressed countries	0.396***	0.054	0.06	0.033	0.09	−0.021	0.064
b.c. x str. Coun.	−0.066***	0.023	−0.061***	0.04	−0.046*	0.037	0.012
Firm demographics							
Independent	0.012	−0.124***	0.017	0.058***	−0.012	0.039***	0.059***
Family-owned	0.040***	−0.035***	−0.008	−0.030**	0.029**	−0.007	0.021*
Size							
Micro	−0.049***	−0.022	−0.164***	0.015	−0.016	−0.033**	−0.081***
Small	−0.020**	−0.015	−0.050***	0.015*	−0.013	−0.023**	−0.042***
Large	0.015	0.035**	0.040***	0.024**	−0.009	−0.005	0.038**
AGE							
< 2 ys	0.090***	0.116***	0.116***	0.019	0.073***	0.049***	0.122***
2 ys & < 5 ys	0.003	0.029*	0.057***	0.008	−0.001	0.021*	0.028**
5 ys & < 10ys	0.01	0.015	0.068***	0.011	0.005	0.028**	0.033***
Turnover							
up to 2 million	−0.079***	−0.027	−0.092***	−0.023*	−0.027*	−0.011	−0.035**
> 2 to 10 mil	−0.034***	−0.014	−0.012	−0.001	−0.006	−0.007	0.004
> 50 million	0.018	0.061***	0	0.049***	0.008	0.034*	−0.005
Financial situation							
Firm outlook	0.034***	0.050***	0.029***	0.009	0.009	0.025*	0.029**
Capital	0.005	−0.015	0.004	−0.018	0.043***	0.005	0.012
Credit history	−0.008	−0.02	0.002	0.017	−0.029**	−0.003	0.005

			Macro economic conditions				
Cost of lending	−0.224	1.949	−6.090***	4.3	6.271**	1.35	1.847
Credit standards	0.011	−0.143***	−0.03	−0.048	−0.051	−0.215***	−0.064**
GDP growth	1.700***	0.561	−0.391	2.233***	2.965***	1.946***	−0.111
Unemployment	−0.526**	−0.751*	0.389	0.884	−0.764*	−0.23	−1.534***
Observations	35,491	25,790	39,949	11,117	18,242	13,942	31,865
R-squared	0.264	0.202	0.156	0.158	0.197	0.201	0.06

Note: The dependent variable is categorical and takes value 1 if the firm has used a specific source of finance in the preceding six months; 0 otherwise. The estimations are based on weighted least squares regressions with calibrated weights that restore the proportions of the economic weight (in terms of number of employees) of each size class, economic activity and country and robust standard errors. Stressed countries are Ireland, Greece, Spain, Italy and Portugal, while non-stressed countries are Belgium, Germany, France, the Netherlands, Austria and Finland. The regressions include country-industry fixed effects and time fixed effects, and errors are robust. Significance levels: *** $p < 0.01$, ** $p < 0.05$, * $p < 0.1$

tive and statistically significant. In particular, very young companies tend more to use all instruments except debt securities, while for firms with an age above 2 years but less than 10 years, the instruments used most are leasing and mezzanine, together with grants. The probability of using non-bank instruments is higher for firms with a better outlook and, in the case of equity, with an improved capital situation. Once firms signal improvements in their credit history, they tend to take less recourse to equity. The signs of the coefficients of the macroeconomic conditions are as expected: if the cost of lending increases, the use of leasing declines and equity increases; whereas, in the case of tightening credit standards, firms make less use of other loans and of mezzanine finance and grants.

1.5 Robustness Checks

The analysis presented above provides clear results on the availability of non-bank financing instruments for companies that are credit constrained. Nevertheless, we run some additional robustness checks to validate them by looking at: (1) a different econometric approach to estimate the relationship and (2) the two main sub-components of the indicator of credit constraints: rejected and discouraged firms.

1.5.1 An Alternative Econometric Specification

The first check is on the econometric specification. We consider a probit model on the same specification presented in Box 1. Chart 1.2 depicts visually the probability of credit constrained firms to use the various non-bank external instruments based on the marginal effects derived from the estimated coefficients of the probit model. The probability of credit constrained firms to use trade credit and other loans is 6% higher than the probability of non-credit constrained firms. In the case of equity, this probability is smaller at 3%. Looking at the use of grants, there is a negative relationship between being credit constraint and access to grants. Overall, for credit constrained firms located in distressed countries, the probability to use trade credit and other loans is much lower than for firms in non-distressed ones.

Box 1 The Empirical Methodology

The empirical analysis is carried out using weighted least squares regressions where the sampling weights adjust the sample to be representative of the population. The dependent variable is a dichotomous variable that takes value 1 if firms report to have used a specific external source of non-bank finance in the preceding six months or 0 otherwise. These external sources of finance are the same depicted in the previous sections: trade credit, other loans, leasing, issued debt, equity, mezzanine and grants.

$$\text{source}_{isct} = \beta_1 CC_{isct} + \beta_2 CC_{isct} \times \text{Stressed}_c + \beta_2 X1_{it} + \beta_3 X2_{ct} + \beta_4 \varphi_{sc} + \beta_5 \eta_t + \varepsilon_{isct} \quad (1.1)$$

where CC_{isct} is a dummy indicating if a firm is credit constrained, X1 is a vector of time-varying firm-level and X2 of time-varying country-level control variables (see also Table 1.12). These variables control for size, age, turnover classes, whether firms are independent or family-owned, their financial situation in terms of sales and profitability, their own capital and their credit history. All variables are derived from the survey. The set of country variables includes the cost of borrowing for non-financial corporations, as well as credit standards, taken from the euro area Bank Lending Survey, which summarize the internal guidelines or criteria that reflect banks' lending policies.[2] Positive figures indicate that more banks were tightening their credit conditions than easing them. We include also two variables to capture real economic activity: real GDP growth and the unemployment rate. Finally, stressed is a dummy variable equal to 1 if firm i is domiciled in country c, which belongs to the group of stressed countries (Greece, Ireland, Italy, Portugal and Spain) and to 0 otherwise. φ_{sc} is an interaction of sector and country fixed effects; η_t is a time fixed effect, which corresponds to each survey wave, and ε_{isct} is an i.i.d. error term.

[2] The variable is calculated as the difference between the sum of the percentages of banks responding 'tightened considerably' and 'tightened somewhat' and the sum of the percentages of banks responding 'eased somewhat' and 'eased considerably'.

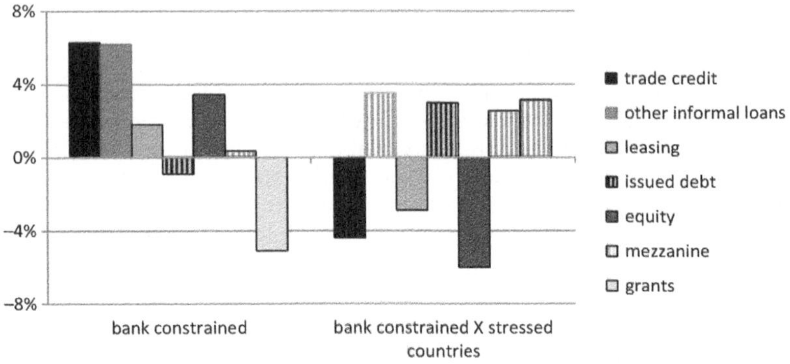

Chart 1.2 Probability of using non-bank external instruments (marginal effects) (Note: each bar represents marginal effects based on a probit regression with the same specification as in Table 1.10.)

1.5.2 Analysis of Sub-Components of the Indicator of Financial Constraints: Rejected Versus Discouraged Firms

Our second robustness check focuses more on the components of the indicator of credit constraints. As explained above, the indicator includes firms that applied for a loan and their applications rejected and firms that did not apply because of fear of rejection. Although previous studies have shown that these two types of borrowers are very similar in terms of riskiness (Ferrando and Mulier 2015b), others stress the importance of considering them also in a distinct way (Ferrando et al. 2015; Ferrando and Rossolini 2015). Indeed, recent evidence lends support to the notion that in some countries informal credit constraints (related to discouragement of borrowers) can be more prevalent than formal ones (related to loan application rejections) (Brown et al. 2011), and that in general such constraints can vary systematically across countries in a way that can yield biased results (Popov 2016). For this reason we modify our probit specification and split the dependent variables into the two sub-components. The first two panels in Table 1.11 report the marginal effects for rejected and discouraged borrowers versus the rest of the companies and the different impact if those categories of firms are in stressed and non-stressed

Table 1.11 Alternative sources of firm financing—estimated results for rejected and discouraged firms (marginal effects)

	1	2	3	4	5	6	7
Variables	Trade credit	Other loans	Leasing	Issued debt	Equity	Mezzanine	Grants
			Panel A: Rejected firms				
Rejected	0.0811***	0179***	0.0852***	−0.00747	0.0218	0.0317	−0.0898**
Rejected X stressed	−0.107***	−0.0485	−0.122***	0.0597	0.00675	−0.02	0.0243
			Panel B: Discouraged firms				
Discouraged	0.00732	−0.00857	−0.017	−0.0314	0.0323	−0.0372*	−0.145***
Discouraged X stressed	−0.0753***	0.0602*	−0.0739***	0.00716	−0.0863***	0.0434	−0.0608*
			Panel C: Rejected versus discouraged firms				
Rejected versus discouraged	0.102***	0.191***	0.103***	0.0335	0.0313	0.0756***	0.164***
Rejc. Versus disc. X stressed	0.00422	−0.100**	0.0102	0.0451	0.0432	−0.0437	0.0729*

Sig.: ***p<0.01, **p<0.05, *p<0.1

countries. All the firm and country control variables of the basic specification (not reported) are confirmed in terms of magnitude and signs. In Panel A, rejected firms are reverting to trade credit, other loans and leasing, but not to grants, and doing so more often than are applied and successful firms and discouraged firms. For discouraged firms the picture is not so clear-cut. Indeed, from panel B it seems that there are no statistical differences between them and the companies that applied for a bank loan, except in the case of the usage of mezzanine and grants.

To further investigate the difference between rejected and discouraged borrowers, we restrict the analysis to the sub-group of rejected and discouraged borrowers only. As a result, our new variable of credit constraints is a dummy variable that takes value 1 when firms signalled that their loan application was rejected and 0 when they were discouraged from applying for a bank loan. This dummy represents the relative importance of formal to informal constraints. Although the sample becomes very small (down from around 40,000 observations to a bit more than 5000), the comparison is quite interesting. The empirical specification shows that rejected firms have a higher probability of using non-bank sources of finance than discouraged ones across the different financial instruments (Panel C in Table 1.11). Overall, the results show that the type of credit constraints that affect firms matters for them when looking for alternative sources of finance.

1.6 Conclusions

Overall, the findings in this analysis confirm that market-based financing sources are used infrequently by euro area non-financial corporations and used to an even lesser extent by SMEs. Although capital markets represent an important alternative source of financing for non-financial corporations, they are accessible mainly to larger firms with high credit ratings and which are generally located in larger countries with more developed financial markets.

Unless non-financial corporations—and especially SMEs—have access to alternative sources of finance, any decline in bank lending is likely to have an adverse impact on corporate ability to finance investment.

By harmonizing financial market policies and supporting a shift towards market-based financing, the European Commission's initiative for a Capital Markets Union (CMU) will make SMEs in Europe more resilient to bank credit supply shocks and will help reduce obstacles to their access to finance. The CMU initiative can play a key role in further reducing fragmentation of the European financial markets, reducing the dependence on banks for financing the economy and thus improving funding to SMEs, strengthening resilience to the shocks of EU financial markets, and hence the initiative can ultimately support economic growth and financial stability in the EU.

CMU will support firms' growth through a range of channels. For example, deeper capital markets can serve a wider set of participants—SMEs, infrastructure projects, international issuers—as they are attractive to global investors for placing long term funds and increasing incentives to strengthen corporate governance. Furthermore, a lower cost of capital can support improved and cheaper access to funding and will in turn aid growth and jobs in the EU. To complement direct bank lending, a greater diversity of financing would expand the range of participants who can benefit, reduce costs and provide 'shock absorption' for different sectors of the economy. An open Europe that leads global regulatory debates and seeks to reduce fragmentation will attract investment and strengthen Europe as a global financial centre and boost competitiveness of EU firms.

Table 1.12 Variables description in the probit model

Variable name	Description
Sources	Dummy variable: with value 1 if firms use one source of non-banking finance in the past 6 months, 0 otherwise
CC (credit firms)	Dummy variable with value 1 in four different cases: (a) the firm's application for a bank loan or credit line in the past 6 months was denied; (b) the firm received less than 75% of the loan amount it requested; (c) the firm refused the loan offer because the rate was too high; or (d) the firm did not apply for a loan because it feared a rejection

(Continued)

Table 1.12 (Continued)

Variable name	Description
Firm size	A series of dummies for firm size as follows: Micro firms are firms with less than 10 employees, small between 10 and 50 employees, medium more than 50 and up to 250. We consider small and medium firms compared to micro firms
Age	A series of dummy variables as follows: 'Age_1' is a dummy variable equal to 1 if the firm is less than 2 years old. 'Age_2' is a dummy variable equal to 1 if the firm is between 2 and 5 years old. 'Age_3' is a dummy variable equal to 1 if the firm is between 5 and 10 years old. 'Age_4' is a dummy variable equal to 1 if the firm is 10+ years old
Family owned	Dummy variable with value 1 for family owned firms, 0 otherwise
Sectors	Industry, construction, trade and services
Profit	Dummy variable with value 1 for firms who reported increased profits over the past six months, 0 otherwise
Turnover	Dummy variable with value 1 for firms who reported increased turnover over the past six months, 0 otherwise
Firm outlook	Dummy variable with value 1 for firms who reported an improvement in their own outlook in terms of sales, profitability and business plan over the past six months, 0 otherwise
Capital	Dummy variable equal to 1 if the firm's capital improved in the past 6 months
Credit history	Dummy variable equal to 1 if the firm's credit history improved in the past 6 months
Cost of lending	It is calculated by aggregating short and long-term bank interest rates for loans to non-financial corporations using a 24-month moving average of new business volumes. The figures are averages of monthly data for each survey round
Credit standards	They summarize the internal guidelines or criteria that reflect a bank's lending policy. They are defined as the difference between the sum of the percentages of banks responding 'tightened considerably' and 'tightened somewhat' and the sum of the percentages of banks responding 'eased somewhat' and 'eased considerably'
GDP growth	The annual growth rate of real GDP based on averages of quarterly data for each survey round
Unemployment rate	The annual unemployment rate based on averages of quarterly data for each survey round

References

Artola, C., & Genre, V. (2011). *Euro area SMEs under financial constraints: Belief or reality?* (CESifo Working Paper No. 3650). Available at: https://www.cesifo-group.de/DocDL/cesifo1_wp3650.pdf. Accessed 25 Feb 2016.

Beck, T., Demirguc-Kunt, A., & Maksimovic, V. (2008). Financing patterns around the world: Are small firms different? *Journal of Financial Economics, 89*(3), 467–487.

Beck, T., Degryse, H., De Haas, R., & Van Horen N. (2014). *When arm's length is too far: Relationship banking over the business cycle* (CentER Discussion Paper Series, 42).

Berger, A. N., & Udell, G. F. (1998). The economics of small business finance: The roles of private equity and debt markets in the financial growth cycle. *Journal of Banking and Finance, 22*, 613–673.

Berger, A. N., & Udell, G. F. (2006). A more complete conceptual framework for SME finance. *Journal of Banking and Finance, 30*(11), 2945–2966.

Berggren, B., Olofsson, C., & Silver, L. (2000). Control aversion and the search for external financing in Swedish SMEs. *Small Business Economics, 15*(3), 233–242.

Bircan G., & De Haas R. (2015). *The limits of lending: Banks and technology adoption across Russia* (CESifo Working Paper No. 5461). Available at: http://www.cesifo-group.de/DocDL/cesifo1_wp5461.pdf. Accessed 25 Feb 2016.

Brown, M., Ongena, S., Popov, A., & Yesin, P. (2011). Who needs credit and who gets credit in Eastern Europe? Economic Policy, 26, 93–130.

Carbo-Valverde, S., Rodriguez-Fernandez, F., & Udell, G. F. (2016). Trade credit, the financial crisis, and SME access to finance. Journal of Money, Credit and Banking, 48, 113–143.

Casey, E., & O'Toole, C. (2014). Bank lending constraints, trade credit and alternative financing during the financial crisis: Evidence from European SMEs. *Journal of Corporate Finance, 27*, 173–193.

Cassar, G. (2004). The financing of business start-ups. Journal of Business Venturing, 19(2), 261–283.

Chavis, L. W., Klapper, L. F., & Love, I. (2011). The impact of the business environment on young firm financing. The World Bank Economic Review, 25(3), 486–507.

Chittenden, F., & Hutchinson, P. (1996). Small firm growth, access to capital markets and financial structure: Review of issues and an empirical investigation. Small Business Economics, 8(1), 59–67.

Cosh, A., Cumming, D., & Hughes, A. (2009). Outside entrepreneurial capital. The Economic Journal, 119(540), 1494–1533.

Drakos, K. (2012). Bank loan terms and conditions for Eurozone SMEs. *Small Business Economics, 41*(3), 717–732.

European Central Bank. (2014a). *Monthly Bulletin July 2014*. Frankfurt. Available at: https://www.ecb.europa.eu/pub/pdf/mobu/mb201407en.pdf. Accessed 25 Feb 2016.

European Central Bank. (2014b). *Financial integration in Europe*. Frankfurt. Available at: https://www.ecb.europa.eu/pub/pdf/other/financialintegrationineurope201404en.pdf. Accessed 25 Feb 2016.

European Central Bank. (2015). *Survey on the access to finance of enterprises in the euro area: April to September 2015*. Frankfurt. Available at: https://www.ecb.europa.eu/pub/pdf/other/accesstofinancesmallmediumsizedenterprises201512.en.pdf. Accessed 25 Feb 2016.

European Investment Fund. (2014). *European small business finance outlook* (Working Paper 24). Luxembourg. Available at: http://www.eif.org/news_centre/publications/eif_wp_24.pdf. Accessed 25 Feb 2016.

Ferrando, A., & Griesshaber, N. (2011). *Financing obstacles among Euro area firms: Who suffers the most?* (ECB Working Paper Series No 1293). Available at: http://www.ecb.europa.eu/pub/pdf/scpwps/ecbwp1293.pdf. Accessed 25 Feb 2016.

Ferrando, A., & Mulier, K. (2015a). Financial obstacles and financial conditions of firms: Do perceptions match the actual conditions? *The Economic and Social Review, 46*(1), 87–118.

Ferrando, A., & Mulier K. (2015b). *The real effects of credit constraints: Evidence from discouraged borrowers in the Euro area* (ECB Working Paper Series No. 1842). Available at: https://www.ecb.europa.eu/pub/pdf/scpwps/ecbwp1842.en.pdf. Accessed 25 Feb 2016.

Ferrando, A., & Rossolini, M. (2015). *Public private partnerships for infrastructure and enterprise funding. Principles, practices and perspectives*. In S. Caselli, G. Corbetta, & V. Vecchi (Eds.), *SMEs access to credit: Are government measures helpful for constrained firms?* Palgrave Publisher, New York.

Ferrando, A., Köhler-Ulbrich, P., & Pál, R. (2007). *Is the growth of Euro area small and medium-sized enterprises constrained by financing barriers?* (Industrial Policy and Economic Reforms Papers No. 6). European Commission, Enterprise and Industry Directorate-General. Available at: http://bookshop.europa.eu/en/is-the-growth-of-euro-area-small-and-medium-sized-enterprises-constrained-by-financing-barriers--pbNBAV08006/downloads/NB-AV-08-006-EN-N/NBAV08006ENN_002.pdf. Accessed 25 Feb 2016.

Ferrando, A., Griesshaber, N., Köhler-Ulbrich, P., Pérez-Duarte, S., & Schmitt, N. (2013). Measuring the opinion of firms on the supply and demand of external financing in the euro area. In *Proceedings of the sixth IFC conference on statistical issues and activities in a changing environment*. Bank for International Settlements. Available at: http://www.bis.org/ifc/publ/ifcb36s.pdf. Accessed 25 Feb 2016.

Ferrando A., Popov A., & Udell G.F. (2015). *The Sovereign debt crisis, non-conventional monetary policy, and their impact on SME access to finance (2015)* (ECB Working Paper Series No. 1820). Available at: https://www.ecb.europa.eu/pub/pdf/scpwps/ ecbwp1820.en.pdf. Accessed 25 Feb 2016.

Gambacorta, L., & Marques-Ibanez, D. (2011). The bank lending channel: Lessons from the crisis. *Economic Policy, 26*(66), 135–182.

Hadlock, C. J., & Pierce, J. R. (2010). New evidence on measuring financial constraints: Moving beyond the KZ index. *Review of Financial Studies, 23*(5), 1909–1940.

Holton, S., Lawless, M., & McCann, F. (2013). SME financing conditions in Europe: Credit crunch or fundamentals? *National Institute Economic Review, 225*(1), R52–R67.

Huyghebaert, N., & Van de Gucht, L. M. (2007). The determinants of financial structure: New insights from business start-ups. *European Financial Management, 13*(1), 101–133.

Jaffee, D., & Russell, T. (1976). Imperfect information, uncertainty, and credit rationing. *The Quaterly Journal of Economics, 90*(4), 651–666.

Mason, C. M. (2009). Public policy support for the informal venture capital market in Europe: A critical review. *International Small Business Journal, 27*(5), 536–556.

Michaelas, N., Chittenden, F., & Poutziouris, P. (1999). Financial policy and capital structure choice in UK SMEs: Empirical evidence from company panel data. *Small Business Economics, 12*(2), 113–130.

Popov, A. (2016). Monetary policy, bank capital and credit supply: A role for discouraged and informally rejected firms. *International Journal of Central Banking, 12*(1), 95–141.

Psillaki, M., & Eleftheriou, K. (2015). Trade credit, bank credit, and flight to quality: Evidence from French SMEs. *Journal of Small Business Management, 53*(4), 1219–1240.

Stiglitz, J. E., & Weiss, A. (1981). Credit rationing in markets with imperfect information. *The American Economic Review, 71*(3), 393–410.

Taketa, K., & Udell, G. F. (2007). Lending channels and financial shocks: The case of SME trade credit and the Japanese banking crisis. *Monetary and Economic Studies, 25*(2), 1–44.

Van Auken, H. E. (2001). Financing small technology-based companies: The relationship between familiarity with capital and ability to price and negotiate investment. *Journal of Small Business Management, 39*(3), 240–258.

Wehinger, G. (2012). Bank deleveraging, the move from bank to market-based financing, and SME financing. *OECD Journal: Financial Market Trends*, 2012(1), 65–79. Available at: http://www.oecd-ilibrary.org/bank-deleveraging-the-move-from-bank-to-market-based-financing-and-sme-financing_5k91hbvfh9g3.pdf. Accessed 25 Feb 2016.

Zecchini, S., & Ventura, M. (2009). The impact of public guarantees on credit to SMEs. *Small Business Economics, 32*(2), 191–206.

2

Neither a Borrower Nor a Lender Be! Loan Application and Credit Decision for Young European Firms

Andrea Moro, Daniela Maresch, Annalisa Ferrando, and Julia Barbar

2.1 Introduction

The default of the English Crown in 1340 drove out of business the Peruzzi family in 1343 and the Compagnia de' Bardi in 1346: not only was the English Crown unable to repay its loans, but both the Peruzzi and Bardi families were unable to implement any strategy which would

---

JEL G21

A. Moro (✉) • J. Barbar
Cranfield University, Bedford, UK
e-mail: andrea.moro@cranfield.ac.uk

D. Maresch
Institute for Innovation Management, Johannes Kepler University Linz, Linz, Austria

A. Ferrando
Capital Markets/Financial Structure Division of the European Central Bank, European Central Bank, Frankfurt, Germany

S.P.S. Rossi (ed.), *Access to Bank Credit and SME Financing*,
Palgrave Macmillan Studies in Banking and Financial Institutions,
DOI 10.1007/978-3-319-41363-1_2

have enabled them to sell English Crown assets and to recover at least part of their loans (Cipolla 1994, 2002). Actually, the history of finance is rich in examples where lenders were not properly protected by laws and the ways in which they are enforced.

In general, the certainty of the law and the probability to recover a loan in case of default affects banks' lending decisions and, as a consequence, firms' access to credit. Banks, as delegated monitors (Diamond 1984), play a vital role in supporting the development of the economy by investing people's savings in reliable firms and projects. The legal context that supports banks in dealing with delinquent customers is important in order to ensure that lenders are able to recover the loan in case of a borrower's default. In countries with strong creditor protection and rigorous law enforcement, banks will find it easier to control borrower risk and recover the loan in the event of a default. Consequently, banks will be more willing to lend *ex ante* (La Porta et al. 1997), which reduces a firm's risk of credit constraint. Likewise, a firm's decision to file for a loan can be affected by the legal context (Demirguc-Kunt and Maksimovic 1999). If the likelihood of a firm to be able to renegotiate the terms of the loan in times of financial distress are low due to strong creditor rights, the demand for loans might decrease since firms are aware they will not be able to escape the repayment of the loan or negotiate better terms.

Our research builds on previous works that examine the role of a country's legal system on firms' debt financing. Empirical evidence suggests that the level of creditor and property rights protection and the rigorousness of law enforcement affect debt ownership concentration (e.g., Esty and Megginson 2003) as well as the terms of the credit, such as size, maturity and interest rate of the loan agreement (Bae and Goyal 2009; Laeven and Majnoni 2005; Qian and Strahan 2007). Research also finds that longer trials increase the probability that credit is less available and that default rates are higher (Jappelli et al. 2005) and shows that the overall supply of credit in developing countries increases subsequent to changes in collateral laws and bankruptcy laws (Haselmann et al. 2010). In line with these findings, Liberti and Mian (2010) suggest that in countries with stronger creditor rights and better information-sharing mechanisms, collateral spreads are smaller. Beck et al. (2005) investigate the impact of the adaptability of a country's legal system and the political independence of the judiciary on the financing obstacles faced by firms. They find that while across-country variations in the legal system's adaptability help to explain the differences in financing obstacles that firms have to face, cross-country variations in the judiciary's independence do not contribute to the explanation of these differences.

Our study aims at expanding on previous research in this area by examining the impact of the recovery rate of delinquent borrowers on both a firm's propensity to file for a loan and a bank's propensity to lend. Our focus is on young firms (younger than nine years) since these firms on the one hand depend more heavily on bank finance to grow (Cassar 2004) and on the other are characterized by greater information opacity (Berger et al. 2001).

We rely on the Survey on the Access to Finance of Enterprises (SAFE) dataset from the European Central Bank, which collects directly information about access to credit, the use of different sources of finance, and liquidity and finance constraints from a sample of European firms. We integrate it with information about the legal systems in Europe by using data from the World Bank. We end up with a dataset containing 11,412 complete observations collected between 2009 and 2012, of which 2665 observations are about firms that applied for a loan.

We test our hypotheses using logit regression and re-test our findings by applying Heckman selection to address potential selection bias in the case of firms that applied for a loan as well as different controls and different estimation techniques.

The results we obtain are robust and suggest that recovery rates affect lenders and borrowers differently. As far as firms (borrowers) are concerned, higher recovery rates reduce the probability that a young firm files for a loan. As far as banks (lenders) are concerned, recovery rates do not affect their decision to provide the loan. However, the picture is more complex when we compare economically weak countries (i.e., those that faced major consequences of the financial crisis and struggled to recover) with economically strong countries (i.e., those that were affected by the financial crisis, but still only faced minor consequences and were able to recover). In economically strong countries, high recovery rates only impact loan applications, whereas in economically weak countries, high recovery rates only impact the bank's decision to provide a loan.

The remainder of the chapter is structured as follows. In Sect. 2.2, we present the theoretical background and develop the hypotheses. Section 2.3 discusses the dataset and the methodology and illustrates the variables used in the analysis. Descriptive statistics are presented in Sect. 2.4. In Sect. 2.5, we present the econometric findings about the impact of recovery rate on credit applications and credit provided to firms, as well as a set of robustness checks. In Sect. 2.6 we discuss the implications. Section 2.7 concludes.

2.2 Theoretical Background and Hypotheses

Firms tend to depend on bank debt in order to finance both their ongoing activities and growth. However, their ability to access bank credit is affected by the limited quantity and accuracy of information available (Berger and Frame 2007; Mason and Stark 2004), which impedes the assessment of their creditworthiness and can adversely affect access to credit (Moro et al. 2014; Petersen and Rajan 1994). Even when the information asymmetry between the bank and the firm is reduced, lending to firms remains an activity that involves the risk of customer default on the credit granted by the bank. Thus, banks have to take into consideration the extent to which creditor rights are protected in determining what kind of loans and what kind of price and non-price terms can be offered to firms since creditor rights affect a bank's monitoring incentives and re-contracting costs, which can be costly when creditor rights are poorly enforced (Bae and Goyal 2009).

Interestingly, the very same aspects that affect banks and their lending decisions can also affect firms and their decision to apply for a loan. Strong creditor protection can increase a firm's perception that taking out a loan in order to finance its operations increases its risk. This is because the bank can credibly commit to liquidate the firm if the firm defaults on the loan. From the firm's point of view, a high level of creditor protection thus reduces the possibility to later renegotiate the terms of payment according to the new situation faced by the firm, which implicitly increases the risk that it can be forced to file for bankruptcy (Berkowitz and White 2004; Cressy 2006).

Prior research suggests that firms benefit from a high level of creditor and property rights protection as well as rigorous law enforcement by accessing credit under more favourable terms. In countries with strong creditor protection, bank loans are associated with more concentrated ownership, longer maturities and lower interest rates (Qian and Strahan 2007), as well as better property rights protection results in higher lending volumes, longer maturities and lower interest rates (Bae and Goyal 2009). Additionally, legal systems that loan managers perceive to be more protective are associated with a higher proportion of banks loans allocated to borrowers characterized by information opacity, such as small and medium-sized enterprises (Haselmann and Wachtel 2010).

Previous empirical papers further suggest a positive relationship between the quality of the legal system and credit access. Credit is found to be less available in Italian provinces with longer trials or large backlogs of pending trials (Jappelli et al. 2005). The loan supply in transition economies increases after changes in collateral laws and bankruptcy laws are enacted (Haselmann and Wachtel 2010). Beck et al. (2005) provide evidence on the relationship between specific characteristics of a country's legal system–i.e., adaptability of the legal system and judicial independence—and firms' access to finance. Their results indicate that despite the fact that across-country variation in the adaptability of the legal system helps to explain the variation in financing obstacles, across-country variation in the political independence of the judiciary does not help explain the variation in financing obstacles.

We add to the research on credit access by investigating how recovery rates impact a firm's decision to apply for a loan and a bank's lending decision. Recovery rates reflect the financial outcome for the bank at the end of insolvency proceedings and therefore also the strength of creditor rights: the better the creditor rights the higher the percentage that the bank will be able to recover on its outstanding loan. A higher certainty to recover most of the principal as well as the interest will increase the bank's willingness to provide *credit ex ante*, as it decreases its risk to incur tremendous losses if the firm defaults on it loan. In turn, the firm's risk to be credit constrained is reduced. Accordingly, we formulate the following hypothesis:

H1 The higher the recovery rate the higher the probability that banks provide credit.

However, what is good for a bank is not necessarily good for a firm. A higher recovery rate can impact the borrower's decision to file for a loan since lender confidence in recovering the large majority of a loan can reduce a bank's interest in renegotiating the loan if a borrower experiences any difficulties. Borrowers can therefore perceive the use of the loan as greater risk. In such a context, the borrower might decide not to apply for a loan. Based on these arguments, we propose the following hypothesis:

H2 The higher the recovery rate the lower the probability that firms apply for a loan.

In addition, the impact of recovery rates might vary in different economic environments. Recovery rates might play a greater role in a bank's decision to lend to firms in weak economic conditions than in strong economic conditions. Similar reasoning applies to a borrower's decision to file for a loan. Thus, we re-test our hypothesis on two sub-samples: one containing countries that have been only marginally affected by the financial crisis and the other containing countries that have faced major issues associated with the financial crisis.

2.3 Data and Methodology

2.3.1 Data

Our research relies primarily on the Survey on the Access to Finance of Enterprises (SAFE) conducted on behalf of the European Commission and the European Central Bank. It collects information about access to finance by firms within the European Union. The SAFE has been run on a given set of questions every six months since 2009 and systematically covers eleven European countries (namely: Austria, Belgium, France, Finland, Germany, Greece, the Netherlands, Ireland, Italy, Portugal and Spain). Firms in the sample are randomly selected from the Dun & Bradstreet database. The sample is stratified by firm size class, economic activity and country. The sample is constructed to offer approximately the same precision for micro (1–9 employees), small (10–49 employees) and medium-sized firms (50–249 employees). A group of large firms (250 or more employees) is also included and it covers less than 10% of the total sample. The sample sizes for each economic activity are selected to ensure adequate representation across the four largest activities: industry, construction, trade and services. Agriculture, forestry, fishing, financial intermediation, public administration, activities of households, extra-territorial organizations, as well as bodies and holding companies are excluded. The person interviewed in each company is a top level executive (Owner, General Manager, Financial Director or Chief Accountant). Since our focus is on young firms, we include in our analysis only firms that are nine years or younger.

We integrate the data provided by the SAFE dataset with information from the quarterly Bank Lending Survey (BLS) run by national central banks on behalf of the European Central Bank. The BLS provides specific data on banks' propensity to lend to large and small/medium-sized firms as well as households. We use the data on large and small/medium-sized firms for the previous three months as controls for the availability of credit in the market.

We also rely on the Eurostat database for general economic data. Eurostat is the statistical office of the European Union located in Luxembourg. Its task is to provide the European Union with statistics at the European level that enable comparisons between countries and regions. We use Eurostat in order to access homogeneous data on GDP growth, unemployment rates, inflation and the Herfindahl-Hirschman Index of bank concentration.

In order to access data about the recovery rate, we use the corresponding variable from the World Bank's 'Doing Business' dataset. This dataset includes economic data from 2003 to the present and is considered highly reliable.

2.3.2 Methodology

Since the dependent variables in our regressions are binary (firm filing for a loan or not, and bank loan obtained or not), we approach the analysis using traditional logit regression (Hosmer and Lemeshow 2000). As we rely on a panel dataset that is unmatched at firm level, we were unable to use fixed effect panel regression. Thus, our analysis relies on pooled logit regressions.

We approach the analysis in two stages. First, we enter the independent variable. Second, in order to examine differences between countries that have been marginally hit by the economic crisis from those that have faced major shock, we re-estimate the specification by splitting the original dataset into two sub-datasets. The first sub-dataset contains observations from Austria, Germany, France, Finland and the Netherlands (i.e., the countries that were only marginally affected by the crisis), and the second contains data from Greece, Belgium, Italy, Portugal, Ireland and Spain (i.e., the countries that were more hard hit by the financial crisis).

In order to check the robustness of our results, we check whether the estimation approach affects our results. We therefore re-run the regressions using the probit estimation. We also re-test our regressions using the bootstrap estimation of the standard errors (Efron and Tibshirani 1998).

2.3.3 Dependent Variables

The SAFE survey comprises numerous questions. One of these questions is whether the firm's manager applied for a loan in the last six months. We use the answer to this question as the dependent variable to examine firms' decision to apply for a loan. The SAFE survey also inquires whether the application was successful, i.e., whether the firm obtained the credit they applied for in the last six months. We use the answer to this question (the firm obtained all the credit = 1; the firm did not obtain the credit = 0) as the dependent variable to explore the bank decision to provide credit.

2.3.4 Independent Variable

In order to test the impact of difficulties in recovering credit from delinquent borrowers, we use the data provided in the 'Doing Business' dataset on 'Resolving Insolvency', published by the World Bank by using the 'Recovery rate'. This index measures the average percentage of the original debt recovered by secured creditors through reorganization, liquidation or debt enforcement proceedings by taking the time, cost and outcome of the insolvency proceedings into account. We collect it for each year considered and for each country in our sample.

2.3.5 Controls

We include a set of variables to control for the firm's characteristics the moment in time when the data was collected, the country and the economic context. In terms of firm characteristics, the SAFE dataset provides some information about the size of the firm by grouping firms into four categories: micro, small, medium and large. We use three dummy variables that identify micro (MICRO), small (SMALL) and medium-sized (MEDIUM) firms. Our expectation is that larger firms are less likely to face a rejection since they are perceived as more secure and successful.

In addition, the SAFE dataset clusters the firms according to age categories. We include in our analysis only firms younger than nine years and control for their age: we use 2_YEARS, and 2_5_YEARS as dummy variables to identify the age group for each observation. According to previous research (Berger and Udell 1995; Petersen and Rajan 1994), we expect older firms more likely to be successful when they apply for a loan: older firms have a more consolidated reputation, which can be helpful when banks have to make lending decisions (Martinelli 1997).

We also control for the performance of the firm in the last six months by including two categorical variables that measure the change in turnover (TURNOVER) and the change in profit (PROFIT). We also control for the financial strategy pursued by the firm by taking into consideration the different sources of finance used during the last period. We use dummies that identify whether the firm used trade credit (TRADE_CREDIT), leasing (LEASING), retained earnings (RETAINED_EARNINGS) or raised additional equity (EQUITY).

Because of the collinearity between our variable of interest (recovery rate) and countries, we do not include any control for the country. However, we consider a set of macroeconomic variables that are country-specific and time-varying to capture the macroeconomic context in which firms operate. In particular, we control for the change in the gross domestic product (GDP), inflation rate (INFLATION) and overall unemployment rate (UNEMPL_OVERALL) for each country and each semester. These data are obtained from the Eurostat dataset. Moreover, we account for the overall financial context by using the European Central Bank's BLS coefficients for small/medium-sized and large firms (BLS). Additionally, we consider the structure of the financial industry by using the Herfindahl-Hirschman Index of bank concentration (HHI) in each country since previous research suggests an impact of bank competition on credit access (Carbó-Valverde et al. 2009; Neuberger et al. 2008).

Finally, the dataset provides unmatched observations for eight semesters, and thus we use seven dummies that identify the semester in which an observation was collected.

2.4 Descriptive Statistics

The dataset we use contains 11,412 observations from eleven countries, covering the period between the first semester of 2009 until the second semester of 2012. Analysis of firms that applied for a loan relies on 2665 observations. The summary statistics are reported in Table 2.1.

Overall, the majority of the firms in the sample are either micro or small, and only 3.5% of them are classified as large. More than three-quarters of the firms in the sample are independent. Only about one-third, 37%, of the firms enjoyed an increase in turnover, 28% experienced no change and 34% suffered a contraction. More than 43% experienced a reduction in profit, whereas only 28% enjoyed an increase. These figures can be explained by the fact that observations were made in the period between 2009 and 2012, thus falling into a period of overall economic stagnation. In terms of financing, firms appear to have used leasing and retained profit quite intensively (31% and 30%, respectively). It is interesting that only 5% of the firms relied on equity. This is not surprising since the observations are from young firms, which do not approach financial markets. The BLS index is +5.29. A positive value of this index is associated with a contraction of the credit provided by the banking system. This implies that, on average, credit is in contraction in the period

Table 2.1 Basic statistics

Variable	Description	Obs	Mean	Std. dev	Min	Max	Obs	Mean	Std. dev	Min	Max
Loan requested	Whether the firm applied for a loan	11412	0.2335	0.4231	0	1					
Loan obtained	Whether the firm obtained a loan	11412	0.1385	0.3455	0	1	2665	0.5932	0.4913	0	1
Micro	Micro firms	11412	0.5066	0.5000	0	1	2665	0.4158	0.4929	0	1
Small	Small firms	11412	0.3017	0.4590	0	1	2665	0.3403	0.4739	0	1
Medium	Medium firms	11412	0.1564	0.3633	0	1	2665	0.1947	0.3961	0	1
<2 years	Firms younger than 2 years	11412	0.0872	0.2821	0	1	2665	0.0949	0.2932	0	1
2 and 5 years	Firms 2–5 years of age	11412	0.3406	0.4739	0	1	2665	0.3280	0.4696	0	1
5 and 9 years	Firms 5–9 years of age	11412	0.5722	0.4948	0	1	2665	0.5771	0.4941	0	1
Independent	Whether the firm is independent	11412	0.7944	0.4041	0	1	2665	0.8203	0.3840	0	1
Change in turnover	Last semester change in turnover	11412	0.0245	0.8487	–1	1	2665	0.0176	0.8687	–1	1
Change in profit	Last semester change in profit	11412	–0.1492	0.8349	–1	1	2665	–0.2146	0.8412	–1	1
Retained_ earnings	Use of retained earnings	11412	0.3024	0.4593	0	1	2665	0.3527	0.4779	0	1
Trade_credit	Use of trade credit	11412	0.2833	0.4506	0	1	2665	0.3760	0.4845	0	1
Leasing	Use of leasing	11412	0.3140	0.4641	0	1	2665	0.4011	0.4902	0	1

(*Continued*)

Table 2.1 (Continued)

Variable	Description	Obs	Mean	Std. dev	Min	Max	Obs	Mean	Std. dev	Min	Max
Equity	Raise of new equity	11412	0.0572	0.2323	0	1	2665	0.0747	0.2629	0	1
BLS	Bank Lending Survey index	11412	5.2948	10.1887	−14	60	2665	4.4858	8.8488	−7	60
GDP	Change in Gross Domestic Product	11412	−0.8327	3.0547	−8.5	4	2665	−1.1265	3.0255	−8.5	
Inflation	Inflation rate	11412	1.7104	1.2317	−1.7	4.7	2665	1.6125	1.2257	−1.7	4.7
Unemp	Unemployment rate	11412	10.5471	5.4953	3.25	25.7	2665	11.1187	5.4472	3.25	25.7
HHI	Herfindahl Index bank concentration	11412	0.0846	0.0729	0.0206	0.3700	2665	0.0724	0.0591	0.0206	0.3700
Rec_rate	Recovery rate (percentage)	11412	67.0844	15.5482	41.8	89.4	2665	64.4672	14.8349	41.8	89.4

Variables presented in the table include: dummy for bank loan application; dummy for bank loan obtained; dummies for firm size (micro, small, medium and large firms); dummy for age (less than 2 years, 2–5 years, 5–9 years); change in turnover and change in profit (reduction −1, unchanged 0, increase, 1); dummies for sources of finance (use of retained earnings, trade credit or leasing; increase in equity); Bank Lending Survey index; GDP growth; inflation rate; unemployment rate; Herfindahl-Hirschman Index of bank concentration; coefficients for recovery rate

Sig.: * <.1; ** <.05; *** <.01

we consider. The BLS index is in line with the more conservative lending policies pursued by banks after the 2008 financial crisis and the introduction of the more stringent Basel III rules.

Turning our attention towards the variable of interest, in the overall dataset the recovery ratio is between 41.8% (Greece) and 89.4% (Finland), with an average of 67.1%. When we turn our attention towards firms that filed for a loan, we see changes in the average, as the average recovery rate goes down to 64%, suggesting that in countries where the recovery rate is lower, firms are more likely to file for a loan.

2.5 Results

Results of each firm's decision to file for a loan are reported in Table 2.2. The first regression reports the results without our independent variable. This allows us to examine the impact of our independent variable by comparing the starting regression with the specification that includes it.

The first specification, which includes only the controls, is significant with an R^2 of 0.0429. The smaller the firm the higher the probability that the firm applied for a loan. In the case of age, younger firms were more likely to file for a loan, possibly because of the lack of alternative sources of finance (e.g., equity or more sophisticated financial tools like leasing). Change in turnover increased the probability to apply for credit, suggesting that growing firms are more likely to rely on bank finance to support their growth. Change in profit is negatively related to filing for a loan. More profitable firms thus seem to rely less on bank financing in line with the argument provided by Myers and Majluf (1984). All the different sources of finance impact positively the filing for a loan, suggesting there is no substitution effect: apparently, firms tend to use a portfolio of sources of finance in a coordinated way. Regarding the macroeconomic context, only the overall unemployment rate (positive) and the Herfindahl-Hirschman Index of bank concentration (negative) are significant, suggesting that firms turn to bank credit in difficult times and prefer to deal with banks in concentrated markets.

The second specification includes the recovery rate (REC_RATE). The regression is significant and R^2 improves marginally to 0.0472. There

Table 2.2 Regressions—applied for a loan

		Number of obs		11412	Number of obs		11412
		LR chi2(22)		532.04	LR chi2(23)		585.11
		Prob > chi2		0.0000	Prob > chi2		0.0000
		Pseudo R2		0.0429	Pseudo R2		0.0472
		Coeff	**Std. dev**	**Sig.**	**Coeff**	**Std. dev**	**Sig.**
Micro	Micro firms	−0.5119	0.1161	***	−0.5162	0.1164	***
Small	Small firms	−0.2022	0.1165	*	−0.1887	0.1168	
Medium	Medium firms	−0.1781	0.1217		−0.1717	0.1220	
<2 years	Firms younger than 2 years	0.1672	0.0830	**	0.1096	0.0838	
2 and 5 years	Firms 2–5 years of age	−0.0359	0.0500		−0.0380	0.0502	
Change in turnover	Last semester change in turnover	0.0700	0.0340	**	0.0654	0.0339	*
Change in profit	Last semester change in profit	−0.1586	0.0350	***	−0.1499	0.0350	***
Retained_ earnings	Use of retained earnings	0.1761	0.0504	***	0.2038	0.0507	***
Trade_credit	Use of trade credit	0.5010	0.0499	***	0.5073	0.0501	***
Leasing	Use of leasing	0.3599	0.0494	***	0.3794	0.0496	***
Equity	Raise of new equity	0.3193	0.0923	***	0.3193	0.0925	***
Wave	Wave of the data collection			***(not reported)***			
BLS	Bank Lending Survey index	0.0006	0.0029		−0.0007	0.0030	
GDP	Change in gross domestic product	−0.0121	0.0114		0.0159	0.0120	

Inflation	Inflation rate	0.0331	0.0263		0.0160	0.0268	
Unemp	Unemployment rate	0.0181	0.0046	***	0.0182	0.0047	***
HHI	Herfindahl Index bank concentration	−3.3851	0.4034	***	−2.5054	0.4253	***
Rec_rate	Recovery rate (percentage)				−0.0123	0.0017	**
_const	Constant	−1.1693	0.1435	***	−0.3313	0.1836	*

Variables presented in the table include: dummy for bank loan application; dummies for firm size (micro, small, medium and large firms); dummy for age (less than 2 years, 2–5 years, 5–9 years); change in turnover and change in profit (reduction −1, unchanged 0, increase, 1); dummies for sources of finance (use of retained earnings, trade credit or leasing; increase in equity); Bank Lending Survey index; GDP growth; inflation rate; unemployment rate; Herfindahl-Hirschman Index of bank concentration; coefficients for recovery rate

Sig.: * <.1; ** <.05; *** <.01

is no change in the significance level of the controls, however SMALL and <2_YEARS turn out to be not significant. The independent variable REC_RATE is highly significant and negative. High recovery rates reduce the number of loan applications, possibly because firms are aware that the legal environment provides a high level of protection for the banks, which enables banks to successfully force firms to repay the loan.

Results of a bank's decision to provide a loan are reported in Table 2.3. In this case as well, the first regression reports the results without our independent variable. Again, this allows us to examine the impact of the recovery rate by comparing the second regression with this specification. Subsequently, we enter the independent variable.

The first specification, which includes only the controls, is significant, and R^2 is 0.0540. Size of firm does not affect access to credit. The age class increase implies a negative impact on credit access as the age of the firm increases: it moves from being not significant to being significant and then being negatively correlated to obtaining a loan. Both change in turnover and change in profit increase the probability to obtain credit, suggesting that banks are more prepared to provide credit to firms that are growing and are more solid in terms of profitability. All the different sources of finance impact negatively on credit access except for LEASING, which is not significant. Equity seems to be the strongest alternative to a loan, whereas leasing is the weakest. As expected, the BLS index is negatively related to credit access: the less prone banks are to lend, the less likely it is that firms are successful in their loan application. Economic expansion (change in GDP) is positively related to credit access, whereas the overall unemployment rate is negatively related.

The second specification investigates the role of the recovery rate (REC_RATE). The specification is highly significant ($p < 0.0001$). R^2 is at 0.0543, suggesting a limited contribution of the variable in explaining the overall variance with respect to the starting specification. There is no change in the significance level of the controls except for INFLATION, which turns out to be marginally significant and negatively related to the probability to obtain a loan. Interestingly, the independent variable is not significant.

Table 2.3 Regressions—obtained a loan

		Number of obs		2665	Number of obs		2665
		LR chi2(22)		194.59	LR chi2(23)		195.45
		Prob > chi2		0.0000	Prob > chi2		0
		Pseudo R2		0.0540	Pseudo R2		0.0543
Variable	**Description**	**Coeff**	**Std. dev**	**Sig.**	**Coeff**	**Std. dev**	**Sig.**
Micro	Micro firms	−0.2511	0.2033		−0.2570	0.2034	
Small	Small firms	0.0265	0.2029		0.0249	0.2030	
Medium	Medium firms	0.1246	0.2118		0.1255	0.2118	
<2 years	Firms younger than 2 years	0.1401	0.1512		0.1249	0.1521	
2 and 5 years	Firms 2–5 years of age	−0.1774	0.0905	**	−0.1771	0.0905	*
Change in turnover	Last semester change in turnover	0.1067	0.0590	*	0.1058	0.0590	*
Change in profit	Last semester change in profit	0.1272	0.0617	**	0.1290	0.0617	**
Retained_ earnings	Use of retained earnings	−0.2210	0.0897	**	−0.2148	0.0899	**
Trade_credit	Use of trade credit	−0.1964	0.0879	**	−0.1941	0.0880	**
Leasing	Use of leasing	−0.0081	0.0882		−0.0061	0.0882	
Equity	Raise of new equity	−0.3696	0.1594	**	−0.3709	0.1593	**
Wave	Wave of the data collection		***(not reported)***				
BLS	Bank Lending Survey index	−0.0194	0.0060	***	−0.0198	0.0060	***
GDP	Change in Gross Domestic Product	0.0811	0.0211	***	0.0873	0.0221	***

Inflation	Inflation rate	−0.0817	0.0517		−0.0856	0.0519	*
Unemp	Unemployment rate	−0.0564	0.0083	***	−0.0558	0.0083	***
HHI	Herfindahl Index bank concentration	−1.1382	0.7741		−0.8929	0.8172	
Rec rate	Recovery rate (percentage)				−0.0030	0.0032	
_const	Constant	1.9627	0.2648	***	2.1554	0.3369	***

Variables presented in the table include: dummy for bank loan obtained; dummies for firm size (micro, small, medium and large firms); dummy for age (less than 2 years, 2–5 years, 5–9 years); change in turnover and change in profit (reduction −1, unchanged 0, increase, 1); dummies for sources of finance (use of retained earnings, trade credit or leasing; increase in equity); Bank Lending Survey index; GDP growth; inflation rate; unemployment rate; Herfindahl-Hirschman Index of bank concentration; coefficients for recovery rate

Sig.: * <.1; ** <.05; *** <.01

2.5.1 Split Dataset

The next level of analysis is about comparing two sub-samples: (i) the weak countries (namely, Belgium, Greece, Ireland, Italy, Portugal, Spain), i.e., those countries that faced major consequences during and after the financial crisis and struggled to recover; and (ii) the strong countries (namely, Austria, France, Finland, Germany, Netherlands), i.e., countries that were affected by the financial crisis, but nevertheless only faced minor consequences and were able to recover quite rapidly. Also in this case, we first investigate for differences in the case of applying for a loan. Then, we move on and look at the bank's decision to provide a loan.

As far as application for a loan is concerned, Table 2.4 reports the results.

The first set of regressions includes only the controls. They are highly significant ($p < 0.0001$). R^2 is higher in the strong countries (0.0502 vs 0.0459). In comparing the two specifications, some differences emerge. Whereas in both weak and strong countries, smaller firms appear to be less likely to file for a loan, only in strong countries do younger firms appear to be more likely to apply for a loan. In both contexts, retained earnings are an alternative to bank finance (Myers and Majluf 1984), and the probability of filing for a loan is positively associated with alternative sources of finance, suggesting that firms tend to diversify the way they finance their operations. Interestingly, in weak countries the macroeconomic context seems to play a very limited role, as only HHI is significant. At the same time, in strong countries, the increase in GDP and the overall unemployment rate are both associated with a greater probability to file for a loan. More interestingly, a lower bank propensity to provide credit is associated with a greater probability to file for a loan, suggesting that banks are not able to respond properly to firm's demand.

The second set of regressions investigates the role of recovery rate in weak and strong countries. In the case of weak countries, the R^2 does not change and there are no changes in the covariates. Interestingly, the recovery rate is not significant. This suggests that in weak economic contexts, the bank's capability to recover the original loan from the firm is not a concern for the firm when taking the decision to borrow. In the

Table 2.4 Applied for a loan (split dataset)

Variable	Description												
		Number of obs		5772	Number of obs		5640	Number of obs		5772	Number of obs		5640
		LR chi2(22)		308.83	LR chi2(22)		280.29	LR chi2(23)		308.84	LR chi2(23)		294.38
		Prob > chi2		0.0000	Prob > chi2		0.0000	Prob > chi2		0.0000	Prob > chi2		0.0000
		Pseudo R2		0.0459	Pseudo R2		0.0502	Pseudo R2		0.0459	Pseudo R2		0.0527
Micro	Micro firms	−0.4429	0.1668	***	−0.5152	0.1646	***	−0.4432	0.1670	***	−0.5540	0.1651	***
Small	Small firms	−0.0733	0.1664		−0.2940	0.1666	*	−0.0736	0.1666		−0.3178	0.1668	*
Medium	Medium firms	−0.0875	0.1724		−0.2245	0.1752		−0.0877	0.1725		−0.2473	0.1754	
<2 years	Firms younger than 2 years	0.0409	0.1389		0.3257	0.1103	***	0.0407	0.1390		0.2507	0.1126	**
2 and 5 years	Firms 2–5 years of age	−0.0621	0.0672		0.0001	0.0772		−0.0622	0.0672		−0.0035	0.0774	
Change in turnover	Last semester change in turnover	0.0934	0.0455	**	0.0446	0.0521		0.0935	0.0456	**	0.0484	0.0521	
Change in profit	Last semester change in profit	−0.1501	0.0500	***	−0.1179	0.0501	**	−0.1502	0.0501	***	−0.1165	0.0500	**
Retained_earnings	Use of retained earnings	0.1913	0.0684	***	0.2929	0.0780	***	0.1912	0.0684	***	0.3044	0.0783	***
Trade_credit	Use of trade credit	0.4680	0.0638	***	0.4197	0.0853	***	0.4681	0.0638	***	0.4110	0.0853	***
Leasing	Use of leasing	0.4353	0.0688	***	0.4148	0.0742	***	0.4352	0.0688	***	0.4390	0.0747	***
Equity	Raise of new equity	0.2966	0.1530	*	0.3524	0.1194	***	0.2967	0.1530	*	0.3995	0.1199	***
Wave	Wave of the data collection												

BLS	Bank Lending Survey index	−0.0039	0.0035		0.0194	0.0078	**	−0.0039	0.0035		0.0077	0.0084	
GDP	Gross Domestic Product	−0.0044	0.0155		0.0553	0.0228	**	−0.0051	0.0226		0.0396	0.0233	*
Inflation	Inflation rate	0.0104	0.0299		0.1186	0.0731		0.0107	0.0308		0.0807	0.0729	
Unemp	Unemployment rate	−0.0071	0.0056		0.1679	0.0193	***	−0.0072	0.0057		0.0786	0.0302	***
HHI	Herfindahl Index bank concentration	−4.3603	0.9562	***	−2.9892	0.5426	***	−4.3745	1.0072	***	−1.8513	0.6227	***
Rec_rate	Recovery rate (percentage)							0.0002	0.0039		−0.0134	0.0036	***
_const	Constant	−0.6732	0.2050	***	−2.6681	0.2836	***	−0.6857	0.3454	**	−1.0430	0.5111	**

Variables presented in the table include: dummy for bank loan application; dummies for firm size (micro, small, medium and large firms); dummy for age (less than 2 years, 2–5 years, 5–9 years); change in turnover and change in profit (reduction −1, unchanged 0, increase, 1); dummies for sources of finance (use of retained earnings, trade credit or leasing; increase in equity); Bank Lending Survey index; GDP growth; inflation rate; unemployment rate; Herfindahl-Hirschman Index of bank concentration; coefficients for recovery rate

Sig.: * <.1; ** <.05; *** <.01

case of strong countries, we notice an increase in the R^2 and no change in the significance of the controls except for BLS, which turns out to be not significant. The variable of interest, namely REC_RATE, is significant and negatively related to applying for a loan. In countries with a strong economic environment, high recovery rates act as constraint on the firm's loan application, possibly because the firm perceives the risk that, if it is not able to repay the loan in the future, the bank will be supported by a strong legal system that enables it to recover the original loan.

As for the bank's decision to provide a loan, the results are reported in Table 2.5.

Both regressions that consider only the covariates are highly significant ($p < 0.0001$). R^2 is again higher in the strong countries 0(.0551 vs 0.0495). In comparing the two regressions, clear differences emerge. Firms in weak countries are less likely to obtain credit when they use alternative sources of finance (namely, retained earnings, trade credit or the issuance of new equity), whereas these variables are not significant in strong countries except for the issuance of new equity. At the same time, in strong countries the growth of a firm's turnover and profit as well as its age seem to matter in a bank's lending decision. Moreover, bigger firms appear to be more likely to access credit in strong countries. In weaker countries, however, these factors do not appear to have an impact on the firm's credit access. Interestingly, the macroeconomic context seems to play a more relevant role in weak countries. Changes in both GDP and the overall unemployment rate are significant and affect the probability to obtain credit (the former increasing the probability, the latter decreasing). In strong countries, only inflation rate is marginally significant. A bank's propensity to lend to firms affects the credit access in weak countries, whereas it is not significant in the strong countries. Overall, the picture we obtain suggests different drivers of credit access based on the impact the financial crisis had on the given country and its ability to recover.

In the next two regressions, we investigate the role of the recovery rate in weak and strong countries. In both countries, R^2 increases with the increase being greater in weak countries. There are no major changes in the covariates except for the change in GDP, which turns out to be not significant in weak countries, and the overall unemployment rate, which

Table 2.5 Obtained a loan (split dataset)

Variable	Description	Weak countries			Strong countries			Weak countries			Strong countries		
		Number of obs		1557	Number of obs		1108	Number of obs		1557	Number of obs		1108
		LR chi2(22)		106.61	LR chi2(22)		76.47	LR chi2(23)		110.47	LR chi2(23)		76.81
		Prob > chi2		0.0000	Prob > chi2		0.0000	Prob > chi2		0.0000	Prob > chi2		0.0000
		Pseudo R2		0.0495	Pseudo R2		0.0551	Pseudo R2		0.0513	Pseudo R2		0.0554
Micro	Micro firms	−0.3706	0.2801		−0.2471	0.3039		−0.4032	0.2807		−0.2658	0.3057	
Small	Small firms	−0.2368	0.2772		0.3431	0.3070		−0.2649	0.2777		0.3264	0.3083	
Medium	Medium firms	−0.2047	0.2857		0.5695	0.3305	*	−0.2271	0.2860		0.5620	0.3308	*
<2 years	Firms younger than 2 years	0.3654	0.2397		−0.1204	0.2116		0.3458	0.2401		−0.1468	0.2162	
2 and 5 years	Firms 2–5 years of age	−0.0387	0.1164		−0.3120	0.1509	**	−0.0498	0.1166		−0.3105	0.1509	**
Change in turnover	Last semester change in turnover	0.0344	0.0780		0.2286	0.0955	**	0.0391	0.0781		0.2297	0.0955	**
Change in profit	Last semester change in profit	0.0671	0.0852		0.2002	0.0939	**	0.0598	0.0854		0.2017	0.0940	**
Retained_ earnings	Use of retained earnings	−0.4160	0.1157	***	0.0763	0.1523		−0.4164	0.1160	***	0.0800	0.1525	
Trade_ credit	Use of trade credit	−0.2027	0.1101	*	−0.0668	0.1580		−0.1994	0.1102	*	−0.0734	0.1585	
Leasing	Use of leasing	0.0289	0.1150		−0.0968	0.1470		0.0263	0.1150		−0.0895	0.1475	
Equity	Raise of new equity	−0.5473	0.2600	**	−0.3808	0.2163	*	−0.5436	0.2609	**	−0.3710	0.2170	*

Wave	Wave of the data collection					*(not reported)*						
BLS	Bank Lending Survey Index	−0.0249	0.0072	**	−0.0211	0.0154		−0.0245	0.0072	***	−0.0242	0.0163
GDP	Gross Domestic Product	0.0922	0.0276	***	0.0674	0.0449		0.0323	0.0412		0.0615	0.0459
Inflation	Inflation rate	−0.0870	0.0588		−0.0189	0.1454		−0.0640	0.0601		−0.0272	0.1463
Unemp	Unemployment rate	−0.0564	0.0096	***	0.0700	0.0369	*	−0.0614	0.0100	***	0.0432	0.0590
HHI	Herfindahl Index bank concentration	1.9553	1.7458		−1.3152	1.0251		0.7261	1.8758		−0.9746	1.1788
Rec rate	Recovery rate (percentage)							0.0144	0.0074	*	−0.0042	0.0071
_const	Constant	1.9595	0.3550	***	0.9114	0.5419	*	0.9518	0.6235		1.4048	1.0058

Variables presented in the table include: dummy for bank loan obtained; dummies for firm size (micro, small, medium and large firms); dummy for age (less than 2 years, 2–5 years, 5–9 years); change in turnover and change in profit (reduction −1, unchanged 0, increase, 1); dummies for sources of finance (use of retained earnings, trade credit or leasing; increase in equity); Bank Lending Survey index; GDP growth; inflation rate; unemployment rate; Herfindahl-Hirschman Index of bank concentration; coefficients for recovery rate

Sig.: * <.1; ** <.05; *** <.01

becomes not significant in strong countries. Interestingly, REC_RATE is significant and positively related to obtaining a loan only in the weak economic context. The results suggest that only in this economic context do banks rely on their capability to recover at least part of their loan in insolvency proceedings when it comes to deciding whether to provide a loan.

2.5.2 Robustness Checks

The analysis presented above provides clear results. Nevertheless, some additional robustness checks are needed before making any generalization.

The first robustness check investigates whether our results are affected by the sample selection bias. In order to deal with this issue, we re-estimate the regressions by relying on the Heckman sample selection model (Heckman 1979). We model the selection process using variables that measure the change in turnover, the change in profit and whether the firm belongs to a group. The results—elaborated using a Heckman probit estimation (Heckman 1979)—are not reported here. All specifications are significant. Additionally, there are no major changes in the sign and the significance level with respect to the regressions presented above. Overall, the results strongly confirm all previous findings in terms of support of the hypotheses.

In the second robustness check, we re-estimate the regressions using a different econometric approach, namely probit regression instead of logit regression. This allows us to check, whether our results are sensitive to the econometric approach used in our estimations. The results are not reported here. Again, there are no changes in the significance and the sign of the variables entered in the regression.

In the third robustness check, we re-estimate the standard errors using a bootstrap estimation of the standard errors (Efron and Tibshirani 1998). Also in this case, there is no change in the significance of the variables entered in the regressions. Finally, we re-estimate the specification including dummy variables that identify the industries (results not reported). Once again, there are no changes with respect to our original results.

To sum up, our robustness checks suggest that our original findings are robust to sample selection, alternative specifications, alternative independent variables and the different estimation techniques.

2.6 Discussion

In Act 1, Scene 3, of *Hamlet* Polonius suggests to his son Laertes, who is about to embark for Paris:

> Neither a borrower nor a lender be;
> For loan oft loses both itself and friend
> And borrowing dulls the edge of husbandry. (Shakespeare 1987)

So, was Polonius right? Or in other words: Are firms right to refrain from applying for a loan based on the recovery rate creditors achieve in case of the firm's insolvency? And, are banks right to refrain from providing credit to firms based on the recovery rate the legal system grants them?

Regarding borrowers, our results suggest that a legal context that increases a bank's ability to credibly commit to liquidate a firm in case the latter defaults on its loan reduces the firm's desire for bank finance. Interestingly, this finding mainly applies when firms operate in economically strong contexts: looking at the analysis for the split dataset, we discover that in strong countries the recovery rate adversely affects the demand for credit, while this variable is not significant in weak countries. If recovery rates are high and creditor protection is thus strict, firms do not have a lot of room to manoeuvre in terms of "escaping" the repayment of the loan. As a consequence, firms might avoid taking out loans. This avoidance will, however, only be a possible strategy when firms have alternative solutions to finance their operations. In weak economic contexts, these solutions might be limited, which might in turn erase the negative impact of the recovery rate on loan applications.

Thus, in terms of Polonius' suggestion not to be a borrower, we conclude that it depends. If the firm operates in a strong economy, it might be better for the firm not to borrow if the bank's expected recovery rate does not leave them room to renegotiate the terms of the loan in times of financial distress. However, in the weak economies, firms often cannot be picky and therefore they do not align their financing strategy with the recovery rate prevalent in the respective country.

Regarding lenders, our results generally suggest that recovery rate does not impact a bank's lending decision. However, looking at our findings for the split dataset, we see that this is only true when banks operate in a strong economic context. In weak economic contexts, however, we find a positive relationship between the recovery rate and the bank's lending decision. Thus, banks seem to only partially exploit the advantage conveyed by high recovery rates: the bank's behaviour might reflect a greater necessity to be able to rely on the legal system in case of a borrower's default when the country's economic situation is generally weak and the likelihood of a firm to fail is higher. This is because the recovery rate provides greater certainty to recover at least part of the outstanding loan in insolvency proceedings. At the same time, the positive impact of the recovery rate on the bank's lending decision can also be a stimulus for the economy by encouraging banks to provide loans to young firms.

In terms of Polonius' suggestion that one not be a lender, we once more conclude that it depends. If the bank operates in a weak economy with a well-functioning creditor protection, it can make its lending decision and rely on the country's creditor protection to ensure that it will at least receive a part of the loan if the firm becomes insolvent. In a strong economy, however, a bank makes its lending decision irrespective of its ability to recover the loan.

Conclusion

Our research investigates the impact of recovery rates—i.e., the percentage of the original debt recovered at the end of insolvency proceedings—on a firm's decision to borrow and a bank's decision to lend. The findings suggest that high recovery rates are negatively related to a firm's decision to borrow but do not have any influence on a bank's decision to lend. However, the findings are not as straightforward as they appear at first sight since the role played by recovery rates differs in strong and weak countries; whereas high recovery rates are negatively associated with the firm's loan application only in strong countries, they turn to have a positive impact on the bank's lending decision in weak countries. These results are robust to a set of econometric tests we pursued.

Our findings have interesting implications for firms, banks and regulators. As far as firms are concerned, the results show that firms are able to benefit in countries with a weak economic environment but well-functioning creditor protection. In this case, firms are more likely to obtain credit, as banks consider the higher recovery rates when making the lending decision. However, firms do not realize this benefit as well-functioning creditor protection does not impact their decision to apply for a loan in weak countries. At the same time, firms refrain from applying for a loan in strong countries with well-functioning creditor protection since they fear the loss of renegotiating power in financially challenging times, even though banks do not consider recovery rates when making their lending decision.

As far as banks are concerned, the results suggest that banks only partially exploit the advantage provided by a well-functioning creditor protection. This is because in the case of strong countries, banks' decisions to lend do not appear to be affected by the level of protection they enjoy, even though banks could reduce the perceived risk by considering recovery rates.

Our findings illustrate the difficult position policymakers may have. If they improve insolvency proceedings in weak countries, they will be able to advance firms' credit access, but they will face the problem of firms being less likely to apply for a loan. If they improve insolvency proceedings in strong countries, they will discourage firms from applying for a loan, even though banks do not consider these improvements when taking the lending decision.

Our research presents some limitations. We examine only European firms because of the characteristics of the dataset used. It would be interesting to replicate the research in other areas to verify the robustness of the role played by our variable around the world. Enlargement of the dataset could also allow for an examination if our variable plays the same role in developing and developed economies.

Notwithstanding the limitations of the dataset and context, the study indicates that recovery rate might play a more important and complex role in lending relationships than has been acknowledged.

References

Bae, K. H., & Goyal, V. K. (2009). Creditor rights, enforcement, and bank loans. *Journal of Finance, 64*, 823–860.

Beck, T., Demirgüc-Kunt, A., & Levine, R. (2005). Law and firms' access to finance. *World Bank Policy Research Working Paper 3194, 7*(1), 211–252.

Berger, A. N., & Frame, S. W. (2007). Small business credit scoring and credit availability. *Journal of Small Business Management, 45*(1), 5–22.

Berger, A. N., & Udell, G. F. (1995). Relationship lending and the lines of credit in small firm finance. *Journal of Business, 68*(3), 351–381.

Berger, A. N., Klapper, L. F., & Udell, G. F. (2001). The ability of banks to lend to informationally opaque small business. *Journal of Banking & Finance, 25*(12), 2127–2167.

Berkowitz, J., & White, M. J. (2004). Bankruptcy and small firms' access to credit. *Rand Journal of Economics, 35*(1), 69–84.

Carbó-Valverde, S., Rodríguez-Fernández, F., & Udell, G. F. (2009). Bank market power and SME financing constraints. *Review of Finance, 13*, 309–340.

Cassar, G. (2004). The financing of business start-ups. *Journal of Business Venturing, 19*(2), 261–283.

Cipolla, C. M. (1994). Uomini Duri. In C. M. Cipolla (Ed.), *Tre Storie Extravaganti*. Il Mulino: Bologna.

Cipolla, C. M. (2002). *Storia economica dell'Europa pre-industriale*. Bologna: Il Mulino.

Cressy, R. (2006). Determinants of small firms survival and growth. In M. Casson et al. (Eds.), *The Oxford handbook of entrepreneurship* (pp. 161–193). Oxford: Oxford University Press.

Demirguc-Kunt, A., & Maksimovic, V. (1999). Institutions, financial markets, and firm debt maturity. *Journal of Financial Economics, 54*, 295–336.

Diamond, D. W. (1984). Financial intermediation and delegated monitoring. *Review of Economic Studies, 51*(3), 393–414.

Efron, B., & Tibshirani, R. T. (1998). *An introduction to the bootstrap*. Boca Raton (FL): Chapman and Hall CRC.

Esty, B. C., & Megginson, W. L. (2003). Creditor rights, enforcement, and debt ownership structure: Evidence from the global syndicated loan market. *Journal of Financial and Quantitative Analysis, 38*, 37–59.

Haselmann, R., & Wachtel, P. (2010). Institutions and bank behavior: Legal environment, legal perception and the composition of bank lending. *Journal of Money, Credit and Banking, 42*, 965–984.

Haselmann, R., Pistor, K., & Vig, V. (2010). How laws affect lending. *Review of Financial Studies, 23*(2), 549–580.

Heckman, J. J. (1979). Selection bias as a specification error. *Econometrica, 47*(1), 153–161.

Hosmer, D. W., & Lemeshow, S. (2000). *Applied logistic regresson*. New York: Wiley.

Jappelli, T., Pagano, M., & Bianco, M. (2005). Courts and banks: Effects of judicial enforcement on credit markets. *Journal of Money, Credit and Banking, 37*, 223–244.

La Porta, R., Lopez-de-Silanes, F., Shleifer, A., & Vishny, R. W. (1997). Legal determinants of external finance. *Journal of Finance, 52*, 1131–1150.

Laeven, L., & Majnoni, G. (2005). Does judicial efficiency lower the cost of credit? *Journal of Banking and Finance, 29*, 1791–1812.

Liberti, J. R., & Mian, A. (2010). Collateral spread and financial development. *The Journal of Finance, 65*(1), 147–177.

Martinelli, C. (1997). Small firms, borrowing constraints, and reputation. *Journal of Economic Behavior & Organization, 33*, 91–105.

Mason, C., & Stark, M. (2004). What do investors look for in a business plan? A comparison of the investment criteria of bankers,venture capitalists and business angels. *International Small Business Journal, 22*(3), 227–248.

Moro, A., Fink, M., & Kautonen, T. (2014). How do banks assess entrepreneurial competence? Public data vs. voluntary information disclosure. *International Small Business Journal, 35*(5), 525–544.

Myers, S. C., & Majluf, N. S. (1984). Corporate finance and investment decisions when firms have information investors do not have. *Journal of Financial Economics, 13*, 187–221.

Neuberger, D., Pedergnana, M., & Räthke-Döppner, S. (2008). Concentration of banking relationships in Switzerland: The result of firm structure or banking market structure? *Journal of Financial Services Research, 33*(2), 101–126.

Petersen, M. A., & Rajan, R. G. (1994). The benefits of lending relationships: Evidence from small business data. *Journal of Finance, 49*(1), 3–37.

Qian, J., & Strahan, P. E. (2007). How laws and institutions shape financial contracts: The case of bank loans. *Journal of Finance, 62*, 2803–2834.

Shakespeare, W. (1987). *Hamlet*. Oxford: Oxford University Press.

3

Legal-Institutional Environment, Social Capital and the Cost of Bank Financing for SMEs: Evidence from the Euro Area

Emma Galli, Danilo V. Mascia, and Stefania P.S. Rossi

3.1 Introduction and Review of the Literature

Access conditions to bank credit in Europe play a decisive role in the survival of small- and medium-sized enterprises (SMEs). The economic literature points out that obstacles to credit access for SMEs mainly derive from their difficulty in producing high quality collaterals and from the opacity of their creditworthiness (Ayadi and Gadi 2013; Öztürk and Mrkaic 2014). The lack of transparency increases asymmetric information, which

---

JEL classification codes: G20, G30, G32

E. Galli
Department of Social and Economic Sciences, Sapienza University of Rome, Rome, Italy

D.V. Mascia • S.P. S. Rossi (✉)
Department of Economics and Business, University of Cagliari, Cagliari, Italy
e-mail: stefania.rossi@unica.it

S.P.S. Rossi (ed.), *Access to Bank Credit and SME Financing*,
Palgrave Macmillan Studies in Banking and Financial Institutions,
DOI 10.1007/978-3-319-41363-1_3

tends to be more severe during times of economic crises and leads to credit rationing and suboptimal lending to viable SMEs. Therefore, factors such as the legal-institutional environment and the quality of social capital may be crucial in increasing level of trust in the credit market, strengthening the relationship between creditors and borrowers, and consequently reducing the cost of financing. In this chapter, we address these issues with respect to European SMEs by using the European Central Bank (ECB) Survey on the Access to Finance of Enterprises (SAFE).[1] Specifically, we employ data on eleven major economies of the euro area for the period 2009–2013.

The literature documents that the efficiency of the enforcement of legal rights (La Porta et al. 1997; Qian and Strahan 2007; Djankov et al. 2008; Maresch et al. 2015) and the competitiveness of the banking market (Cavalluzzo et al. 2002; Alesina et al. 2013) affect banks' lending decisions and thereby the cost of funding for SMEs. Some studies investigate the impact of a country's legal system on the terms of credit—such as size, maturity and interest rate of a loan agreement; however, these studies do not directly discuss whether firms are able to obtain bank loans at lower costs (Laeven and Majnoni 2005; Qian and Strahan 2007; Bae and Goyal 2009). Recently, Maresch et al. (2015) investigated the impact of the legal environment (i.e., creditor rights protection and judicial enforcement) on credit access (i.e., whether or not a firm obtained the credit it applied for) by using SAFE data related to firms chartered in eleven European countries. They used an objective measure of credit constraints that was not based on firms' perceived difficulties in access to finance. Rather, by employing rejected loan applications and other measures of credit constraints, they found that the better the judicial enforcement system (reduced costs, reduced time, limited number of procedures) and the higher the creditor protection (high overall strength of the legal system, high property rights protection), the lower the probability that the firms were credit constrained.

Another strand of literature stresses the importance of social capital[2] in the credit market. By increasing the level of trust and reducing the

---

[1] The Survey is available at: https://www.ecb.europa.eu/stats/money/surveys/sme/html/index.en.html.

[2] Social capital can be defined as the advantages and opportunities that people obtain through membership in certain communities or as the resources of individuals that emerge through social

asymmetric information characterizing credit contracts, the existence of social capital makes access to bank loans easier and less costly (see Uzzi 1999; Guiso et al. 2004; Ostergaard et al. 2009; Guiso et al. 2013) and diminishes the use of real guarantees for mortgages (Moro and Fink 2013; Mistrulli and Vacca 2015). Indeed, on the borrower side, social capital affects individual behaviour, thus causing the firm to be less inclined to engage in opportunistic conduct that is against moral and social rules. On the creditor side, social capital facilitates the collection of soft information, which in turn reduces adverse selection and moral hazard. Moreover, by stimulating peer monitoring and other social collateral, social capital more efficiently allocates resources in the credit market, thereby reducing transaction and credit costs, especially for small firms. In areas where social capital is high, the access to bank credit is easier for people and firms that generally use informal financing channels, such as friends and families (Guiso et al. 2004), and the ability to reimburse the mortgage is higher (Guiso et al. 2013). By controlling for financial viability before and after an unexpected shock, such as the 2008 financial crisis, Mistrulli and Vacca (2015) and Lozzi and Mistrulli (2014) show that social capital, together with business networking, played an important role in increasing trust and reducing asymmetric information. Indeed, in areas characterized by high social capital the negative effect of the 2008 financial crisis on credit access was significantly less pronounced. Alesina et al. (2013) consider social capital across different provinces in Italy and find that interest rates are lower where social capital is higher. Finally, other studies have emphasized the role of cooperative banks in reducing asymmetric information between banks and borrowers, and consequently in increasing trust and cooperation in credit markets. More specifically, the role of cooperative banks is more relevant and the quality of the credit supply is greater where social capital is higher, given that the latter positively affects cooperation in credit markets by reducing the free-rider phenomenon (Albertazzi and Marchetti 2010; Catturani et al. 2014).

Our study combines two strands of the literature, one that considers the effects of legal-institutional factors and the other the impact of social

ties. For a wide discussion of the different dimensions of social capital, see Coleman (1994) and more recently Putnam (2001); De Blasio et al. (2012).

capital in credit markets, in order to examine the determinants (other than the economic and financial aspects) of funding cost for SMEs in the euro area.

Our hypotheses are aimed at verifying whether, in countries characterized by an efficient legal system, a competitive bank market and higher social capital, SMEs can benefit from a better cost of funding. Indeed, a higher level of trust, which reduces the asymmetries in credit contracts, makes it easier for lenders to control for firms' risk and reduces the cost of bank financing. After controlling for standard firm characteristics as well as for micro and macro features, our empirical investigations support these hypotheses.

The rest of this chapter is organized as follows. In Sect. 3.2, we present the data and the methodology. In Sect. 3.3, we discuss our empirical results. Sect. 3.4 draws the main conclusions.

3.2 Data and Methodology

3.2.1 Data

Our main source of data is represented by the SAFE, which is jointly administrated by the ECB and the European Commission and conducted every six months (so-called 'waves'). Starting from 2009, this survey gathers information about SMEs access to finance as well as a series of the firms' characteristics (e.g., size, age, sector). Non-financial firms are interviewed; however, enterprises in agriculture, public administration and financial services are intentionally excluded from the survey. The enterprises in the sample are randomly selected from the Dun & Bradstreet business register. The sample is stratified by country, firm size and activity (inter alia, Moritz et al., 2016).

Although the SAFE is biennially extended to a wider number of countries (even outside the euro area), we limit our analysis to the eleven largest euro area economies (i.e., Austria, Belgium, France, Finland, Germany,

Greece, Italy, Ireland, the Netherlands, Portugal and Spain).[3] Such countries pertain to different European macro areas, where divergences in micro- and macroeconomic features as well as in the institutional and social environment are not negligible. Table 3.1 shows the number of sample observations according to the various waves that were considered in our analysis. The distribution of our observations by country is presented in Table 3.2, with France, Spain and Italy displaying the highest values.

Table 3.1 Observations by wave

Wave	Freq.	%
1	1519	6.81
2	1586	7.11
3	1857	8.33
4	2514	11.28
5	2352	10.55
6	2545	11.42
7	2427	10.89
8	2503	11.23
9	2535	11.37
10	2457	11.02
Total	22,295	100.00

Table 3.2 Observations by country

Country name	Freq.	%
Austria	1249	5.60
Belgium	1171	5.25
Finland	706	3.17
France	3897	17.48
Germany	2919	13.09
Greece	1144	5.13
Ireland	984	4.41
Italy	4251	19.07
Netherlands	729	3.27
Portugal	1134	5.09
Spain	4111	18.44
Total	22,295	100.00

[3] In this respect it is worth noting that the ECB intentionally excludes from the survey the smallest countries (i.e., those representing less than 3% of the total number of employees in the euro area), as they would only marginally affect the results.

3.2.2 Dependent Variable

To test our hypothesis, we rely on information about price terms and conditions of bank financing (specifically, interest rates) available at the level of respondent firms.[4]

More specifically, our dependent variable is qualitative and ordinal and is based on the question:

> *'For each of the above-mentioned terms and conditions, could you please indicate whether they were increased, remained unchanged or were decreased over the past 6 months?'*

The answers to this question in the SAFE dataset were initially coded 1/2/3 for increased/unchanged/decreased, respectively. However, we inverted the original coding as 1/2/3 for decreased/unchanged/increased to give an easier and more intuitive interpretation to our dependent variable. In fact, since the labelling is ordinal, any monotonic transformation of the labels gives an equally valid labelling (Öztürk and Mrkaic 2014).

3.2.3 Empirical Methodology, Key Variables and Controls

As described in Sect. 3.1, we investigate whether the country's legal-institutional and social environment has an impact on the level of trust in credit markets and reduces the asymmetric information in financial contracts, consequently affecting the cost of SME financing as measured by the level of interest rates. As our dependent variable is qualitative and ordinal and the covariates are both continuous and categorical variables, we use an ordered logit model (see Öztürk and Mrkaic 2014).

More formally, the general specification of our model is the following:

$$\Pr(LIR_{it}) = F\left(\theta LI_{jt} + \phi SC_{jt} + \beta X_{it} + \gamma Q_{it} + \delta Z_{jt} + \mu T_t\right) \quad (3.1)$$

[4] The SAFE also collects information on the cost of financing other than interest rates (e.g., fees and commissions) and some non-price terms and conditions of bank financing such as (i) available size of loan or credit line; (ii) available maturity of the loan; (iii) collateral requirements; (iv) others (e.g., loan covenants and required guarantees) that are not investigated here.

for $t = 1, \ldots, T$, indicating the time period; $i = 1, \ldots, N$, representing the number of firms interviewed; and $j = 1, \ldots, J$, denoting the different countries involved. Therefore, the subscripts i and t refer to firm i at time t, whereas the subscripts j and t refer to country j at time t. LIR_{it} indicates the change in the level of interest rates experienced by each firm. LI_{jt} is a vector accounting for a set of legal-institutional features, and SC_{jt} is a vector of variables that proxies for the social capital.

X_{it} is a vector of standard firm controls such as size, age and sector. Q_{it} is a vector of additional controls of the firm accounting for the demand of credit and the level of indebtedness. Z_{jt} is a vector of macroeconomic controls, that is, GDP growth, inflation and unemployment rate. T_t controls for time effects across the observed period. All variable descriptions and sources are provided in detail in Table A.3.1 in the Appendix.

Specifically, we would like to test two major hypotheses:

1. In countries where the efficiency of judicial systems and/or the enforcement of law is lower SMEs are more likely to face, *ceteris paribus*, an increase in the cost of bank financing; and
2. In countries where the social capital is higher SMEs are more likely to obtain a better cost of funding.

Therefore, the coefficients of our variables of interest are the θ, which refer to the legal-institutional features, and the φ, which refer to the social capital indicators.

Our hypothesis on the effects of the legal-institutional context on the level of interest rates would imply a positive θ for the proxies of the efficiency of a country's legal system (namely, the costs to resolve insolvencies, briefly called 'cost of claim', and the number of steps to enforce a contract, identified as 'procedures number') and for the concentration of the banking system, all of which are supposed to positively affect the levels of interest rates. Indeed, a high level of the cost of claim and a high number of procedures to enforce a contract may be perceived by banks as a source of risk, since both imply complications and delays in loans being paid back in the case of litigations. In this respect it is worth noting that Italy, Ireland and the Netherlands are characterized by high levels of cost of claims compared to the rest of the euro area countries (see Fig. 3.1).

Not surprisingly, Italy also stands out for the high number of steps needed to enforce a contract, together with Spain, Greece and Portugal (see Fig. 3.2). The concentration of the banking system is also supposed to lead to higher levels of interest rates, since the lower the competition among banks, the higher the incentives to keep interests high—thus penalizing firms. Figure 3.3 shows the Herfindahl-Hirschman Index (HHI) of bank concentration by country and year, with Finland and the Netherlands being characterized by the highest concentration levels. Interestingly, it also highlights a steep increase of the HHI in Greece in 2013, which captures the important wave of bank mergers undertaken because of the ongoing Greek crisis.

As for the second hypothesis, we would anticipate a negative φ for our proxies of social capital since a higher level of trust reduces the asymmetric information in credit contracts, thus lowering the expected cost of bank financing. As highlighted in the literature, measuring social capital is not an easy task (OECD 2001). Social capital is usually based on

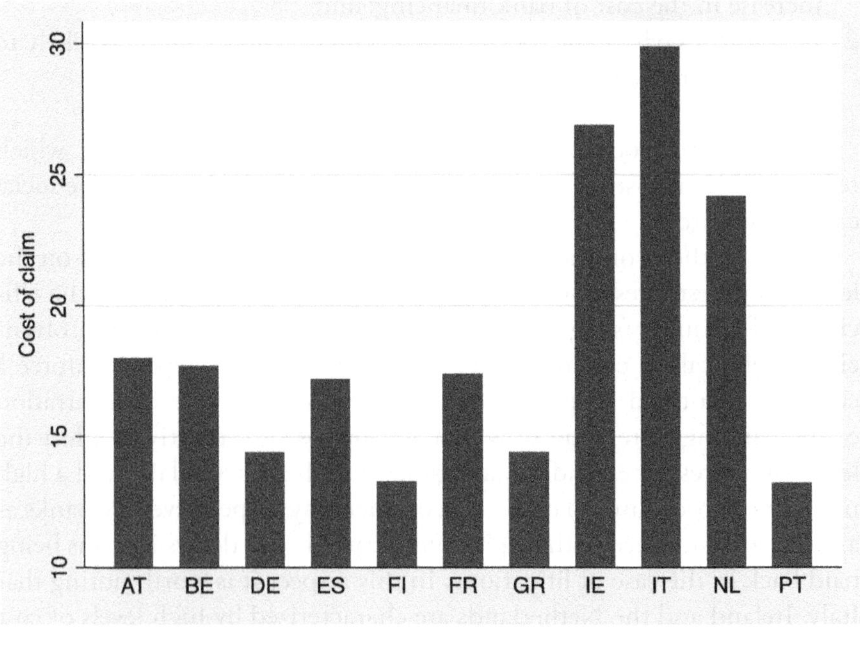

Fig. 3.1 Cost of claim

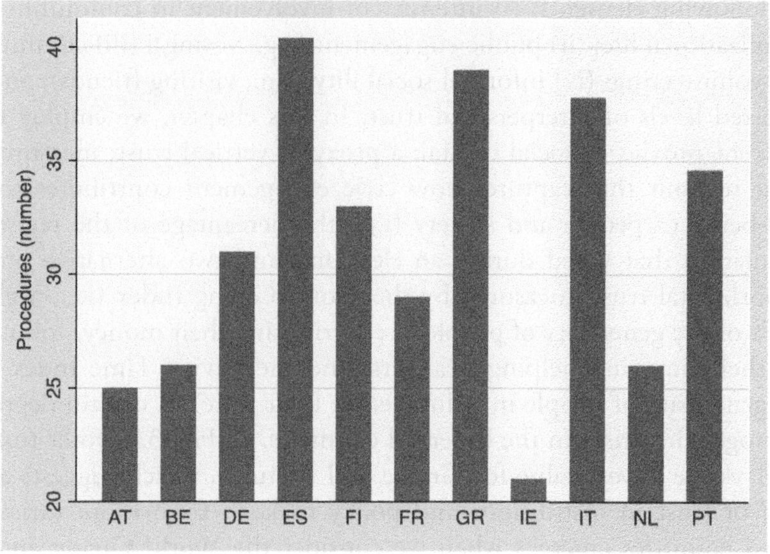

Fig. 3.2 Number of procedures

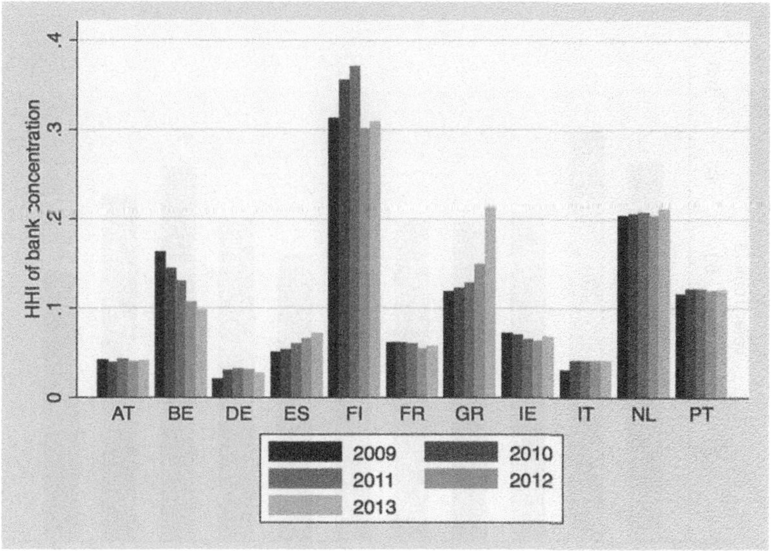

Fig. 3.3 HHI of bank concentration

the following elements: (i) intensity of involvement in community and organizational life; (ii) public engagement (e.g., voting); (iii) community and volunteering; (iv) informal sociability (e.g., visiting friends); and (v) reported levels of interpersonal trust. In this chapter, we employ three different proxies of social capital: a proxy of vertical trust, measured by voter turnout that captures how civic engagement contributes to the well-being of people and society (i.e., the percentage of the registered population that voted during an election); and two alternative proxies of horizontal trust, measured by the World Giving Index (i.e., a global index of the generosity of people in contributing their money, volunteering their time and helping strangers) and the Giving Time Index (i.e., the generosity of people in volunteering their time). A certain degree of heterogeneity arises in the observed countries. In Fig. 3.4, voter turnout displays the lowest value for Greece and Portugal, which suggests a low level of trust in institutions and policy makers. Even more variability across countries emerges when we consider the World Giving and the Giving Time indexes in Figs. 3.5 and 3.6, respectively. Here, data show that Greece, Portugal and Spain present the lowest level of generosity, while the Netherlands and Ireland are ranked as the best in our sample.

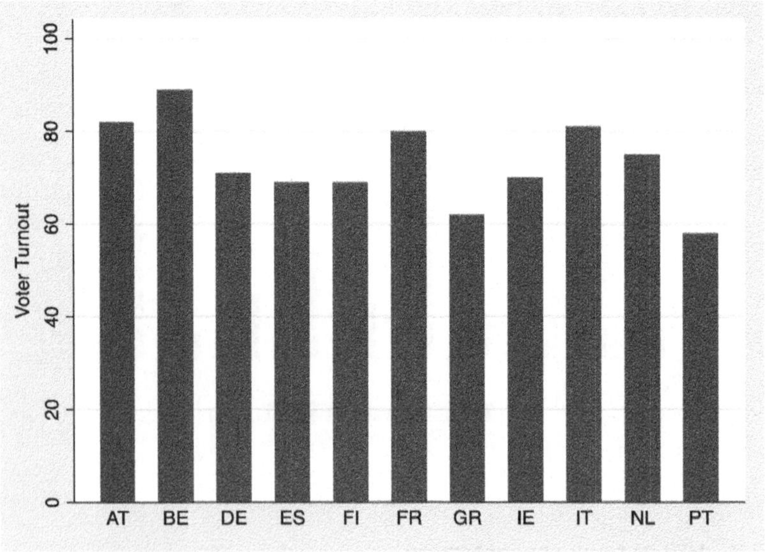

Fig. 3.4 Voter turnout

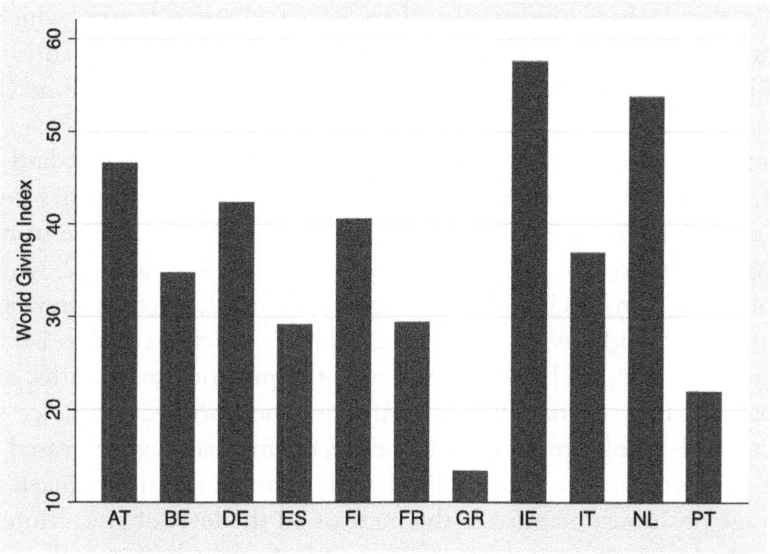

Fig. 3.5 World Giving Index

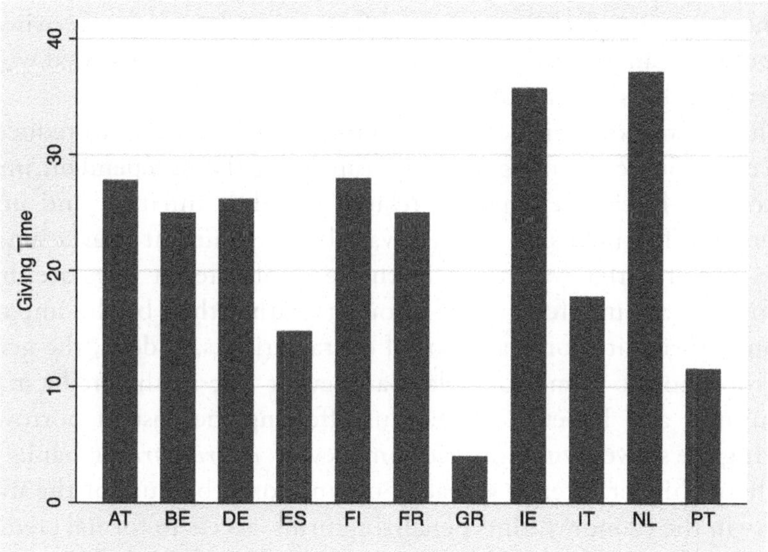

Fig. 3.6 Giving Time Index

We also include the market share of cooperative banks, which (as pointed out in literature) are expected to increase credit quantity and quality, given also the mutualistic nature of such organizations (Lang et al., 2016).

For the other covariates included in our model, the standard firm controls (vector X_{it}) and the additional firm-level characteristics (vector Q_{it}) are meant to reduce sources of endogeneity that may arise from the analysis. In particular, we include two dummies: 'leverage up', which is equal to 1 if firms declare that leverage has increased over the previous six months, and 0 otherwise; and 'leverage down', which is equal to 1 if firms declare that leverage has decreased over the previous six months, and 0 otherwise. They capture how a change in the borrower's balance sheet affects the level of interest rates. We expect firms that have increased their debt-to-asset ratios to be penalized more than those that reduced their leverage positions, because of the increase in the level of risk. Moreover, it is important to control for the demand of credit by firms. Therefore, we build two dummies: 'demand up', which takes the value of 1 when the firm has increased its demand for external credit in the previous six months, and 0 otherwise; and 'demand down', which takes the value of 1 when there is a decline in external finance needs, and 0 otherwise. We suppose that an increased need for external funding is associated with an increase in the interest rates.

The macroeconomic controls (vector Z_{jt}) are expected to reduce the potential source of endogeneity by capturing the independent impact of country-level heterogeneity related to GDP, inflation and unemployment. The inclusion of these variables is aimed at alleviating possible concerns that variations in the level of interest rates are driven by macroeconomic features of a country rather than by the impact of a country's institutional and social characteristics. Indeed, the general macroeconomic framework plays a relevant role in the credit market (Bouvatier and Lepetit 2008), thus affecting the cost of borrowing. During the slowdown of the economic cycle, *ceteris paribus*, banks tend to charge higher interest spreads on bank loans because of the uncertainty in the economy, thus penalizing firms' access to formal credit. In contrast, during booms, firms are more likely to benefit from a lower level of interest rates. Inflation and unemployment, on the other hand,

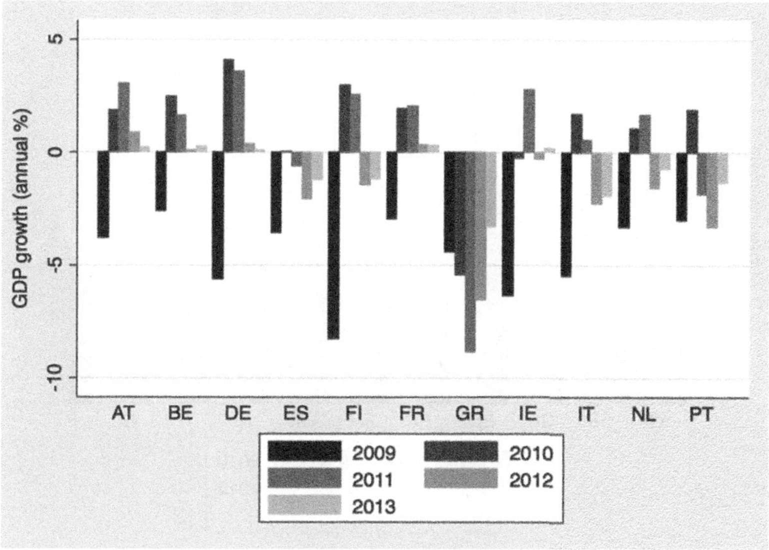

Fig. 3.7 Annual percentage change of GDP growth

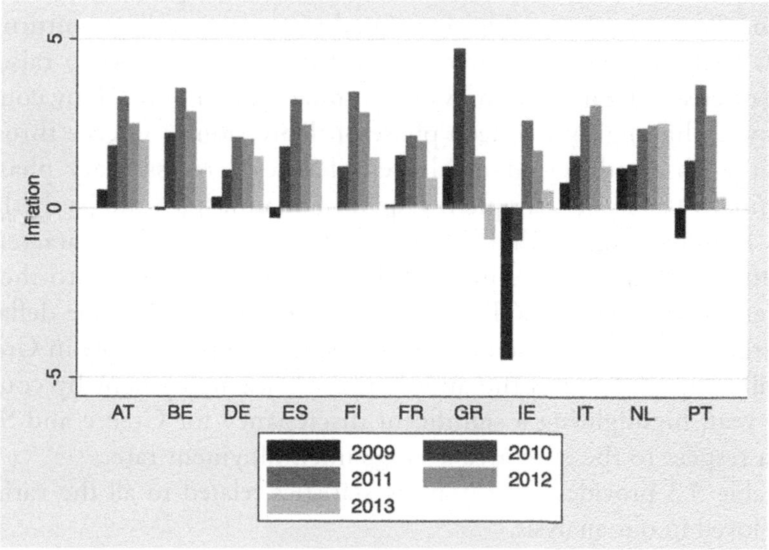

Fig. 3.8 Inflation rate

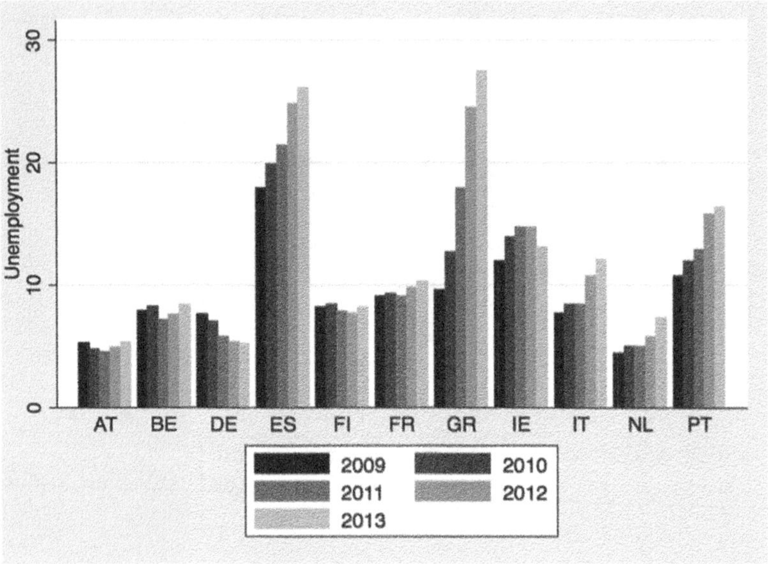

Fig. 3.9 Unemployment rate

are expected to positively affect the cost of financing for firms. Indeed, an increase in both variables is a signal of an economic downturn and is, as such, a potential source of risk that induces banks to raise the cost of credit. Figure 3.7 shows the annual growth of GDP by country and year, highlighting a deep phase of depression in Greece throughout the observed period. It also emphasizes a recessionary phase in the final years of our sample for Spain, Finland, Italy, the Netherlands and Portugal. Again, the final years of our sample are characterized by an important decline in the inflation rate with respect to the 2% target pursued by the ECB (see Fig. 3.8). Interestingly, some deflation emerges as well, in particular, in the last year of our sample in Greece. Finally, Fig. 3.9 shows the annual rate of unemployment by country and year, highlighting a significant discrepancy for Greece and Spain with respect to the euro area average unemployment rate.

Table 3.3 provides the summary statistics related to all the variables employed in our analysis.

Table 3.3 Summary statistics

Variable	Obs.	Mean	Median	St. Dev.	p1	p99
Dependent variable						
Level of interest rates (LIR)	22,295	2.292	2.000	0.760	1.000	3.000
Key variables						
Cost of claim	22,295	19.543	17.400	5.815	13.000	29.900
Procedures number	22,295	33.093	33.000	5.839	21.000	41.000
Concentration	22,295	0.075	0.057	0.062	0.021	0.355
Cooperatives	22,295	23.770	20.600	18.189	0.000	60.300
Voter turnout	22,295	74.573	75.000	7.645	58.000	89.000
World Giving Index	22,295	34.956	33.000	10.358	13.000	60.000
Giving Time Index	22,295	21.316	22.000	8.017	3.000	38.000
Firm-level controls						
Demand up	22,295	0.405	0.000	0.491	0.000	1.000
Demand down	22,295	0.122	0.000	0.328	0.000	1.000
Leverage up	22,295	0.331	0.000	0.470	0.000	1.000
Leverage down	22,295	0.275	0.000	0.447	0.000	1.000
Other firm-level characteristics						
Micro	22,295	0.259	0.000	0.438	0.000	1.000
Small	22,295	0.340	0.000	0.474	0.000	1.000
Medium	22,295	0.302	0.000	0.459	0.000	1.000
Very recent	22,295	0.018	0.000	0.132	0.000	1.000
Recent	22,295	0.062	0.000	0.241	0.000	1.000
Old	22,295	0.121	0.000	0.327	0.000	1.000
Construction	22,295	0.099	0.000	0.299	0.000	1.000
Manufacturing	22,295	0.241	0.000	0.428	0.000	1.000
Wholesale/Retail	22,295	0.296	0.000	0.457	0.000	1.000
Macroeconomic controls						
GDP growth	22,295	−0.614	0.014	2.627	−8.864	4.091
Inflation	22,295	1.745	1.800	1.102	−0.921	4.713
Unemployment	22,295	11.789	9.300	6.177	4.600	27.500

3.3 Results

The empirical results of our estimations are presented in Table 3.4, where we report the coefficients of the ordered logit estimates of Eq. (3.1). We rely on a sample of 22,295 firm-level observations pertaining to SMEs in eleven euro-area countries, obtained by pooling together the first ten waves of the SAFE (from the first half of 2009 to the second half of 2013).

In Table 3.4, model specifications vary across the different columns for the progressive inclusion of our key variables. Since the ordered logistic coefficients cannot be read as normal elasticities like the OLS coefficients, we only comment here on the related signs of the various regressors.

The empirical evidence supports our hypotheses. The positive and significant coefficients of the legal covariates, namely the 'cost of claim' and the 'procedures number', show that the cost of financing for SMEs is more likely to increase in countries characterized by a lower efficiency of judicial systems, where the costs to resolve insolvencies and the steps to enforce a contract are higher. We also find a positive and highly significant coefficient of the bank concentration index, suggesting that firms are more likely to experience increased costs of financing in countries characterized by a higher concentration of the banking industry. As far as social capital is concerned, we find a negative and significant coefficient for each of the employed proxies signalling that, all else being equal, the cost of bank financing decreases when SMEs belong to countries characterized by a high level of trust. More specifically, the proxy for civic engagement turns to be always negative, in line with expectations. Moreover, the generosity indexes that we use alternatively in columns 4 and 5, because of the high correlation, present the expected negative sign. Consistent with our hypothesis, the coefficient of the market share of cooperative banks is negative and highly significant as well.

Now we look at the other variables used in our model to control for some sources of potential endogeneity at the micro level (firm characteristics, level of risk, demand) and at the macro level (GDP, unemployment, inflation). The dummy 'leverage up' shows a positive and significant sign, suggesting that firms which have increased their leverage over the previous six months are more likely to face an increase in interest rates compared to firms that reported no change or a decrease in the leverage ratios. Consistent with this evidence, the dummy 'leverage down' reports a negative sign, confirming that SMEs that have decreased their leverage over the previous six months are more likely to experience a decrease in the cost of financing. It is also worth noting that the sign of the dummy 'demand up' is positive and highly significant, suggesting

Table 3.4 Impact of legal-institutional and social factors on interest rates

	Change in the level of interest rates				
	(1)	(2)	(3)	(4)	(5)
Cost of claim	0.047***	0.050***	0.069***	0.082***	0.072***
	(0.00)	(0.00)	(0.00)	(0.00)	(0.00)
Procedures number	0.011***	0.013***	0.006*	−0.004	−0.002
	(0.00)	(0.00)	(0.00)	(0.00)	(0.00)
Concentration		1.044***	0.629***	0.699***	0.722***
		(0.22)	(0.23)	(0.23)	(0.23)
Cooperatives			−0.002***	−0.004***	−0.002**
			(0.00)	(0.00)	(0.00)
Voter turnout			−0.028***	−0.034***	−0.029***
			(0.00)	(0.00)	(0.00)
World giving index				−0.012***	
				(0.00)	
Giving time index					−0.009**
					(0.00)
Standard firm-level controls	YES	YES	YES	YES	YES
Demand up	0.167***	0.160***	0.168***	0.170***	0.169***
	(0.03)	(0.03)	(0.03)	(0.03)	(0.03)
Demand down	0.002	−0.002	−0.005	0.001	−0.003
	(0.04)	(0.04)	(0.04)	(0.04)	(0.04)
Leverage up	0.235***	0.229***	0.243***	0.237***	0.243***
	(0.03)	(0.03)	(0.03)	(0.03)	(0.03)
Leverage down	−0.077**	−0.080**	−0.074**	−0.072**	−0.073**
	(0.03)	(0.03)	(0.03)	(0.03)	(0.03)
GDP growth	−0.087***	−0.075***	−0.039***	−0.017	−0.029**
	(0.01)	(0.01)	(0.01)	(0.01)	(0.01)
Inflation	0.229***	0.223***	0.291***	0.312***	0.297***
	(0.02)	(0.02)	(0.03)	(0.03)	(0.03)
Unemployment	0.092***	0.092***	0.083***	0.078***	0.083***
	(0.00)	(0.00)	(0.00)	(0.00)	(0.00)
Constant 1	1.685***	1.869***	−0.260	−1.285***	−0.756**
	(0.12)	(0.12)	(0.23)	(0.30)	(0.31)
Constant 2	3.518***	3.706***	1.587***	0.564*	1.092***
	(0.12)	(0.13)	(0.23)	(0.30)	(0.31)
Observations	22,295	22,295	22,295	22,295	22,295
Pseudo R-squared	0.100	0.1000	0.103	0.104	0.103
LR chi2	4579	4601	4748	4779	4754
Prob > chi2	0.00	0.00	0.00	0.00	0.00
Time dummies	YES	YES	YES	YES	YES

*** indicates significance at the 1% level, ** at the 5% level, and * at the 10% level.

that SMEs that have increased their need for financing in the previous six months are more likely to face an increase in interest rates. Although not shown, our models also control for other firm characteristics (i.e., size, age and sector). Interestingly, all the macroeconomic controls show the expected sign: negative for the GDP growth rate and positive for inflation and unemployment rates.

3.4 Conclusions

This chapter investigates the role that the legal-institutional context as well as the stock of social capital has on the cost of bank financing experienced by SMEs. We perform an empirical analysis using the ECB SAFE survey conducted on a large sample of SMEs across eleven European countries during the period 2009–2013. The hypotheses under investigation are twofold. First, we test whether SMEs are more likely to face higher price terms for bank financing (i.e., interest rates) when they pertain to countries characterized by a less efficient legal system and a higher concentration of the bank market. Second, we verify whether a higher stock of social capital improves the price conditions of bank financing for SMEs. After controlling for firm-level characteristics and country features, our estimates confirm both hypotheses. On the one hand, the higher the cost to settle a dispute for a claim, the higher the number of procedures to enforce a contract; and the higher the concentration of the banking system in a country, the higher the cost of bank financing faced by SMEs. On the other hand, the higher the stock of social capital and the higher the market share of cooperative banks in a country, the lower the cost of financing experienced by the European SMEs. Our findings suggest that all else being equal, the legal-institutional system and the social environment play a pivotal role in affecting the cost of financing for enterprises.

Acknowledgments We thank the ECB for the use of data from the Survey on the Access to Finance of Enterprises (SAFE). Additionally, Danilo V. Mascia and Stefania P.S. Rossi gratefully acknowledge research grants from the Autonomous Region of Sardinia, *Legge Regionale 2007, N. 7* [Grant Number CRP-59890, year 2012].

The evidence presented in this chapter has been discussed at several seminars. In particular, we would like to thank the conference participants of the International Workshop 'Access to bank credit and SME financing'—satellite session of the CLADAG Annual Meeting held in Pula (Sardinia), on 8–10 October 2015—for useful comments and suggestions. The usual disclaimer applies.

3.5 Appendix

Table A.3.1 Variable descriptions and sources

Variables	Description	Source
Dependent variable		
Level of interest rates (LIR)	Ordinal variable that equals 1/2/3 if the level of interest rates—experienced by each firm—decreased/remained unchanged/increased during the previous six months, respectively	ECB: SAFE
Key variables		
Cost of claim	Costs for settling a dispute (as % of the debt claim)	World Bank: Doing Business database
Procedures number	Number of steps to enforce a contract	World Bank: Doing Business database
Concentration	Herfindahl–Hirschman Index (HHI) of bank concentration	ECB: Statistical Data Warehouse
Cooperatives	Market share of cooperative banks	European Association of Co-operative Banks

(*continued*)

Table A.3.1 (continued)

Variables	Description	Source
Voter turnout	Percentage of the registered population that voted during an election	OECD: Better Life dataset
World Giving Index	A global index about the generosity of people in giving their money, volunteering their time and helping strangers	Charities Aid Foundation (CAF)
Giving Time Index	Generosity of people in volunteering their time	Charities Aid Foundation (CAF)
Standard firm-level controls		
Micro	Dummy variable that equals 1 if the firm has between 1 and 9 employees	ECB: SAFE
Small	Dummy variable that equals 1 if the firm has between 10 and 49 employees	ECB: SAFE
Medium	Dummy variable that equals 1 if the firm has between 50 and 249 employees	ECB: SAFE
Very recent	Dummy variable that equals 1 if the firm is less than 2 years old	ECB: SAFE
Recent	Dummy variable that equals 1 if the firm is between 2 and 5 years old	ECB: SAFE
Old	Dummy variable that equals 1 if the firm is between 5 and 10 years old	ECB: SAFE
Construction	Dummy variable that equals 1 if the firm's main activity is construction	ECB: SAFE
Manufacturing	Dummy variable that equals 1 if the firm's main activity is manufacturing	ECB: SAFE
Wholesale/Retail	Dummy variable that equals 1 if the firm's main activity is wholesale or retail trade	ECB: SAFE
Other firm-level characteristics		
Leverage up	Dummy variable that equals 1 if a firm experienced an increase in debt-to-assets ratio in previous six months	ECB: SAFE
Leverage down	Dummy variable that equals 1 if a firm experienced a decrease in debt-to-assets ratio in previous six months	ECB: SAFE

(*continued*)

Table A.3.1 (continued)

Variables	Description	Source
Demand up	Dummy variable that equals 1 if a firm experienced an increase in bank loans needs in previous six months	ECB: SAFE
Demand down	Dummy variable that equals 1 if a firm experienced a decrease in bank loans needs in previous six months	ECB: SAFE
Macroeconomic controls		
GDP growth	Annual growth rate of real GDP	World Bank
Inflation	Annual inflation rate	World Bank
Unemployment	Annual unemployment rate	Eurostat

References

Albertazzi, U., & Marchetti, D. J. (2010). *Credit supply, flight to quality and evergreening: An analysis of bank-firm relationships after Lehman. Temi di Discussione* (Working paper no. 756/April). Bank of Italy. Available at: https://www.bancaditalia.it/pubblicazioni/temi-discussione/2010/2010-0756/en_tema_756.pdf

Alesina, A., Lotti, F., & Mistrulli, P. E. (2013). Do women pay more for credit? Evidence from Italy. *Journal of the European Economic Association, 11*(1), 45–66.

Ayadi, R., & Gadi, S. (2013). Access by SMEs to finance in the Southern and Eastern Mediterranean: What role for credit guarantee schemes. European Commission, MEDPRO Technical Report No. 35.

Bae, K. H., & Goyal, V. K. (2009). Creditor rights, enforcement, and bank loans. *Journal of Finance, 64*(2), 823–860.

Bouvatier, V., & Lepetit, L. (2008). Banks' procyclical behavior: Does provisioning matter? *Journal of International Financial Markets, Institutions and Money, 18*(5), 513–528.

Catturani, I., Kalmi, P., & Stefani, M. L. (2014). Social Capital and the Credit Cooperative Banks. In *Capitale sociale, economia, politica economica*. Bank of Italy, Workshops and Conferences No. 17/November.

Cavalluzzo, K. S., Cavalluzzo, L. C., & Wolken, J. D. (2002). Competition, small business financing, and discrimination: Evidence from a new survey. *Journal of Business, 75*(4), 641–679.

Coleman, J. S. (1994). *Foundations of social theory*. Cambridge, MA: Harvard University Press.

De Blasio, G., Scalise, D., & Sestito, P. (2012). *Universalism vs. Particularism: A round trip from economics to sociology*. Bank of Italy, *Questioni di Economia e Finanza,* No. 212.

Djankov, S., La Porta, R., Lopez-de-Silanes, F., & Shleifer, A. (2008). The law and economics of self-dealing. *Journal of Financial Economics, 88*(3), 430–465.

Guiso, L., Sapienza, P., & Zingales, L. (2004). The role of social capital in financial development. *American Economic Review, 94*(3), 526–556.

Guiso, L., Sapienza, P., & Zingales, L. (2013). The determinants of attitudes toward strategic default on mortgages. *Journal of Finance, 68*(4), 1473–1515.

La Porta, R., Lopez De-Silanes, F., Shleifer, A., & Vishny, R. W. (1997). Legal determinants of external finance. *Journal of Finance, 7*(3), 1131–1150.

Laeven, L., & Majnoni, G. (2005). Does judicial efficiency lower the cost of credit? *Journal of Banking and Finance, 29*(7), 1791–1812.

Lang, F., Signore, S., & Gvetadze, S. (2016). The role of cooperative banks and smaller institutions for the financing of SMEs and small midcaps in Europe. (Working paper no. 36). European Investment Fund.

Lozzi, M., & Mistrulli, P. E. (2014). Loan Applications and Social Capital in the Great Recession. In *Capitale sociale, economia, politica economica*. Bank of Italy, Workshops and Conferences No. 17/November.

Maresch, D., Ferrando, A., & Moro, A. (2015). *Creditor protection, judicial enforcement and credit access*. ECB working paper series, no 1829/July.

Mistrulli, P. E., & Vacca, V. (2015). *Social capital and the cost of credit: Evidence from a crisis. Temi di Discussione* (Working paper no. 1009/April). Bank of Italy. Available at: https://www.bancaditalia.it/pubblicazioni/temi-discussione/2015/2015-1009/en_tema_1009.pdf

Moro, A., & Fink, M. (2013). Loan managers' trust and credit access for SMEs. *Journal of Banking and Finance, 37*(3), 927–936.

Moritz, A., Block, J.H., & Heinz, A. (2016). Financing patterns of European SMEs – an empirical taxonomy. Venture Capital, 18(2), 115-148.

OECD. (2001). The well-being of nations. The role of human and social capital. ISBN 92-64-18589-596 2001 01 1 P. Available at: http://www.oecd.org/site/worldforum/33703702.pdf

Ostergaard, C., Schindele, I., & Vale, B. (2009). *Social capital and the viability of non-profit firms: Evidence from Norwegian savings banks*. (Working paper no. 14). Norges Bank.

Öztürk, B., & Mrkaic, M. (2014). *SMEs' access to finance in the Euro area: What helps of hampers?* (Working paper no. 14/78). IMF.

Putnam, R. (2001). Social capital: Measurement and consequences. In J. F. Helliwell (Ed.), *The contribution of human and social capital to sustained economic growth and well-being*. International Symposium Report, Human Resources Development Canada and OECD.

Qian, J., & Strahan, P. E. (2007). How laws and institutions shape financial contracts: The case of bank loans. *Journal of Finance, 62*(6), 2803–2834.

Uzzi, B. (1999). Embeddedness in the making of financial capital: How social relations and the networks benefit firms seeking financing. *American Sociological Review, 64*, 481–505.

4

Credit Access for Small Firms in the Euro Area: Does Gender Matter?

Maria Lucia Stefani and Valerio Vacca

4.1 Introduction[1]

There is ample evidence of significant differences in the financial structure of male and female firms and of major challenges faced by female firms in access to financing (for a survey, see Cesaroni 2010). Specifically, female

[1] This chapter was originally published with the title 'Small Firms' Credit Access in the Euro Area: Does Gender Matter?' as an article in *CESifo Economic Studies* (2015), 61(1), pp. 165–201. The views expressed therein are those of the authors and do not necessarily reflect those of the Bank of Italy. For their very useful comments, we would like to thank: Renée Adams, Magda Bianco, Marcello Bofondi, Giovanni D'Alessio, Leandro D'Aurizio, Silvia Del Prete, Annalisa Ferrando, Giovanni Ferri, Francesca Lotti, Vincenzo Mariani, Paolo Mistrulli, Miriam Wetter, two anonymous referees and the participants at the Conference 'Women and the Italian Economy' organized by the Bank of Italy (March 2011), at a seminar at the University of Bari (May 2012) and at the CESifo Workshop on 'The Determinants of Gender Gaps: Institutional Design and Historical Factors' (July 2013). The usual disclaimer applies.

JEL classification: G32, G21, J16

M.L. Stefani
Structural Economic Analysis Directorate, Bank of Italy, Rome, Italy

V. Vacca (✉)
Financial Stability Directorate, Bank of Italy, Rome, Italy
e-mail: Valerio.Vacca@bancaditalia.it

S.P.S. Rossi (ed.), *Access to Bank Credit and SME Financing*,
Palgrave Macmillan Studies in Banking and Financial Institutions,
DOI 10.1007/978-3-319-41363-1_4

firms tend to use a smaller variety of sources of external financing and to rely more frequently on their own capital. This could be due to structural differences between female and male firms because the former are, on average, smaller and younger; they are also more frequently active in the services sector and organized as single proprietorship, and they are more frequently part of a group. From the point of view of a bank or, more generally, of a finance provider, these characteristics are less desirable and may therefore contribute to an explanation of the observed gender differences in firms' access to finance. However, whether some pure gender effect remains after controlling for these firm-specific features is still an open question. This question is relevant because access to finance is one of the most pressing problems firms have to tackle, especially if they are small and medium enterprises (SMEs). Female firms' difference in access to external financing may hamper their profitability and growth.

From a policy point of view, it is important to understand whether women-led firms find access to credit tougher *due to* the gender of their directors or due to other intrinsic features of the firms themselves; in the former case, gender-focused policies would be required, while in the latter they would be minimally effective.

This paper enters this debate by using a unique firm-level dataset built on the Survey on the Access to Finance of SMEs in the Euro Area (SAFE), which is conducted by the European Central Bank (ECB) and the European Commission. In the dataset, firms are classified as male or female according to the answer given to a specific survey question. The SAFE dataset is particularly valuable because it enables one to distinguish between demand and supply effects in firms' access to finance, and control for certain firm characteristics, such as size, age, sector of activity and proprietorship type; because the survey also collects information on firms that do not apply for external financing (for various reasons), sample selection bias problems are reduced. The survey is run at the euro area level, and the sample is representative of the four largest countries (Germany, France, Italy and Spain), thus enabling one to highlight, within a homogeneous framework, country specificities that have been little investigated to date.

After describing the main differences between male and female European SMEs based on their financing structure as it emerges from the survey data, this paper addresses its main research question, which is whether female enterprises face more difficult credit access than their male counterparts due to demand effects (i.e., self-restraint in asking for credit due to fear of rejection) or significantly tighter credit supply conditions (i.e., lower credit availability and/or less favourable cost conditions upon application).

The analysis is based on the four waves of the SAFE that cover the second half of 2009 to the first half of 2011. It considers different sources of finance and focuses on bank credit, because SMEs, which represent over 99 % of European firms, heavily rely on the latter; the study is run both at the euro area level and for each of the four countries for which there is a representative sample.

We find that the firm-specific features which make female firms structurally different from male ones largely explain why women-led enterprises seek less financing, and why—once an application is made—they experience a higher rejection rate. However, some significant gender effects arise at the country level.

The paper is organized as follows. Sect. 4.2 offers a review of the related literature; Sect. 4.3 describes the dataset used in the analysis and the main characteristics of the interviewed firms; Sect. 4.4 provides some stylized facts on the access to finance of female firms, identifying characteristics of the largest euro area countries; Sect. 4.5 presents an econometric analysis run through multinomial logistic models; Sect. 4.6 concludes.

4.2 Related Literature

Female firms display significant differences in financial structure from their male counterparts. Specifically, women-led enterprises tend to start with less capital and rely more heavily on personal, rather than external, finance for follow-on investments (Carter and Show 2006; Coleman and Robb 2009). Additionally, some sources of finance, such as venture capital, are used by female enterprises only to a very limited extent (Aspray and McGrath Cohoon 2007). Female firms are, on average, younger and smaller than male businesses; they are more concentrated in the commerce and service sectors, and they are more likely to be organized as proprietorships rather than corporations. Each of these specific features could affect the relationship of female firms with providers of external financing. Even after controlling for age, size and sector, female-led firms are characterized by a different financial structure. The literature focuses on two possible explanations: demand-side debt aversion and supply-side discrimination (Cesaroni 2010).

On the demand side, apart from possible discrepancies rooted into the structural characteristics of the female firm, differences are often linked to a higher level of risk aversion in women,[2] which may imply a lower propensity to leverage a firm via external funds.[3] Differences in demand behaviour may also arise from a possibly lower propensity to negotiate on the part of women, as compared to men (Babcock and Laschever 2003). In finance markets, differences in risk preferences and attitudes may involve differences in approach towards application for external financing between male and female enterprises. Women tend to feel more financially constrained than men and are less likely to get involved in a business start-up (Roper and Scott 2007). In the US, Cavalluzzo et al. (2002) find significant evidence of female firms being less likely to apply for credit as the lender market concentration increases, as measured by the Herfindahl-Hirschman Index. Some authors find that women show different demand patterns even when their applications do not display a significantly higher probability of being denied (Coleman 2000; Cole and Mehran 2009). Robb and Wolken (2002) find that women are more likely to borrow through credit cards (which do not typically require a bank negotiation) because they fear a denial mainly for reasons linked to their credit history. Marlow and Carter (2006) find that women tend

[2] See Croson and Gneezy (2009) for a survey on experimental literature and Dohmen et al. (2005). Among the recent studies that do not confirm the results regarding the higher risk aversion of women is Adams and Funk (2012).

[3] This result is not confirmed by Verheul and Thurik (2000), who find that women-led start-ups have a smaller amount of capital made by a smaller proportion of equity and a higher share of bank loans with respect to their male counterparts.

to demand less funding because, on the one hand, they prefer to run smaller enterprises (that allow a better work-life balance through flexible or part-time work) and, on the other hand, they are more reluctant to assume the burden of debt [see also Carter and Show (2006)]. A lower rate of application by females may be due to discouragement resulting from past discrimination (Cavalluzzo and Cavalluzzo 1998).

Turning to the supply side, evidence from the existing literature is not clear-cut on whether female entrepreneurs face tighter credit conditions. Using survey data from the US National Survey of Small Business Finance (NSSBF), Cavalluzzo and Cavalluzzo (1998) exclude gender discrimination, while Cavalluzzo et al. (2002), by using more recent data, find significant evidence of a gap in lenders' denial rates between male and female firms. Moreover, Coleman (2000) establishes cases of discrimination on price (interest rates) and non-price (collateral) conditions, but not on the availability of credit, while Blanchflower et al. (2003) do not find any. Turning to evidence from outside the United States, Madill et al. (2006) find that Canadian female firms do not display different application rates or bank rejection rates than their male counterparts, but that their relationships with banks are shorter. Using firm survey data (Business Environment and Enterprise Performance Survey, BEEPS) for a number of countries, including Eastern and some Western European economies, Muravyev et al. (2009) provide evidence of higher prices and lower probability of obtaining a loan when the entrepreneur is a woman. Using banking data from Italy, Alesina et al. (2013) find that female entrepreneurs pay higher interest rates (after controlling for different borrower characteristics and the structure of the credit market) without any evidence of higher riskiness. Analyzing credit lines to individual firms made available by one major Italian bank in a specific area, Bellucci et al. (2010) do not find significant differences in prices, but they do find lower credit availability.

Table 4.1 summarizes the main features of the empirical literature reviewed above and a few literature surveys.

Table 4.1 Empirical literature: survey

Author(s)	Year	Countries	Period	Main finding
Alesina et al.	2013	Italy	2004–2006	Women pay more, are not riskier
Adams and Funk	2012	Sweden	2005	Women in top corporate officer positions are slightly more risk-prone than men
Aspray and Cohoon	2007	Lit. survey		
Babcock and Laschever	2003	Survey evidence (US)		Women initiate negotiations less often than men. When they do negotiate, they ask for and obtain less since they are pessimistic about how much it is possible to get
Bellucci et al.	2010	Italy (part)	2004 and 2006	Women are more credit constrained, do not pay more
Blanchflower et al.	2003	US	1993 and 1998	No gender discrimination in credit markets (loan denials)
Carter and Shaw	2006	Lit. survey		Survey on business ownership by women; women have less access to capital, debt finance, pay more; roots: (i) structural differences in enterprises, (ii) supply, (iii) demand; little evidence on gender-discrimination by banks
Cavalluzzo and Cavalluzzo	1998	US	1988–1989	Women not discriminated in credit markets, favoured in concentrated credit markets
Cavalluzzo et al.	2002	US	1993–1994	Women do not pay more, but receive more loan denials
Cesaroni	2010	Lit. survey		
Cole and Mehran	2009	US	1987–2003	Women not more credit constrained if firm features are controlled for
Coleman	2000	US	1993–1994	Female firms use less external financing, pay more interest rates and are required to provide more collateral
Coleman and Robb	2009	US	2004–2006	Female start-up more external financing constrained
Croson and Gneezy	2009	Lit. survey		Women are different in risk, social and competitive attitude

(*continued*)

Table 4.1 (continued)

Author(s)	Year	Countries	Period	Main finding
Madill et al.	2006	Canada	2001–2002	Female firms: 1. are not more constrained; 2. do not pay more; 3. have shorter bank-firm relationship
Marlow and Carter	2006	UK (part)		Women prefer to run smaller firms; they ask less finance also because of more caution towards finance choices
Muravyev et al.	2009	34 (transition) countries, mainly East Europe	2005	Women are more credit constrained, pay more
Robb and Wolken	2002	US	1998	Gender does not matter in financing patterns, with the only exception of credit card borrowing
Roper and Scott	2009	UK	2004	Women are more financially constrained and discouraged to start up business
Verheul and Thurik	2000	NL	1994	Direct and indirect effect (via firm features) of gender. Women's start-ups: less capital, less equity, more bank debt

4.3 Description of Data

4.3.1 The SAFE Survey

The following analysis is carried out by using data from the Survey on the Access to Finance of SMEs in the Euro Area (SAFE), which is conducted by the ECB every six months, beginning in the first half 2009.[4] This dataset allows one to perform breakdowns by economic activity and firm size and to compare results for the four largest European countries (Germany, France, Italy and Spain), for which the sample is also representative.

[4] See http://www.ecb.europa.eu/stats/money/surveys/sme/html/index.en.html. In particular, the whole questionnaire is available at: http://www.ecb.europa.eu/stats/pdf/surveys/sme/SME_survey_Questionnaire_publication201104.pdf.

The survey addresses several finance-related features of firms: growth and profitability, levels of debt, internal and external financing, credit applications and outcomes, credit availability, and conditions. The aim of the survey is to track the evolution of access to finance for European SMEs; therefore, entrepreneurs are questioned on the changes over time of relevant phenomena and not on the level of the latter. More specifically, the answers collected at each wave of the survey refer to improvement or deterioration, increase or decrease, or use or lack of use of the different aspects of external financing by a firm during the previous six months or, in some cases, to expectations for the following six months. Accordingly, the statistics used in this analysis should not be interpreted as referring to the *amount* of external financing used, but rather to its *change* over time.

In this paper, four waves of the survey were used, beginning with the second (covering the second half of 2009), which introduced a question on gender of owner, director or CEO (thus allowing one to distinguish female from male firms) and going to the fifth (covering the first half of 2011). The four waves are homogeneous for questions relevant to this study and, via pooling of their data, a sample of about 24,000 observations is used.[5] Female firms account for 14.4 % of the total sample.[6]

The formulation of the questions asked in the survey changed over time; additionally, every two years the survey has been conducted by the ECB jointly with the European Commission (as in the first and fifth wave), which entails a richer questionnaire and a slightly different sampling procedure.

The number of interviewed firms for the total sample and by representative country is presented in Table 4.2.

The analysis is entirely based on the survey evidence, which should allow one to detect whether the gender dimension of the firm has an

[5] The inclusion of the sixth wave of the survey (second half 2011) would not change the findings of this paper in a meaningful way.

[6] In the dataset used in this paper, the answer about gender is missing for about 5 % of firms. In the basic descriptive and econometric analysis, these firms have been added to male ones, but this inclusion does not affect the primary results.

Table 4.2 Number of interviewed firms

Wave	Total	*Of which*:			
		Germany	France	Italy	Spain
2009H2	5,320	1,001	1,001	1,004	1,004
2010H1	5,312	1,000	1,003	1,000	1,000
2010H2	7,532	1,000	1,004	1,000	1,000
2011H1	8,316	1,006	1,002	1,001	1,001

Source: ECB SAFE; waves from the second half of 2009 to the first half of 2011
Note: Unless differently specified, data in the following tables refer to firms with less than 250 employees, surveyed in the four SAFE waves run from the second half of 2009 to the first half of 2011

impact on the relevant phenomena (credit conditions and financial structure), after controlling for firm-specific features.[7]

The survey sample features a complicated panel dimension, and the number of firms interviewed in more than one survey is small (Osiewicz and Pérez-Duarte 2011). Consequently, as in other papers,[8] the panel component has not been exploited in this study; possible underestimation of variance that this may entail is negligible.[9]

Finally, given that the proportions of firms in the sample are distorted with respect to the reference population, all statistics used in this paper are weighted in order to restore the proportions of the economic weight of each size class, economic activity and country. Weights are provided by the ECB.

[7] Even if the identification codes of the surveyed firms were made available by the ECB, it would be difficult to retrieve comparable information from external databases (e.g., about balance sheets, bank credit and so forth) for small firms belonging to different countries. Additionally, classification variables (such as size and age) are made available in discrete classes rather than continuous variables. These facts have to be considered in interpretation of survey results.

[8] Öztürk and Mrkaic (2014) observe that, even considering the SAFE panel component, fixed effects cannot be used when the time dimension is quite small and the sample size rather large because the 'incidental parameters problem' arises.

[9] The error in disregarding the panel component depends on the share of the panel firms and on the correlation among answers provided by the same firm in subsequent survey waves (Fabbris 1989). In the case at hand, given the share of the panel firms in the SAFE survey and realistic values of possible auto-correlation among the answers of the same firm across different survey waves, it can be assumed that the estimated variance should be augmented, at most, by about 10 % in order to arrive at the true variance. Moreover, econometric estimates display variances that are generally so large as to reject coefficient significance, thus rendering any correction irrelevant.

4.3.2 Characteristics of Female Firms in the Sample and Differences at Country Level

Female SMEs demonstrate significant structural differences when compared to other firms (Table 4.3). Female firms are smaller than average and are systematically over-represented in the size class going from 1 to 9 employees, while being under-represented in the upper size classes. In addition, their ventures are younger and more often operate in the sectors of trade or other services.[10]

Some (expected) structural dissimilarities arise at the country level (Table 4.4); for example, German enterprises are larger than the average euro area firm, while in Italy the proportion of family firms is much higher. Such differences generally apply to both male and female firms within the country. Italy and Germany, however, display smaller gender discrepancies in the size distribution of firms than the euro area as a whole. By contrast, France is by far the country with the highest gender differences in the size and age of firms.[11]

These findings support certain facts about female firms that could have an impact on the relationships between firms and providers of external financing; for example, since young and small firms are perceived as riskier, this structural feature helps explain why female firms are more financially constrained than others. Accordingly, after a description of differences that can be observed in answers by firms regarding their gender and access to finance (see Sect. 4.4), an econometric analysis tries to determine whether differences in credit access can be confirmed after controlling for firm-specific features.

[10] The same pattern occurs when firm size is represented by turnover (total revenues), with over-representation of female firms in the lowest class (up to 2 million) and under-representation in the others.

[11] More precisely, the percentage of French female firms in the smallest size class (1–9 employees) is more than 30 percentage points higher than the percentage of male firms, which is the largest gap among the four countries considered here. The same effect occurs for age, where the share of French female firms belonging to the oldest class (10 years or more) is around 11 percentage points less than the proportion of corresponding male enterprises.

Table 4.3 General characteristics of the firms in the sample *(percentage frequencies)*

	Gender of the owner/director/CEO			
	Male	Female	t-statistic (1)	Overall
Memo: Total firms	*85.56*	*14.44*		*100.00*
Size (employment)				
From 1 to 9 employees	43.46	62.60	***	46.28
From 10 to 49 employees	30.96	24.64	***	30.03
From 50 to 249 employees	25.57	12.76	***	23.69
Total	*100.00*	*100.00*		*100.00*
Size (annual turnover in euros)				
Up to 2 million	56.65	76.90	***	59.55
More than 2 and up to 10 million	26.48	17.07	***	25.13
More than 10 and up to 50 million	14.25	5.12	***	12.94
More than 50 million	2.62	0.92	***	2.37
Total	*100.00*	*100.00*		*100.00*
Financial autonomy				
Part of a profit-oriented firm (2)	10.92	7.08	***	10.36
Autonomous profit-oriented firm	89.08	92.92	***	89.64
Total	*100.00*	*100.00*		*100.00*
Main activity				
Construction	10.97	6.09	***	10.27
Manufacturing	17.72	9.42	***	16.52
Wholesale or retail trade	19.40	23.34	***	19.97
Other services to bs or persons	51.90	61.15	***	53.24
Total	*100.00*	*100.00*		*100.00*
Age (years)				
10 years or more	71.01	61.14	***	69.59
5 years or more but less than 10	16.19	18.86	***	16.58
2 years or more but less than 5	10.20	15.44	***	10.95
Less than 2	2.60	4.56	***	2.88
Total	*100.00*	*100.00*		*100.00*
Ownership				
Public (the company is listed)	3.92	1.77	***	3.61
Family or entrepreneurs	53.29	53.60		53.34
Other firm or business associates	12.71	7.39	***	11.94
Venture capital firms	1.35	0.59	***	1.24
A natural single person	26.68	35.28	***	27.92
Other	2.05	1.36	**	1.95
Total	*100.00*	*100.00*		*100.00*

(1) *** = difference is statistically significant at 1 %; ** = at 5 %; * = at 10 %.
(2) An enterprise that does not make fully autonomous financial decisions (e.g., a subsidiary or a branch)

Table 4.4 General characteristics of firms in the sample by country *(percentage frequencies)*

	Germany			*France*			*Italy*			*Spain*		
	Male	Female	(1)	Male	Female	(1)	Male	Female	(1)	Male	Female	(1)
Memo: N. firms	84.43	15.57		85.54	14.46		86.00	14.00		84.72	15.28	
Size (employment)												
From 1 to 9 employees	30.95	48.66	***	35.35	66.81	***	58.10	71.78	***	49.01	68.10	***
From 10 to 49	34.73	33.43		34.83	22.44	***	26.14	18.16	***	30.23	21.36	***
From 50 to 249	34.32	17.91	***	29.82	10.75	***	15.77	10.05	***	20.76	10.54	***
Total	*100.00*	*100.00*		*100.00*	*100.00*		*100.00*	*100.00*		*100.00*	*100.00*	
Size (annual turnover in euros)												
Up to 2 million	51.30	72.60	***	50.99	80.35	***	65.30	77.75	***	62.05	78.50	***
2 to 10 million	28.40	20.69	***	29.56	14.81	***	21.52	15.60	**	25.19	16.51	***
10 to 50 million	18.03	5.75	***	17.20	3.80	***	10.87	5.82	***	10.40	4.23	***
More than 50 million	2.27	0.97	*	2.26	1.04	**	2.31	0.84	**	2.36	0.76	***
Total	*100.00*	*100.00*		*100.00*	*100.00*		*100.00*	*100.00*		*100.00*	*100.00*	
Financial autonomy												
Part of a profit-oriented firm	12.57	11.62		12.08	4.92	***	5.42	1.13	***	9.28	7.62	
Autonomous profit-oriented firm	87.43	88.38		87.92	95.08	***	94.58	98.87	***	90.72	92.38	
Total	*100.00*	*100.00*		*100.00*	*100.00*		*100.00*	*100.00*		*100.00*	*100.00*	
Main activity												
Construction	6.62	5.21		11.11	4.00	***	11.87	8.55		17.06	7.40	***
Manufacturing	20.70	13.08	***	16.55	4.45	***	22.59	13.21	***	14.20	7.38	***
Wholesale or retail trade	17.20	20.21	*	19.23	23.27	**	18.62	24.57	***	18.84	25.19	***
Other services	55.48	61.50	**	53.11	68.28	***	46.92	53.67	**	49.91	60.03	***
Total	*100.00*	*100.00*		*100.00*	*100.00*		*100.00*	*100.00*		*100.00*	*100.00*	

	Germany			France			Italy			Spain		
Age (years)												
10 years or more	73.76	66.10	***	66.52	45.61	***	66.42	62.34		72.27	63.99	***
5 years or more but less than 10	13.66	16.43		16.07	22.30	***	20.65	19.99		15.94	20.37	**
2 years or more but less than 5	10.32	13.16	*	11.74	21.91	***	10.59	14.91	**	10.69	13.20	
Less than 2	2.27	4.31	**	5.68	10.19	***	2.36	2.76		1.10	2.45	**
Total	*100.00*	*100.00*		*100.00*	*100.00*		*100.00*	*100.00*		*100.00*	*100.00*	
Ownership												
Public (listed company)	2.56	0.70	**	2.82	1.98		2.39	1.22		4.36	2.06	***
Family or entrepreneurs	45.59	43.06		39.77	41.07		68.33	73.35	*	57.74	62.00	
Other firm or business associates	11.08	4.52	***	24.53	17.98	***	7.88	0.66	***	13.58	9.37	**
Venture capital firms	1.66	0.27	***	0.80	0.65		1.23	0.00	**	1.42	1.18	
A natural single person	37.04	50.09	***	29.99	36.36	**	18.48	22.87	*	21.53	25.06	
Other	2.07	1.35		2.09	1.96		1.69	1.90		1.37	0.33	**
Total	*100.00*	*100.00*		*100.00*	*100.00*		*100.00*	*100.00*		*100.00*	*100.00*	

(1) t-statistic: *** = difference is statistically significant at 1 %; ** = at 5 %; * = at 10 %

4.4 Access to Credit by Female Firms: Statistical Evidence

4.4.1 Financing the Firm

According to the SAFE, access to finance is identified by female firms as their most pressing problem at a frequency that is not significantly different from that of their male counterparts.[12] Consequently, over the period of time covered in this study, access to finance is not perceived to be an issue that typically hinders the development of female firms.[13]

By contrast, the evolution of income and financial situation highlights some important differences. First, women-led companies experienced a more negative trend in turnover (i.e., total revenue) in the 2009–2011 period; second, they saw a greater deterioration in profitability; and, finally, the debt-to-asset ratios for female indebted firms decreased less and more often remained stable when compared with their male counterparts. The evolution of leverage raises the question of whether the higher stability of female firms is driven entirely by these firms' choices or, at least in part, by the differing attitude of financiers towards male and female firms, especially during a credit slowdown.

Figure 4.1 sheds some light on this issue: the share of female firms that did not use external financing is around 25 %, compared to 18.5 % for other firms. This difference is statistically significant at the 1% confidence level and appears consistent with the literature's finding that female firms make less use of external financing (see Sect. 4.2). Furthermore, and more importantly, the less frequent use of external financing by female firms' is not offset by a wider recourse to internally generated funds. On the one hand, this might suggest a significant share of these enterprises experience financial constraints that hinder their investment capacity and ultimately their growth and development; however, it is also consistent with the evidence

[12] See the working paper version of this study for details on the descriptive SAFE results used in this paragraph (Stefani and Vacca 2013).

[13] By using the question in which SAFE asks which is the most pressing problem for the firm, Ferrando and Griesshaber (2011) find that only firm age and ownership matter in detecting which enterprises are more likely to report financial obstacles. Their results partially differ from the ones of Beck et al. (2006), who state that size is also relevant in this respect. Neither work, however, investigates the role of the gender of the entrepreneur in predicting financially constrained firms.

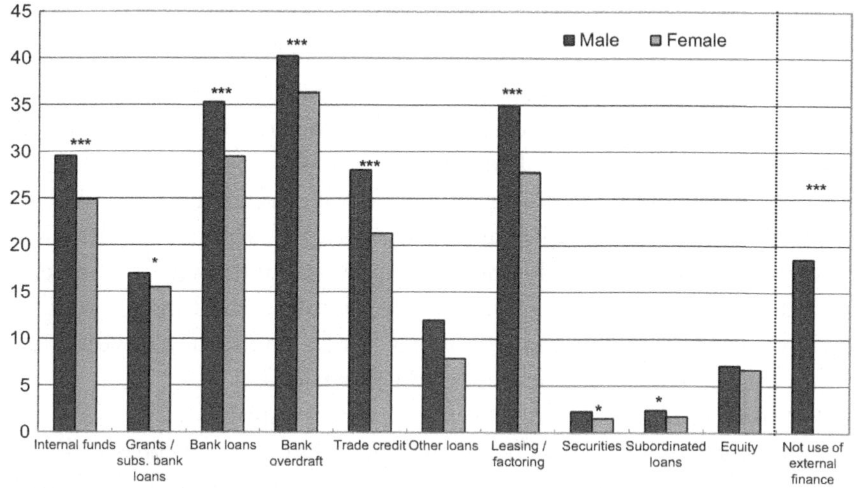

Fig. 4.1 Sources of financing (1) *(percentage frequencies)*
(*Source*: ECB SAFE survey; waves are from the second half of 2009 to the first half of 2011. (1) *** = difference is statistically significant at 1 %; ** = at 5 %; * = at 10 %)

that female entrepreneurs tend to maintain a smaller venture size (consequently, they require less external financing, despite less internal resources).

When they use external financing, women-led enterprises display a narrower range of sources of funds, with markedly less funding via bank loans, trade credit, leasing, hire purchasing and factoring.

Gender differences also arise as factors affecting financing needs. Specifically, female firms display a weaker demand to finance fixed investments, which could be interpreted as a harsh consequence of the cyclical downturn on female firms.

4.4.2 Availability of External Financing: Application and Results, Terms and Conditions

In the period covered by the analysis, the proportion of female firms that reported an improved availability of external financing was significantly lower than that of their male counterparts for each of the financing sources considered in the SAFE. With respect to demand-related factors that can affect a company's recourse to external financing, a significantly higher proportion of female firms reported deterioration in their general or firm-specific outlook and in the firm's own capital. As for supply-related factors, a lower share of female enterprises reported an improved willingness of banks to lend, of business partners to provide trade credit, or of investors to invest in equity or debt securities issued by the firm. Female firms appear to be less optimistic than firms led by men about the future availability of external funds.

A crucial issue in assessing access to finance is whether gender differences affect a company's likelihood of approaching providers of external funds and the probability of success in obtaining the funds. Table 4.5, panel (a), addresses demand side issues (credit application), while panel (b) focuses on supply side issues (credit provision).

The share of female enterprises, which did not apply for external funds, is higher than that of other firms; gender differences are statistically significant when the non-application is due to fear of rejection, especially for bank loans (Fig. 4.2).

Table 4.5, panel (b), shows that, of those firms that applied for financing, the ratio of firms obtaining the full amount requested does not dis-

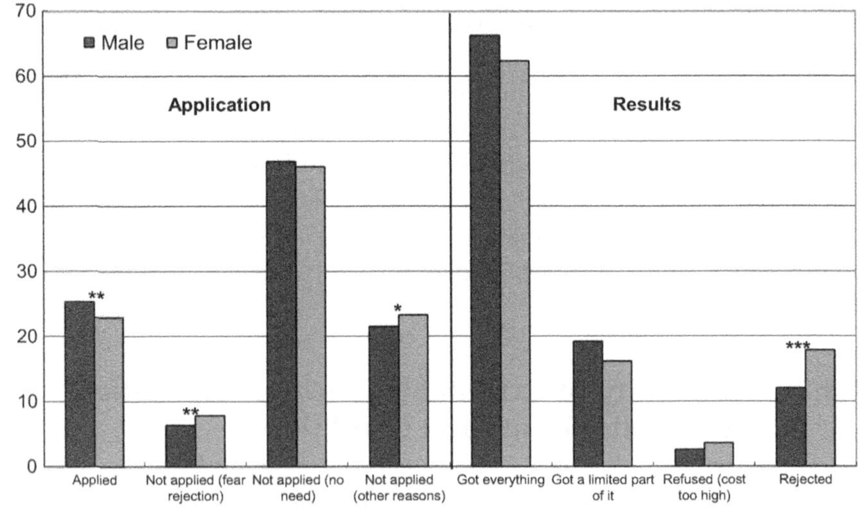

Fig. 4.2 Application for bank loans and results (1) *(percentage frequencies)* (*Source*: ECB SAFE survey, waves from the second half of 2009 to the first half of 2011. (1) *** = difference is statistically significant at 1 %; ** = at 5 %; * = at 10 %)

Table 4.5 Application for external funds and results from application *(percentage frequencies)*

	Bank loan			Bank overdraft, credit line or credit card overdraft			Trade credit			Other		
	Male	Female	(1)	Male	Female	(1)	Male	Female	(1)	Male	Female	(1)
a) Application												
Applied	25.29	22.87	**	21.20	19.82		14.00	9.92	***	10.80	8.34	***
Not applied (fear rejection)	6.36	7.85	**	5.80	6.20		3.91	5.53	***	3.79	4.54	*
Not applied (no need)	46.88	46.01		51.58	51.27		44.89	44.48		46.24	46.49	
Not applied (other reasons)	21.48	23.27	*	21.42	22.71		37.20	40.07	**	39.17	40.62	
b) Results												
Got everything	66.18	62.31		61.16	59.31		65.03	70.73		75.51	76.41	
Got partial	19.19	16.18		24.84	23.99		24.94	20.85		13.74	11.79	
Refused (cost too high)	2.59	3.63		3.17	4.05		1.16	2.37	*	2.18	0.96	
Rejected	12.04	17.88	***	10.83	12.65		8.87	6.05		8.56	10.84	

(1) t-statistics: *** = difference is statistically significant at 1 %; ** = at 5 %; * = at 10 %

Table 4.6 Terms and conditions of the bank financing (1) *(percentage frequencies)*

	Increased by bank			Unchanged			Decreased by bank		
	Male	Female	t-statistic (2)	Male	Female	t-statistic (2)	Male	Female	t-statistic (2)
Level of interest rates	50.73	54.56	*	34.44	34.57		14.82	10.88	***
Level of cost of financing other than interest rates	50.83	55.80	**	44.96	41.43		4.21	2.77	*
Available size of loan or credit line	19.59	19.34		61.13	60.43		19.28	20.23	
Available maturity of loan	8.48	7.90		82.57	83.88		8.95	8.21	
Collateral requirements	37.73	38.75		59.24	58.99		3.04	2.26	
Other (e.g., loan covenants)	34.73	36.06		62.52	61.26		2.75	2.68	

(1) Evolution of the indicators over the previous six months. (2) *** = difference is statistically significant at 1 %; ** = at 5 %; * = at 10 %

play gender differences; in the case of bank loans, though, female firms reported a significantly higher bank rejection rate (17.9 versus 12 %).

Regarding the terms and conditions under which banking finance is granted, in the period addressed by this study, a slight relative deterioration emerges for female enterprises vis-à-vis other firms (Table 4.6). In particular, the share of female firms that reported a decrease in interest rates is comparatively low (10.9 versus 14.8 %).

4.4.3 Differences at Country Level

The use of a narrower set of financing sources by female firms is common to each of the four countries addressed individually (i.e., Germany, France, Italy and Spain).

The share of female enterprises which did not apply for bank loans over the previous six months due to fear of rejection is higher than the share of male enterprises in every country, but this difference is statistically significant only in Germany and France (see Table 4.7, panel (a)). On the supply side, the proportion of firms that reported a bank loan rejection is significantly higher for female firms in Germany and Italy. German female firms obtained all the bank funds they requested less often than did their male counterparts, and they more often refused a loan proposal because its cost was too high. Data from Spain revealed that a lower proportion of female firms obtained at least part of a requested loan (see Table 4.7, panel (b)).

Regarding the terms and conditions of bank financing, Italy was the only country where the share of female firms that faced an increase in bank interest rates, in the period covered by the analysis, was significantly higher than did the share of male firms. This evidence is particularly negative for Italian female firms when one considers that they pay more for bank credit, *ceteris paribus*, as found by Alesina et al. (2013). According to SAFE, Italian female firms were also more often asked to increase collateral. In contrast, Spanish female firms less frequently experienced an increase in both interest rates and collateral requirements than their male counterparts. German and French female firms were charged

Table 4.7 Application for bank loans and results from application by country *(percentage frequencies)*

	Germany			*France*			*Italy*			*Spain*		
	Male	Female	(1)	Male	Female	(1)	Male	Female	(1)	Male	Female	(1)
a) Application												
Applied	20.97	20.09		30.64	24.20	**	29.19	27.00		31.34	27.13	*
Not applied (fear rejection)	7.15	9.81	**	5.65	9.08	**	3.87	3.94		8.03	9.44	
Not applied (no need)	58.13	54.66		43.78	42.47		43.95	47.46		36.00	33.09	
Not applied (other reasons)	13.75	15.44		19.93	24.25	*	22.99	21.60		24.63	30.34	**
b) Results												
Got everything	77.44	64.36	***	78.82	78.78		64.82	58.15		52.64	56.39	
Got partial	13.49	9.58		9.94	9.29		22.40	19.10		27.85	19.19	**
Refused (cost too high)	2.04	5.35	*	1.58	1.76		1.99	2.47		2.84	4.33	
Rejected	7.03	20.71	***	9.66	10.17		10.79	20.29	**	16.67	20.09	

(1) t-statistics: *** = difference is statistically significant at 1 %; ** = at 5 %; * = at 10 %

higher financing costs other than interest rates; German female firms were less frequently allowed an extension on the maturity of their loan. Interestingly, in virtually no country did significant gender differences arise for variations in the available size of loans or credit lines.

In summary, according to SAFE's descriptive evidence, German and French female firms more frequently refrain from seeking bank loans than their male counterparts, but once an application has been made, only German firms display differences in the likelihood of obtaining such a loan. Therefore, Germany is the only country where self-restraint in loan demand is coupled with relatively higher credit rejection for female firms. In Italy and Spain, some significant gender effects appear in the results of loan application; specifically, there is a higher frequency of credit rejection for female firms in Italy and a lower frequency of partial success in obtaining credit in Spain.

4.5 Econometric Analysis

4.5.1 Baseline Specification

As suggested above, differences detected in the attitude of female firms towards seeking external financing might result from firm-specific characteristics, such as structural differences between male and female enterprises that are unrelated to the gender of the directors (e.g., business age, size, sector and ownership). To investigate whether female firms experience more difficulty in obtaining external financing *because* they are directed or owned by women, one must control for these confounding factors.

This analysis is applied to the two primary questions regarding the capability of women-led firms to access financing (i.e., the likelihood of applying for external funds and the outcome of such applications). Because our dependent variables are qualitative and non-ranked, we apply a multinomial logistic analysis to the answers provided in the survey. The baseline analysis is:

$$P_i(\text{applying for external funds}) = f(\text{female, size, age, sector, country, type, ownership, wave}) \quad (4.1a)$$

$$P_i(\text{getting external funds}) = f(\text{female, size, age, sector, country, type, ownership, wave}) \quad (4.1b)$$

The dependent variable, $P(\cdot)$, is the probability that firm i applies for external financing (Eq. [4.1a]) or, conditional on application, the probability of obtaining the funds (Eq. [4.1b]). Because possible answers can include more than two unordered values, coefficients from the estimation indicate whether each independent variable entails an increase or decrease in the likelihood of eliciting the different answers from a firm as compared to the reference answer (base case); a positive coefficient means that the factor under consideration will make it, *ceteris paribus*, more likely to get that answer from the respondent firm. The independent variables are dummies; specifically, *female* is a dummy variable, which takes the value of 1 if the firm is directed by a woman, and 0 otherwise.[14]

Table 4.8 reports the results for the probability of applying for external financing (Eq. [4.1a]). For the variable of interest (dummy for female firms), the marginal effects evaluated at the means are shown. For the control variables, the sign and the statistical significance of the dummy variables are reported. Panel (a) refers to bank loans and panel (b) to trade credit.

The control variables enable us to identify which structural features reduce the ability of firms to succeed with financiers and must be addressed in order to isolate the female firm effect, if any. Regarding bank loans in panel (a), the likelihood that a firm will refrain from applying for financing (due to fear of rejection or any other reason) decreases, not surprisingly, with an increase in the firm's size, both in terms of employees and turnover (revenues). Being part of a larger group also results in a lower likelihood of refraining from applying for financing. In other

[14] Dummies are constructed following the general characteristics of the firms collected in the survey and displayed in Table 4.3. Specifically, there are 4 dummies for size assessed through the number of employees and 4 dummies for size measured by turnover; 4 dummies are for age classes; 4 dummies are for the sector of activity (construction, manufacturing, trade, or other services), 11 dummies for country; 2 dummies for type (financial autonomy) and 6 for ownership; 4 dummies denote the survey wave (i.e., from the second to the fifth wave).

Table 4.8 Econometric analysis: application for bank loans and trade credit (1) *(multinomial logistic estimates)*

	(a) Bank loans			(b) Trade credit		
	Did not apply because of possible rejection	Did not apply because of sufficient internal funds	Did not apply for other reasons	Did not apply because of possible rejection	Did not apply because of sufficient internal funds	Did not apply for other reasons
Female firm (2)	.062	.008	.014	.428***	.215**	.205
	[.108]	[.068]	[.079]	[.139]	[.091]	[.091]
	.003	*–.001*	*.001*	*.010*	*.009*	*.004*
Controls: (3)						
SAFE survey wave (base = 2)						
Wave 3		+***		–*	+***	–*
Wave 4	+***	+***		–**	+**	–***
Wave 5	+***	+***		–**	+*	–***
Size (employees) (base = micro firm)						
Small	–***	–***	–***	–***	–***	–***
Medium-sized	–*	–***	–***	–***	–***	–***
Financial autonomy (base = autonomous firm)						
Non autonomous firm	–**	–***	–***		–**	–*
Main activity (base = industry)						
Construction						–*
Trade		+***	+**			
Services		+***	+*		+***	+***
Size (turnover) (base = up to 2 million)						
2 to 10 million	–***	–***	–***	–***	–***	–***
10 to 50 million	–***	–***	–***	–***	–***	–***
More than 50 million	–***	*	–***	–***	–***	–***
Age (base = old, i.e., more than 10 years)						
Middle-aged						
Young	+***				–***	
New			–*			–***
Ownership (base = shareholders)						
Family/ entrepreneurs	–**	–***		–***	–***	–*
Other firm/bs associates				–***	–***	

(continued)

Table 4.8 (continued)

	(a) Bank loans			(b) Trade credit		
Venture capital/B angels					−**	−*
A single person		−**		−*	−***	
Other						
Country (base = Germany)						
Austria	−***			−***		−**
Belgium		−**			−**	−***
Spain	−***	−***		−***	−***	−***
Finland	−***	+***	+***	−**	+***	
France	−***	−***		+***	−*	
Greece		−***	+***	−*	−***	−***
Ireland	+***			−***	−***	−***
Italy	−***	−***		−***	−***	−***
Netherlands	+***	+***	+***	+***	−*	−***
Portugal	−**	−***	+***	−***	−***	−***
N. observations	22,744			22,501		
Pseudo R2	0.045			0.056		

(1) The base-case answer is not reported ('Applied'). *** = coefficient is statistically significant at 1%; ** = at 5%; * = at 10%. (2) Robust standard errors are reported in square brackets under the coefficient estimate. Estimated marginal effects evaluated at the mean are reported in italics. (3) The sign and the statistical significance of the dummy coefficient are reported. For each control variable the base case is excluded

words, a larger size and inclusion in a group make firms more likely to ask for credit. Firms active in the trade or services sectors are also less likely to refrain from applying for loans. Age, by contrast, does not have a clear-cut impact, because only 'young' firms display a higher likelihood of restraining from applying due to rejection fears as compared to both newer and more seasoned firms. Finally, country effects suggest that self-restraint due to possible rejection is higher in Ireland and the Netherlands than in Germany, while it is even lower in six other countries. Regarding trade credit in panel (b), both size effect and, though weaker, industry effect are confirmed, while ownership of the firm is apparently more crucial than for bank loans; single-owner and family firms display a lower likelihood of refraining from application than do shareholder-owned firms. Again,

Dutch and French firms display a higher likelihood than German firms of refraining from applying for loans due to fear of rejection.

The key finding of Table 4.8 is that, after controlling for a set of firm features, no significant differences emerge for female firms as opposed to their male counterparts, as far as application for bank loans is concerned. Specifically, the sign of the coefficient could suggest that female firms more often refrain from applying for bank loans due to fear of rejection, but the coefficient is not statistically significant. The same result is found in considering the application for bank overdraft or for other loans (not displayed). Nevertheless, some evidence of gender-based differences, evidence which remains after controlling for structural features, emerges when looking at non-bank sources of external financing and, specifically, trade credit (panel (b)). The estimated marginal effect is 1.0 percentage point, which represents the increase in likelihood of obtaining this outcome due solely to the fact that the respondent firm is directed or owned by a woman. This differential should be compared with the original 1.6 percentage point gap that was derived from descriptive evidence (see Sect. 4.2). Other motivations for refraining from applying for trade credit are also significantly higher for female firms, with lower marginal effects (e.g., 'sufficient funds' displays a marginal effect of 0.9 percentage point, while 'other reasons' displays a marginal effect of 0.4 percentage point).

Regarding the supply side and the outcomes of credit applications, the estimates from Eq. [4.1b] for bank loans (Table 4.9, panel (a)) show again a size effect and an industry effect. Middle-aged and young firms have a greater probability of being denied a bank loan, and the same is true for French, Greek and Italian firms. According to the estimates for trade credit (Table 4.9, panel (b)), both the size and age effect are weaker than for bank loans, while a stronger country effect emerges; in almost all countries, the likelihood of being denied trade credit is statistically higher than in Germany, and in no country is it significantly lower. Interestingly, according to Table 4.9, female firms do not display a significantly higher likelihood of having their bank loan applications rejected, after controlling for the above factors. The coefficient of the female dummy is positive, but not significant. Only a weak significant effect emerges regarding applications for trade credit, where female firms appear more likely than their male

Table 4.9 Econometric analysis: results from application for bank loans and trade credit (1) *(multinomial logistic estimates)*

	(a) Bank loans			(b) Trade credit		
	Applied and got part of it	Applied but refused because cost too high	Applied but was rejected	Applied and got part of it	Applied but refused because cost too high	Applied but was rejected
Female firm (2)	–.154	.109	.172	–.260	.814*	–.549
	[.166]	[.306]	[.174]	[.189]	[.478]	[.257]
	–.026	*.003*	*.022*	*–.037*	*.015*	*–.031*
Controls: (3)						
SAFE survey wave (base = 2)						
Wave 3			–***			–**
Wave 4		–*	–***			–**
Wave 5			–**			–**
Size (employees) (base = micro firm)						
Small			–***		+***	
Medium-sized		–*	–***			–**
Financial autonomy (base = autonomous firm)						
Non autonomous firm		–***				+**
Main activity (base = industry)						
Construction					–*	–*
Trade	–**	–**	–***	–**		–***
Services	–*		–**			
Size (turnover) (base = up to 2 million)						
2 to 10 million						
10 to 50 million		–*	–***			–***
More than 50 million			–**			–**
Age (base = old, i.e., more than 10 years)						
Middle aged			+**			–**
Young			+***			
New						
Ownership (base = shareholders)						
Family/entrepreneurs						
Other firm/bs associates						–*
Venture capital/B angels			+*	+**	–***	
A single person						
Other		–***				–***

(continued)

Table 4.9 (continued)

	(a) Bank loans			(b) Trade credit		
Country (base = Germany)						
Austria				−**	−***	
Belgium			−**	−**		+**
Spain	+***		−***	+***		+***
Finland	−***			−*	−***	+*
France	−**					+***
Greece	+***	+**	+***	+***	+**	+***
Ireland	+***	+**	+***	+**		+**
Italy	+***				−***	
Netherlands	+***	+***	+***			+***
Portugal	+***					+**
N. observations	5,650			3,354		
Pseudo R2	.076			.084		

(1) The base-case answer is not reported ('Applied and got everything'). *** = coefficient is statistically significant at 1%; ** = at 5%; * = at 10%. (2) Robust standard errors are reported in square brackets under the coefficient estimate. Estimated marginal effects evaluated at the mean are reported in italics. (3) The sign and the statistical significance of the dummy coefficient are reported. For each control variable the base case is excluded

counterparts to refuse proposed arrangements due to their cost (with a marginal effect of 1.5 percentage points, which is even higher than the 1.2 percentage points derived from the descriptive analysis). The same results apply to other sources of external financing.

In summary, differences in access to external financing for female firms that emerge from the descriptive analysis seem to be widely explained by firm-specific structural features (such as size, age and proprietorship), which are generally different from the features of male enterprises and are plausibly less desirable to financiers.

4.5.2 Differences at Country Level

In light of the differences in both structural features and attitudes towards external financing in the major European countries (see Sect. 4.4), baseline econometric specifications have been run for the subsets of the four major countries, for which the sample is also representative. Specifically, the objective is to investigate whether differences exist between German, Spanish, French and Italian enterprises in companies' attitudes towards bank loan applications and the results of such applications. In Table 4.10 the coefficients of the female dummy are reported, while the estimation results referring to control variables are omitted for the sake of brevity.

Regarding applications for bank loans, Table 4.10 suggests that results obtained for the whole sample generally hold for each of the four countries, and no gender-based differences are detected once structural differences in the characteristics of the enterprises are taken into account. Some weak evidence suggests that French female firms experience a higher likelihood of abstaining from applying for loans than their male counterparts for reasons other than fear of rejection or availability of sufficient funds (panel (c)). The relevant coefficient, barely significant at a 10 % confidence level, has a marginal effect of 3.2 percentage points: in other words, after controlling for respective features, French female firms still have a likelihood of refraining from application for unspecified reasons that is 3.2 percentage points higher than other firms (4.3 percentage points without controlling for structural features).

Regarding outcomes from bank loan applications, results obtained for the entire sample generally hold true at the country level, but some countries display evidence of a lower likelihood of female firms having their applications accepted, as compared to comparable male businesses (Table 4.11). For Spanish firms, weak evidence suggests that female entrepreneurs are less likely to secure at least part of the loan sought (panel (b)). German and Italian firms show a higher frequency of rejected applications, even after controlling for non-gender-related differences; marginal effects suggest that female firms have a higher probability than their male counterparts of denial, with probabilities as large as 6.6 and 8.8 percent-

Table 4.10 Country analysis. Econometric analysis: application for bank loans (1) *(multinomial logistic estimates)*

	Applied	Did not apply because of possible rejection	Did not apply because of sufficient internal funds	Did not apply for other reasons	
			a. Germany		
Female firm (2)	[base]	−.035	−.104	−.161	
		[.218]	[.137]	[.179]	
		.004	*-.011*	*-.010*	
N. observations	3,363				
Pseudo R2	.037				
			b. Spain		
Female firm (2)	[base]	.131	−.072	.118	
		[.217]	[.153]	[.157]	
		.009	*−.029*	*.025*	
N. observations	3,389				
Pseudo R2	.032				
			c. France		
Female firm (2)	[base]	.362	.152	.315	*
		[.256]	[.154]	[.176]	
		.012	*-.000*	*.032*	
N. observations	3,497				
Pseudo R2	.030				
			d. Italy		
Female firm (2)	[base]	−.102	−.007	−.046	
		[.358]	[.171]	[.198]	
		−.003	*.004*	*−.006*	
N. observations	3,400				
Pseudo R2	.035				
Memo: Controls for every specification					
size (employees)	Yes				
size (turnover)	Yes				
age	Yes				
type of firm	Yes				
ownership	Yes				
country	Yes				

(1) Robust standard errors are reported in square brackets under the coefficient estimate. *** = coefficient is statistically significant at 1%; ** = at 5%; * = at 10%.
(2) Estimated marginal effects are reported in italics. Marginal effects are evaluated at means

Table 4.11 Country analysis. Econometric analysis: results from application for bank loans (1) *(multinomial logistic estimates)*

	Applied and got everything	Applied and got part of it	Applied but refused because cost too high	Applied but was rejected
		a. Germany		
Female firm (2)	[base]	−.378	.870	.874 ***
		[.398]	[.623]	[.318]
		−.057	*.019*	*.066*
N. observations	696			
Pseudo R2	.110			
		b. Spain		
Female firm (2)	[base]	−.486 *	.600	.000
		[.291]	[.532]	[.295]
		−.096	*.020*	*.019*
N. observations	1122			
Pseudo R2	.054			
		c. France		
Female firm (2)	[base]	−.235	−.300	−.738
		[.406]	1.170	.453
		−.012	*−.003*	*−.057*
N. observations	1015			
Pseudo R2	.095			
		d. Italy		
Female firm (2)	[base]	.029	−14.636 ***	.755 *
		[.361]	.606	.455
		.039	*−.205*	*.088*
N. observations	1067			
Pseudo R2	.100			
Memo: Controls for every specification				
size (employees)	Yes			
size (turnover)	Yes			
age	Yes			
type of firm	Yes			
ownership	Yes			
country	Yes			

(1) Robust standard errors are reported in square brackets under the coefficient estimate. *** = coefficient is statistically significant at 1%; ** = at 5%; = at 10%.
(2) Estimated marginal effects are reported in italics. Marginal effects are evaluated at means

age points in Germany and Italy, respectively (panel (a) and (d)).[15] By contrast, in France the general descriptive findings for the entire sample are fully confirmed, and the dummy for female firms turns out not to be statistically significant (panel (c)).

4.5.3 Robustness Checks and Further Research

Existing literature has found that the differing attitudes towards applications for external financing might depend on the personal characteristics of female directors and owners, such as a generally higher risk aversion, lower propensity to negotiate and higher inclination to be discouraged based on past denials (see Sect. 4.2). The dataset used in this paper permits us to shed some light on these hypotheses by relying on a SAFE survey question that addresses future prospects for the availability of financing. Answers show that, on average, women have more negative expectations. Although this variable is likely to be correlated with a firm's performance, we have added to the baseline specification (Eq. [4.1a]) and, in order to reduce possible endogeneity, we have used the answer on prospects for internal funds. The new specification (not reported) yields results very similar to the baseline, and the possibility that a firm will refrain from applying for a loan because it is led by a woman does not demonstrate statistical significance. An additional specification of the supply-side (Eq. [4.1b]) has been obtained by adding discouraged borrowers (i.e., those who refrained from application due to fear of rejection) to the applicants that were denied loans. This procedure should provide, according to Muravyev et al. (2009), an upper bound for possible discrimination. The estimation (not reported) yields the same results as the baseline.

Regressions based on several alternative specifications have also been run (results not reported) by adding explanatory variables that might capture the idiosyncratic riskiness of a firm, as perceived by third parties. The objective is to test the impact on the demand and supply of credit on the different perceptions that providers of funds may have regarding

[15] For Italian female firms, there also emerges a lower likelihood of refusing loans because their cost is considered too high, but the estimated coefficient is driven by just one observation in the entire sample.

the riskiness of female versus male firms. The risk variables that have been used are retrieved from the survey questions that refer to recent evolution in (i) firm-specific outlook, (ii) credit history, (iii) willingness of business partners to provide trade credit, (iv) willingness of investors to invest in equity or debt securities issued by the firm, and (v) profitability. The results of these extended specifications confirm the main outcomes of the baseline equation.

Although the analysis provides consistent evidence, other factors may also explain this result. The dataset cannot be matched with other sources of information on small firms, so an omitted variables problem cannot be tackled. A possible improvement of this study might be to account for the demand and supply determinants of bank credit variations by using the results of the ECB Bank Lending Survey at the country level in order to explain possible differences in the situation of female firms over different time periods, during different waves of the SAFE survey.

The latter point is relevant because previous results have been obtained, as stated, by pooling four waves of the survey that are homogenous in the questions that are relevant to this analysis, with the aim of enlarging the sample to make results as robust as possible. During the period dealt with in this paper, however, there might have been relevant changes, for instance in bank lending policy, that deserve to be considered. Therefore, further research should seek to understand why econometric results are, in some cases, different across survey waves. The fourth wave (covering the second half of 2010), for instance, presents some strong econometric evidence of more difficult access to credit for female firms, after having taken firms' characteristics into account; the fifth wave, relating to the first half of 2011, by contrast, shows the opposite in some cases (not reported).[16]

From a theoretical perspective, more precise estimations may be obtained by exploiting the panel component of the dataset. Extending the analysis to a panel econometric exercise, in principle, might shed

[16] Note that these results from a single survey wave (unpooled) are not affected by the downward bias in variance estimation, originating from the use of pooled survey waves with an unexploited panel component. See Sect. 4.3.1.

light on the partly contrasting outcomes in different periods. Due to the small SAFE panel component, however, the key results of this paper should not change significantly. Finally, a subsample of male firms might be drawn from the whole sample, mirroring the same structural features as the female subsample (matching sample), and the subsequent analysis might be focused on comparing the access to credit by these similar firms in order to remove the confounding effects of the different (and more diverse) features of the male firms.

4.6 Conclusions

Access to finance is one of the most serious issues that firms face, especially smaller firms. This paper contributes to the discussion of whether gender influences firms' access to various sources of external financing and, therefore, their financing structure. The existing literature is not definitive on whether observed differences between male and female firms in the probability of seeking and obtaining loans are fully explained by firm characteristics or whether some gender effect exists. When access to credit is found to be more limited for female firms, previous literature is inconclusive regarding whether this limitation is the outcome of a pessimistic attitude or self-restraint on the part of female entrepreneurs, as opposed to gender-related discrimination. Finally, empirical evidence is scarce for European countries. To shed further light on these issues, this paper uses the ECB SAFE survey, which is particularly valuable in assessing credit access conditions across the euro area with firm-level data.

The main results of this paper are as follows. From a descriptive point of view, we find that, first, firms in the euro area do not display significant gender differences in how relevant they believe credit constraints to be as an obstacle to their activity. Second, women-led enterprises tend to operate with a narrower variety of sources of financing compared to enterprises led by men, and they are less likely to use external financing. Third, even though banks are the major source of financing for female small firms, such firms have greater difficulty in obtaining credit than their male counterparts, due to both demand-side and supply-side factors. Regarding the demand side, female firms tend to apply less frequently for bank loans; specifically, they more frequently decline to apply for bank loans out of anticipation of rejection. Regarding the supply side, female firms' loan applications are more frequently rejected.

The econometric analysis suggests that this evidence is almost completely explained by firm-specific features (e.g., size, age, sector and proprietorship); female firms are significantly smaller and younger than male ones; a single entrepreneur is often the owner and they operate mostly in trade or other services. These characteristics may explain the lower need for external financing and, on the supply side, they are less desirable characteristics from a bank's perspective. In summary, female enterprises do experience more difficulty in financing; however, this is not merely *because* they are led by women.

Our results are robust to various different regression specifications. However, the dataset we have used cannot be matched with other sources of firm-level data and the omitted variable issue cannot be addressed. Additionally, results appear to be sensitive to the subperiod considered, identifying a disadvantage in credit access for female firms in some periods while providing no evidence of such a disadvantage in other periods. This apparent discrepancy could be due to significant changes that occurred during the period considered in this paper (e.g., in bank lending policies). This issue could be more effectively studied over a longer period of time using a larger number of survey waves, and we leave that approach to further research.

Last, but not least, an additional contribution of this paper is the exploitation of the SAFE advantage of being representative of the four largest euro area countries. This advantage has enabled us to compare country-level results in a homogenous setting. In particular, we found that even after controlling for firm characteristics, some significant gender differences remain. German and Italian female firms are more likely to have their loan applications rejected, whereas Spanish women-led firms experience a lower probability of obtaining at least a part of their requested loans. French female firms are more likely not to apply for loans due to reasons other than fear of rejection and sufficient internal funds.

The findings of this paper are relevant in identifying the roots of the difficulties of small European firms in accessing external financing. Factors hindering access to credit might limit the growth of some firms and, ultimately, the growth of the economy as a whole; therefore, it is crucial from the perspective of possible policy implications to understand whether differences in access to financing stem from gender-related stigma or, as our findings suggest, from other structural features of the firm.

References

Adams, R. B., & Funk, P. (2012). Beyond the glass ceiling: Does gender matter? *Management Science, 58*(2), 219–235.

Alesina, A., Lotti, F., & Mistrulli, P. E. (2013). Do women pay more for credit? Evidence from Italy. *Journal of the European Economic Association, 11*(1), 45–66.

Aspray, W., & McGrath Cohoon, J. (2007). Access to finance capital: A review of research literature on women's entrepreneurship in the information technology field, *Entrepreneurial Report Series*, National Center for Women and Information Technology.

Babcock, L., & Laschever, S. (2003). *Women don't ask. Negotiation and the gender divide*. Princeton: Princeton University Press.

Beck, T., Demirgüç-Kunt, A., Laeven, L., & Maksimovic, V. (2006). The determinants of financing obstacles. *Journal of International Money and Finance, 25*, 932–952.

Bellucci, A., Borisov, A., & Zazzaro, A. (2010). Does gender matter in bank-firm relationships? Evidence from small business lending. *Journal of Banking and Finance, 34*, 2968–2984.

Blanchflower, D. G., Levine, P. B., & Zimmerman, D. J. (2003). Discrimination in the small-business credit market. *The Review of Economics and Statistics, 85*(4), 930–943.

Carter, C., & Show, E. (2006). *Women's business ownership: Recent research and policy developments*. Report to the Small Business Service, UK Minister of State for Industry and the Regions.

Cavalluzzo, K. S., & Cavalluzzo, L. C. (1998). Market structure and discrimination: The case of small businesses. *Journal of Money, Credit and Banking, 30*(4), 771–792.

Cavalluzzo, K. S., Cavalluzzo, L. C., & Wolken, J. D. (2002). Competition, small business financing and discrimination: Evidence from a new survey. *Journal of Business, 75*(4), 641–679.

Cesaroni, F. (2010). Donne imprenditrici e banche. Le ragioni di un rapporto difficile. In G. Calcagnini & I. Favaretto (Eds.), *L'economia della piccola impresa*. Milano: FrancoAngeli.

Cole, R. A., & Mehran, H. (2009). *Gender and the availability of credit to privately held firms: Evidence from the surveys of small business finances*. Staff Report, Federal Reserve Bank of New York.

Coleman, S. (2000). Access to credit and terms of credit: A comparison of men- and women-owned small businesses. *Journal of Small Business Management, 38*, 37–52.

Coleman, S., & Robb, A. (2009). A comparison of new firm financing by gender: Evidence from the Kaufman Firm Survey data. *Small Business Economics, 33*, 397–411.

Croson, R., & Gneezy, U. (2009). Gender differences in preferences. *Journal of Economic Literature, 47*, 1–27.

Dohmen, T., Falk, A., Huffman, D., Sunde, U., Schupp, J., & Wagner, G. G. (2005). *Individual risk attitudes: New evidence from a large, representative, experimentally-validated survey*. (DP no. 1730). IZA.

Fabbris, L. (1989). *L'indagine campionaria: metodi, disegni e tecniche di campionamento*. Roma: NIS.

Ferrando, A., & Griesshaber, N. (2011). *Financing obstacles among Euro area firms who suffers the most?* (Working paper no. 1293). European Central Bank.

Madill, J. J., Riding, A. L., & Haines, G. H. (2006). Women entrepreneurs: Debt financing and banking relationships. *Journal of Small Business and Entrepreneurship, 19*(2), 121–142.

Marlow, S., & Carter, S. (2006). *If you don't ask you don't get! Women, self-employment and finance*. Warwick Business School small firm finance conference, Warwick.

Muravyev, A., Talavera, O., & Shäfer, D. (2009). Entrepreneurs' gender and financial constraints: Evidence from international data. *Journal of Comparative Economics, 37*, 270–286.

Osiewicz, M., & Pérez-Duarte, S. (2011). Measuring the access to finance of small and medium enterprises across the euro area through a flexible survey, mimeo available in www.ecb.europa.eu/events/pdf/conferences/ws_survey-data/Session_3paper_Perez-Duarte_Osiewicz.pdf?57eb075495c674780df69d6b078c451d

Öztürk, B., & Mrkaic, M. (2014). *SMEs access to finance in the Euro area: What helps or hampers?* (Working paper no. 78). IMF.

Robb, A., & Wolken, J. (2002). *Firm, owner, and financial characteristics: Differences between female and male-owned small businesses*. Federal Reserve working paper series. Washington, DC: Federal Reserve Board of Governors.

Roper, S., & Scott, J. M. (2009). Perceived financial barriers and the start-up decision: An econometric analysis of gender differences using GEM data. *International Small Business Journal, 27*, 149–171.

Stefani, M. L., & Vacca, V. (2013). *Credit access for female firms: Evidence from a survey on European SMEs*. (Occasional papers no. 176). Bank of Italy.

Verheul, I., & Thurik, R. (2000). *Start-up capital: Differences between male and female entrepreneurs "Does Gender Matter?"*. Erim Report Series 'Research in Management', Erasmus Universiteit Rotterdam.

5

The Small Firm Financing Premium in Europe: Where and When Do Small Firms Pay the Most?

Sarah Holton and Fergal McCann

5.1 Introduction

One of the defining characteristics of the recent euro area financial crisis has been a breakdown in the smooth transmission of monetary policy to segments of the economy. Firstly, both the cost of credit and the probability of a successful credit application have diverged greatly *across countries*, with borrowers in stressed economies (those having suffered the most severe shocks to banking and sovereign debt markets) facing a more severe credit contraction than those in "non-stressed" economies. Secondly, there has been a divergence in financing conditions *across firm types*, with small and medium-sized enterprises (SMEs) experiencing a disproportionate

JEL Codes: G21, G30

S. Holton
Monetary Analysis Division, European Central Bank, Frankfurt, Germany

F. McCann (✉)
Financial Stability Division, Central Bank of Ireland, Dublin, Ireland
e-mail: fergal.mccann@centralbank.ie

S.P.S. Rossi (ed.), *Access to Bank Credit and SME Financing*,
Palgrave Macmillan Studies in Banking and Financial Institutions,
DOI 10.1007/978-3-319-41363-1_5

increase in borrowing costs and decline in credit access relative to larger firms.[1] This deterioration has been particularly acute in stressed economies.

It is crucial to point out at the outset that across country types and across all states of the economy, one should expect smaller firms to pay an interest rate premium relative to larger firms when borrowing from banks. This premium, which we denote the Small Firm Financing Premium (SFFP), is to be expected for a multitude of reasons: higher observed default and a higher degree of idiosyncratic risk among SMEs[2]; more acute asymmetric information problems, which lead to an increased need for lender investment in screening; the fixed cost of making a loan must be covered out of interest rate payments leading to higher rates on smaller loans[3]; a higher reliance on the domestic economy among SMEs than larger corporates display, leading to less diversification against fluctuations in the local business cycle[4]; banks' reliance on larger corporate borrowers for deposits. In our data, the rate paid by small and large firms is proxied by the interest rate charged on loans below and above €1 million, respectively. Rather than exploring the relative impacts of the above drivers of the premium, this chapter is motivated by the large degree of *variation* in the SFFP across euro area economies during the crisis, and the heterogeneous response of the premium to macroeconomic developments and stress in banking markets, both across countries and banks.

Our chapter documents the evolution of the SFFP in the euro area from 2007 to 2015. Using monthly bank-level panel data, we show that in a benign economic environment in 2007, SMEs were paying an average premium of around 40–70 basis points on their bank borrowings in (future) non-stressed and stressed economies, respectively.[5] While there was variation across countries in the average premium charged in 2007,

[1] See Holton et al. (2013) and (2014) for evidence of divergence in credit access for SMEs during the euro area financial crisis.

[2] Past literature highlights these factors which tend to make SME loans riskier than larger corporate loans [see, for instance, Saurina and Trucharte (2004), Dietsch and Petey (2002) and Altman and Sabato (2013)].

[3] This is referred to as a 'multiplier' effect by Banerjee and Duflo (2010).

[4] See 'The Impact of the Global Crisis on SME and Entrepreneurship Financing and Policy Responses', OECD report, 2009.

[5] In this chapter, stressed countries are defined as Greece, Ireland, Italy, Portugal, Slovenia and Spain.

this variation increased markedly as the crisis unfolded.[6] In Ireland, for example, the SFFP increased from about 30 basis points (bps) before the collapse of Lehman Brothers and the onset of the financial crisis to around 150 bps in 2012. On the other hand, in countries less affected by the sovereign debt crisis such as Austria and France, SMEs were paying only 20 bps more than domestic larger corporates for bank financing, even at the height of the difficulties experienced in the euro area in 2012.

A time series depiction of the SFFP across stressed and non-stressed economies highlights the dramatic fragmentation in credit markets for firms in the euro area. In non-stressed economies, the period from late 2008 to mid-2013 was characterized by a 20 bps increase in the SFFP (from 40 to 60 bps). However, in stressed economies the picture was markedly different. In the period from late 2008 to early 2011, the premium hovered on average between 80 and 100 bps, and from late 2011 to mid-2012 a further increase was experienced, with SMEs paying a full 120 bps more than larger corporate borrowers in these economies in June 2012. On a loan of €1 million at a term of ten years, such a differential would equate to an increase in the loan lifetime interest bill of between €60,000 and €70,000,[7] simply by virtue of being in a country where banks are charging a higher premium.

We document an important role for macroeconomic developments and country factors in explaining variation in the SFFP. We show that at the lowest unemployment levels seen in the sample, the SFFP averages 40 bps, while at unemployment rates above the 75th percentile of all country-month observations in the sample, the average premium is 120 bps. We are agnostic on the precise drivers of this pattern, which may include the relatively low productivity and domestic orientation of the SME sector, which leads to them being more vulnerable than large firms to the impacts of large domestic macroeconomic shocks; however, the trend does suggest that in a deteriorating economic environment smaller borrowers are more prone to financing obstacles, which may serve to exacerbate the negative effects of a downturn.

[6] Even in stable times, differences in economic and banking structures across countries—including regulatory and fiscal regulations, collateral policies, non-interest expenses, maturity and market structure—can lead to natural and expected differences in interest rate pricing (ECB 2006).

[7] For a base interest rate ranging from 3 to 11%.

To provide another perspective on the heterogeneity underlying the aggregate observation of increasing cost of credit for SMEs, we use bank balance sheet information on all lenders in our data set to document supply side correlates of high premiums. The impact of bank balance sheet strength and weakness (as distinct from the characteristics of borrowing firms) on the supply of credit is generally referred to as the 'bank lending channel'.[8] SMEs' reliance on banks for finance makes the bank lending channel all the more relevant for them (Mishkin 1995). Moreover, the fact that SMEs depend on banks may mean that banks with balance sheet impairments may price interest rates to SMEs higher to improve their margins, given the lack of outside options available to small firms. For the US, Santos (2011) finds that banks with large subprime losses increased interest rates on loans to bank-dependent borrowers by more than the amounts they increased rates for borrowers that were not dependent on them. Balduzzi et al. (2013) find that in Italy increased bank funding costs lead to smaller and younger firms hiring fewer workers, investing less and reducing their bank lending. Moreover, there is evidence that during the crisis, the impact of factors reflecting bank balance sheet weakness hampered the pass-through of policy cuts more for smaller loans than for larger loans (Holton and Rodriguez d'Acri 2015). Consistent with the proposition that high premiums are partially a result of impaired profitability and bank funding stresses, we show that banks with high non-performing loan (NPL) ratios and high credit default swap (CDS) spreads charge higher premiums to SMEs.

Combining these country and bank-level factors, it is also plausible that when macroeconomic or financial shocks occur, banks that are under more intense funding and profitability pressure charge the highest cost of credit to segments of their borrower base with the narrowest set of outside options. In many economies, SMEs precisely fit this category of borrower. These type of effects are analyzed more formally in Holton and McCann (2016).

Finally, we highlight the importance of country heterogeneity in the link between bank-side characteristics and the SFFP. We plot fitted relationships

[8] For an overview of the bank lending channel, see Bernanke and Gertler (1995) and Gertler and Kiyotaki (2011).

between the SFFP and NPL, CDS, bank market share, and SME specialization and banks' holdings of domestic sovereign bonds for the two largest stressed economies (Spain and Italy) and non-stressed economies (France and Germany).

The results for bank market share are of particular interest, highlighting the importance of the structure of banking markets for SME funding. In both Spain and Italy, there is a linear and strong relationship whereby banks with larger market share charge SMEs a larger premium. In France, a similar relationship exists, but the levels of market power of individual banks are significantly lower than in Spain or Italy. In Germany, on the other hand, we show that there is in fact a negative unconditional relationship between bank market power and the SFFP, suggesting a different dynamic is at play, possibly in line with predictions of the 'information hypothesis' of Petersen and Rajan (1994). These results highlight the importance of the interaction between banking market structure and macroeconomic performance: the combination of weak bank competition and weak macroeconomic performance provide the perfect backdrop for an increasing cost of credit for SMEs.

The country-by-country analysis also shows that the strongest relationships between bank balance sheet weakness (proxied by either CDS spread or NPL) and the SFFP are also exhibited in stressed economies.

The findings presented in this chapter are in line with previous literature, which has highlighted that borrowers like SMEs pay a higher cost of credit than larger firms, at least partially due to their bank dependence, and that bank balance sheet weakness exacerbates this effect.[9] The implication that bank-level characteristics affect the SFFP suggests that the bank lending channel affects SMEs more than large firms. This is in line with Disyatat's (2011) reformulation of the bank lending channel, whereby variations in the health of banks and perceptions of risk affect the propagation of monetary policy. In this framework, financial frictions at the level of financial intermediaries and variations in their external finance premium are reflected in the cost and quantity of loans to borrowers that are dependent on these institutions. Theoretical literature offers an explanation for this phenomenon. Rajan (1992) suggests

[9] Santos (2011) and Balduzzi et al. (2013).

that banks' informational advantage over other outside lenders makes it more difficult for SMEs to switch to alternative finance as a response to increased bank interest rates. Our chapter fits into these strands of literature by providing an explicit bank-side treatment of the factors associated with the relative interest rate charged by banks on small versus large loans, highlighting the importance of macro-financial stresses, bank balance sheet weakness and bank market power.

The chapter proceeds as follows: Sect. 5.2 introduces the iBSI dataset, Sect. 5.3.1 discusses macroeconomic correlates of the SFFP; Sect. 5.3.2 introduces bank-level measures associated with the SFFP; Sect. 5.4 concludes.

5.2 Data and Aggregate Statistics

The dataset used in this chapter includes balance sheet and interest information on 176 euro area banks over 95 months from August 2007 to June 2015. It comprises information on the iMIR (Individual MFI Interest Rates) and iBSI (Individual Balance Sheet Items) datasets collected by the ECB, and data from market sources. The four largest economies in the euro area—Germany, Italy, Spain and France—account for around 65% of observations, shown in Table 5.1. This section describes both the bank-level variables and the macro variables used in the analysis and shows how they developed across the euro area over different periods.

Our key variable of interest is the spread between loans up to and over €1 million, which we denote as the Small Firm Financing Premium (SFFP). This measure is commonly used to analyze the cost of funds for SMEs relative to larger firms.[10] The measure used is for short term loans up to 1 year, for which we have most information. The increasing spread between small and large loans, particularly in stressed countries, has been well documented at the country level using aggregate data (as shown in Fig. 5.1 for the four largest economies), but this chapter allows us to investigate factors at the bank level that have contributed to this increase.

[10] See the Box in ECB Monthly Bulletin, July 2013 entitled: 'Small and Medium-Sized Enterprises in the Euro Area: Economic Importance and Financing Conditions'.

Table 5.1 Breakdown of bank-month data by country

Country	Freq.	%	# Banks
Austria	855	5.11	9
Belgium	665	3.98	7
Germany	5510	32.9	58
Spain	1805	10.8	19
Finland	570	3.41	6
France	1805	10.8	19
Greece	380	2.2	4
Ireland	760	4.55	8
Italy	1900	11.3	20
Luxembourg	760	4.5	8
Netherlands	665	3.9	7
Portugal	570	3.4	6
Slovenia	475	2.8	5
Total	16,720	100	176

Figure 5.2 shows the distribution of the SFFP across all bank-month observations in our dataset.[11] The first noteworthy observation is that in 15% of cases, the SFFP is in fact negative, that is, the lender charged a lower interest rate on its loans below €1 million than on those above €1 million. The median SFFP is 60 basis points, while a long right tail exists whereby at the 90th, 95th and 99th percentiles we see premiums of 170, 220 and 300 basis points, respectively.

Figure 5.3 shows that across the entire sample period 2007–2015, there are important differences in the average SFFP across countries. At the high end, SMEs have been paying an average premium of 120 basis points relative to large firms in both Ireland and Portugal. These are followed by average premiums of roughly 80 basis points in Spain and Slovenia. At the other end of the spectrum, we see extremely low average premiums in Austria (25 basis points), Finland and France (45–50 basis points).

Figure 5.4 shows the SFFP across countries for two selected years: 2007, when economic conditions in the euro area were relatively benign; and 2012, at the height of the banking and sovereign debt crisis in 'peripheral' euro area countries. The chart clearly shows that even in the

[11] The shape of the distribution reflects the effect of winsorizing the 1% tails.

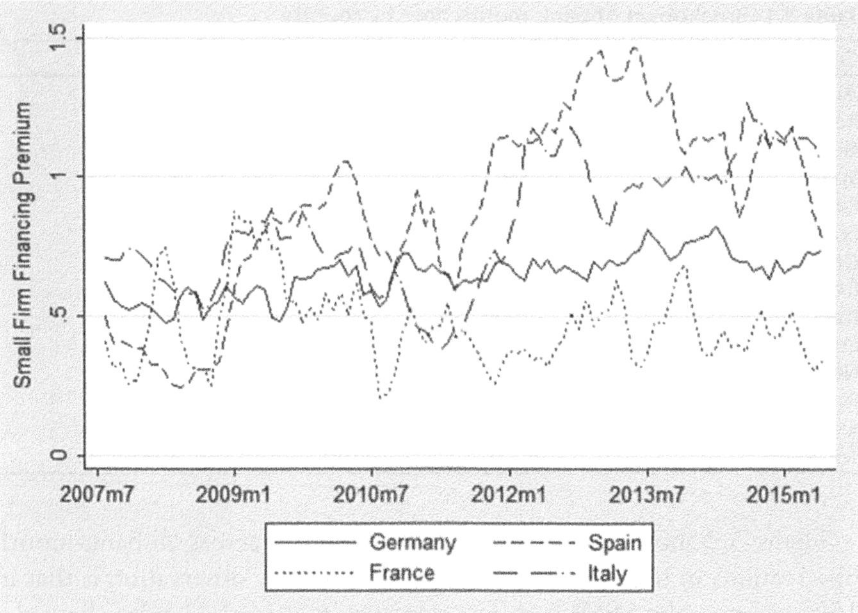

Fig. 5.1 Spread between loans up to and over 1 million euro (up to 1-year interest rate fixation, 3-month average)

pre-crisis era, there were significant structural differences in the relative cost of credit for SMEs across the euro area economies. Portuguese SMEs were paying a premium of 150 basis points, with Greek SMEs paying 120 basis points more than larger firms. At the other extreme, it appears that Finnish SMEs had an almost identical cost of credit to larger Finnish corporates in 2007.

The chart also depicts large differences in the shock to the SFFP induced by the crisis. Irish SMEs appear to have suffered the most extreme shock relative to their larger counterparts, with the SFFP rising from 55 to 155 basis points. Other countries with sharp increases include Spain, Italy, Netherlands and Slovenia. Meanwhile countries with a high SFFP over the whole sample period such as Greece and Portugal show little evidence of suffering an adverse shock to the SFFP as a result of the crisis: in both countries, the premium in fact appears to have decreased. This could be related to a compositional change in lending and a flight to quality.

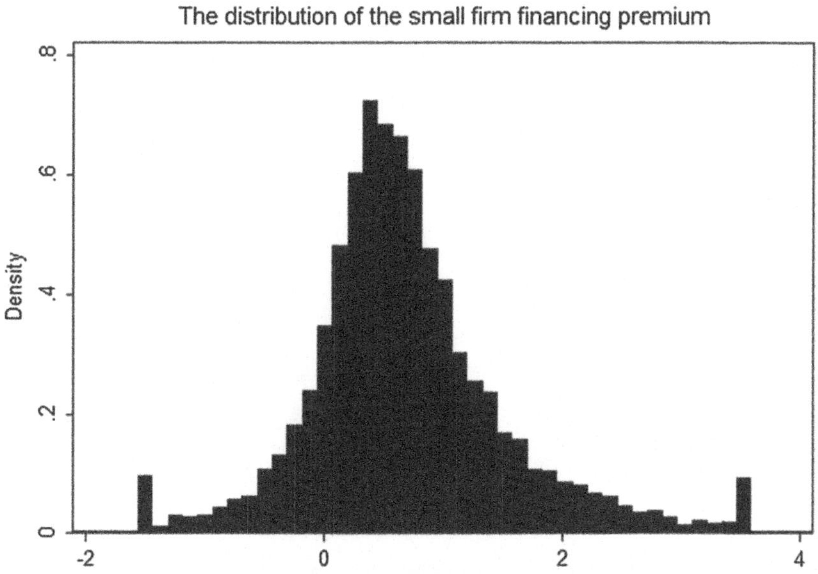

Fig. 5.2 Histogram of SFFP values, 2007–2015

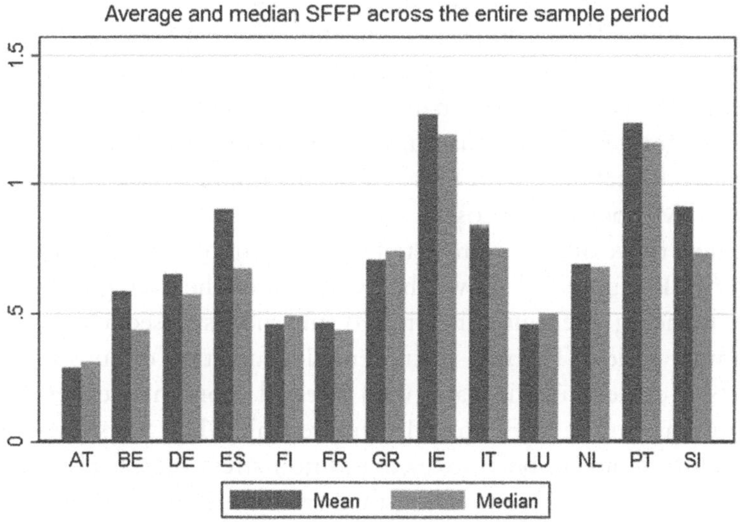

Fig. 5.3 Average and median SFFP across countries, 2007–2015

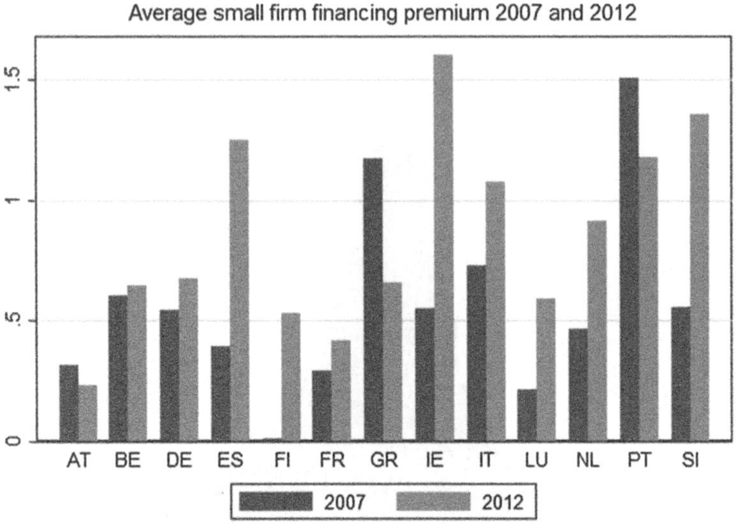

Fig. 5.4 Average SFFP across countries, 2007 and 2012

In Portugal, for instance, lending to state-owned companies increased over the period. These companies generally receive more favourable interest rates than private companies, and there is evidence (from 2012 at least) that loans to these companies tended to be smaller (Santos 2013). 'Core' economies such as Austria, Germany, France and Belgium exhibit a remarkable stability, with close to no disproportionate impact of the crisis on SME borrowing costs.

We now move on to a more detailed treatment of the timing of changes to the SFFP. Figure 5.5 shows the evolution of the average value of the SME financing premium in stressed and non-stressed countries over the sample period. The well-documented bifurcation of euro area credit markets is evident in the data, with stressed economies experiencing a huge increase in the SFFP in 2011. Interestingly, Fig. 5.6 shows that the standard deviation in both stressed and non-stressed areas also increased in late 2010 and 2011, providing further evidence of the breakdown in smooth transmission of monetary policy across the euro area during the recent crisis.

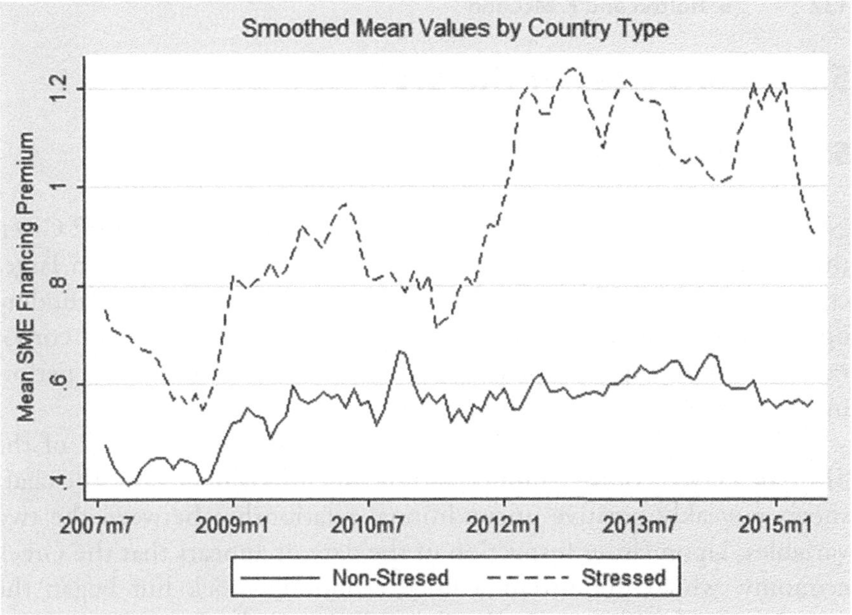

Fig. 5.5 Average monthly SFFP, stressed and non-stressed economies

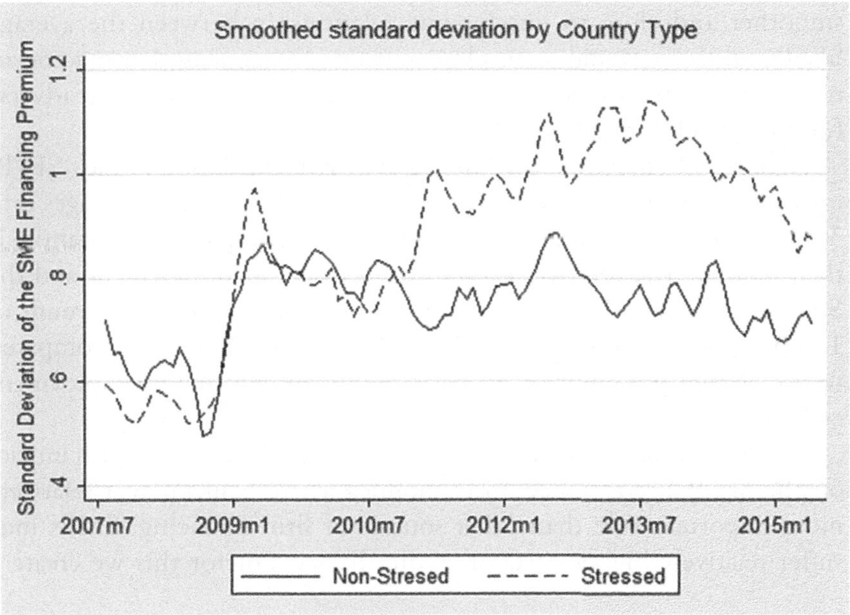

Fig. 5.6 Monthly standard deviation in the SFFP, stressed and non-stressed economies

5.3 Correlates of the SFFP

5.3.1 Country Level

Numerous macroeconomic factors are likely to influence the SFFP. Given that SMEs are more dependent on the domestic economy than larger corporates, combined with the fact that a wider set of alternative funding options are available domestically and internationally for larger corporates, it is to be expected that a deterioration in macroeconomic performance will be associated with higher levels of the SFFP.

Figure 5.7 plots the relationship between the average level of the SFFP in a given country-month and the unemployment rate. The chart shows a weakly positive unconditional relationship between the two variables. Upon closer inspection of the data, it appears that the Greek economy, which underwent a huge economic shock but began the sample period with an already high SFFP, and the Spanish economy are outliers in this relationship. Figure 5.8 plots the relationship for all country-months without Spain and Greece. We now observe a much smoother and close to one-for-one relationship between the average SFFP and the national unemployment rate, suggesting that macroeconomic developments are associated with a disproportionately adverse funding shock for SMEs.

Figure 5.9 presents an alternative visualization of the SFFP-unemployment relationship, splitting the monthly country averages into 50 quantiles. The average SFFP within each unemployment quantile is then plotted. The positive relationship between unemployment and the SFFP is again clearly exhibited using this method, with a premium of 120 basis points around the 40th to 45th of the 50 quantiles compared to an average premium of 40 basis points among low-unemployment economies.

Factors relating to the structure of the financial sector may also impact on the SFFP. For instance, in economies where banks play a relatively more important role than other sources of firm financing, SMEs may suffer relatively higher costs of credit. To account for this we create a

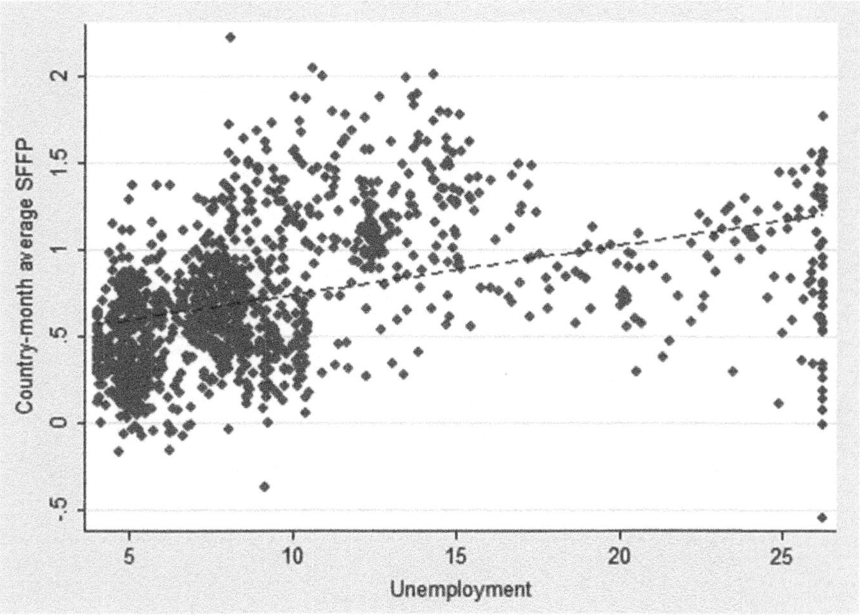

Fig. 5.7 Relationship between national unemployment and the SFFP

variable, 'bank dependence', which is the ratio of private sector bank credit to the sum of private bank credit and stock market capitalization (both available from the World Bank). While the stock market is not relevant for most SMEs, this ratio provides a macroeconomic overview of the importance of banks in the funding mix of firms. Figure 5.10 plots the relationship between annual country averages for the SFFP and annual measures of bank dependence. The chart provides tentative evidence that more bank dependence is indeed associated with higher levels of the SFFP.

5.3.2 Bank Level Correlates of the SFFP

We use a number of bank balance sheet characteristics that capture the general balance sheet composition of banks and those that are more

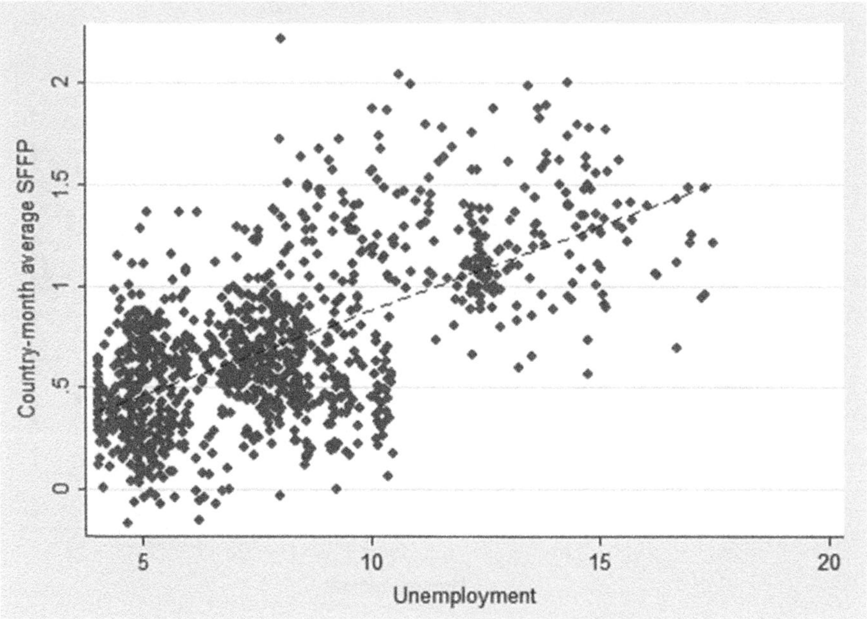

Fig. 5.8 Relationship between national unemployment and the SFFP, Greece and Spain excluded

related to cyclical developments. In line with the bank lending channel literature, these variables could affect credit provision and propagate shocks through the financial system. The three more general balance sheet characteristics we are concerned with are: market share, SME share and holdings of domestic sovereign bonds. The cyclical variables that we include are the non-performing loan (NPL) ratio and the credit default swap (CDS) spread. Table 5.2 provides a definition of these variables.

We begin by cutting the distribution of banks' within-country, within-time period market share into 50 quantiles and plotting the average SFFP within each group (Fig. 5.11). We observe relatively little by way of a systematic relationship in the first 60% of the market share distribution (up to quantile 30). However, in the top 40% of banks, there is clearly a tendency for banks with higher within-country market shares to charge disproportionately higher interest rates to SMEs. Such a finding is in line with bank market power literature, which suggests that firms experience

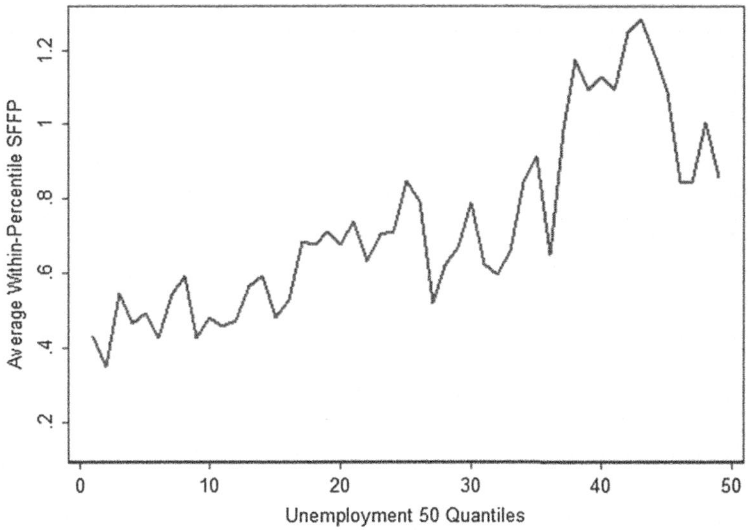

Fig. 5.9 SFFP within 50 quantiles of national unemployment

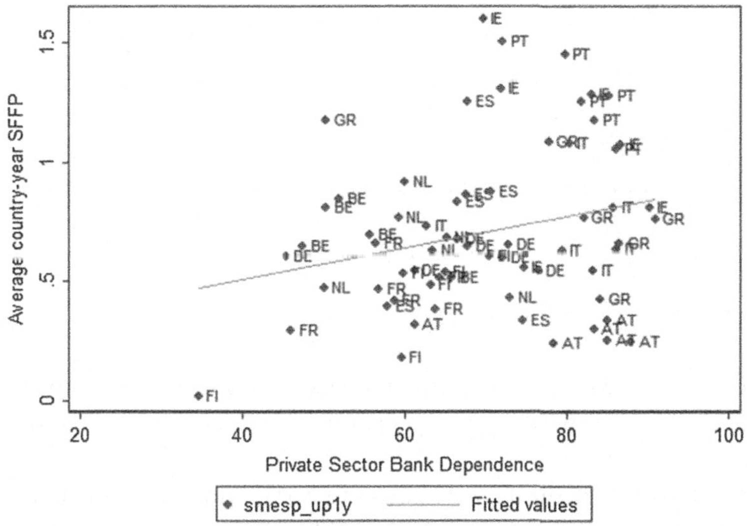

Fig. 5.10 Yearly average SFFP and bank dependence (2007–2012)

Table 5.2 Definition of bank-level explanatory variables

Market share	Main assets over total main assets at a country level	iBSI and BSI
SME share	Small loan new business flows over total flows	iBSI
NPL	Non-performing loans over risk-weighted assets	SNL
CDS	CDS spreads	Datastream
Dom GB	Holdings of domestic sovereign bonds over main assets	iBSI

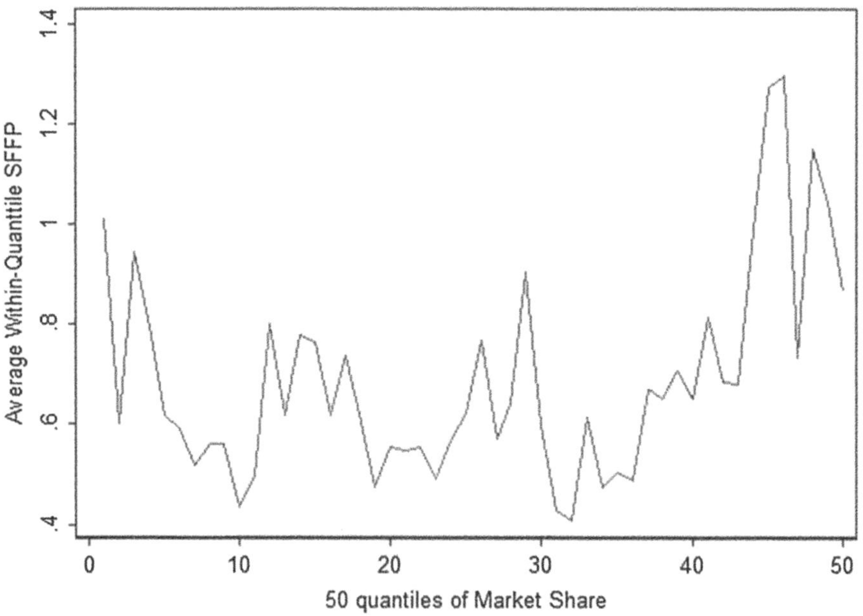

Fig. 5.11 SFFP across the distribution of market share

greater credit constraints in countries where bank concentration is higher and competition is weaker [see for example Ryan et al. (2014) and Carbó-Valverde et al. (2009)].

The relative specialization of banks in SME and corporate lending is a potentially important driver of the SFFP. Figure 5.12 provides a histogram of our measure of SME specialization, which is calculated as the ratio of non-financial corporate (NFC) loans below €1million to all NFC loans. The share of SME lending in all corporate lending is relatively small at

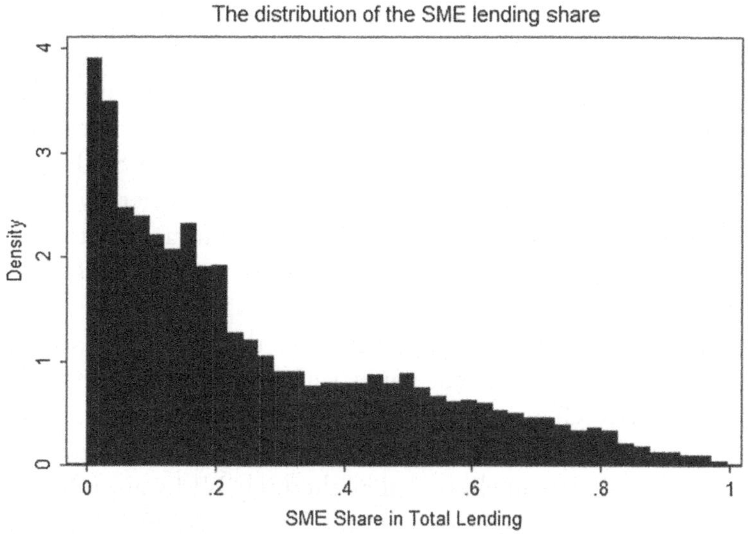

Fig. 5.12 Histogram of the share of SME loans in banks' total corporate lending

most banks in the sample, with the median share being around 20%. Banks with an SME share higher than 50% are relatively rare in the data. This partially reflects the focus of the iBSI data set on large euro area banks, with cooperative and local banks not being included in the data.

A priori, there could be alternative interpretations regarding the impact of banks' SME specialization on the SME premium. As information can reduce agency costs and frictions in credit markets, theories emphasizing that there are economies of scale in information production and that information is not easily transferred would suggest that developing specialization in lending to a certain sector would reduce the cost of lending and, consequently, the interest rates to this sector (Petersen and Rajan 1994).

On the other hand, banks with a high degree of specialization in SME lending may 'capture' SME borrowers by offering a broader and more tailored range of banking services and a stronger relationship with the borrower. This may lead to an informational monopoly and a bargaining power that could allow the specialized SME lender to charge a higher interest rate for this service [in line with Sharpe (1990) and Rajan (1992)]. Alternatively, it may be the case that SME-specialized lenders operate in countries experiencing more macroeconomic stresses. For these reasons, we may also expect a positive relationship. Figure 5.13 presents the simple unconditional relationship between SME specialization and the SFFP; it shows a positive relationship whereby banks with SME specialization rates above the sample median appear to charge an SFFP of 20–30 bps higher than those below the median. This would suggest that the informational monopoly may be operating.

Figure 5.14 plots the average SFFP across the NPL ratio distribution. A priori, we would expect that banks suffering from higher NPL ratios are more likely to charge higher levels of SFFP for a number of reasons: (i) their need to repair profitability after suffering provision-related losses on the NPLs; (ii) the likelihood that the high NPLs are reflective of a weak macroeconomic environment; and (iii) the likely riskier profile of borrowers at banks with a high stock of NPLs. The chart confirms that in general, banks with higher NPLs do indeed charge a higher SFFP, but the relationship is neither linear nor without noise. The increase in

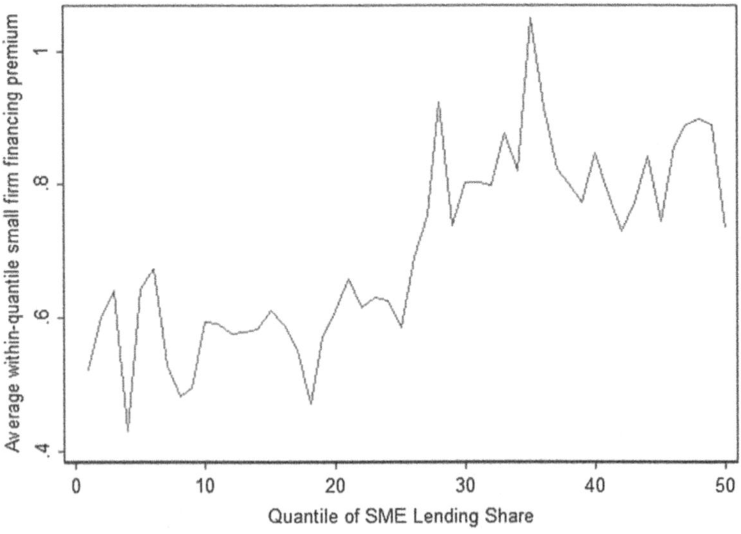

Fig. 5.13 SFFP across the distribution of SME specialisation

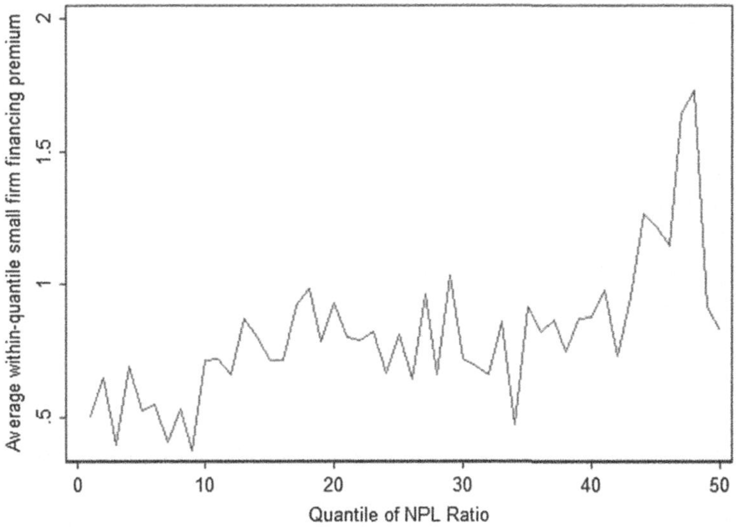

Fig. 5.14 Average SFFP across the distribution of banks' non-performing loan ratio

SFFP associated with higher NPLs only appears at the 20% of the NPL distribution.

Another way in which bank stress can be measured is through the credit default swap (CDS) spread, a quantification of the perception in financial markets that the bank is likely to default. Figure 5.15 plots the average SFFP across the distribution of CDS spreads in the data, with a strong tendency to charge significantly higher SFFP exhibited among the most risky banks. Banks in the top decile of CDS spreads charge an average SFFP of roughly 120–130 bps, while around the median the premium charged is 60–70 bps.

Finally, we measure banks' domestic sovereign debt holdings as a percentage of total assets. In 'normal' or non-crisis times, sovereign bonds are considered a close-to-risk-free and very liquid asset. However, during the sovereign debt crisis experienced in peripheral euro area economies since 2010, higher holdings of domestic sovereign bonds may have amplified the co-movement of sovereign and banking market stresses. Figure 5.16 plots a non-linear relationship between holdings of domestic sovereign

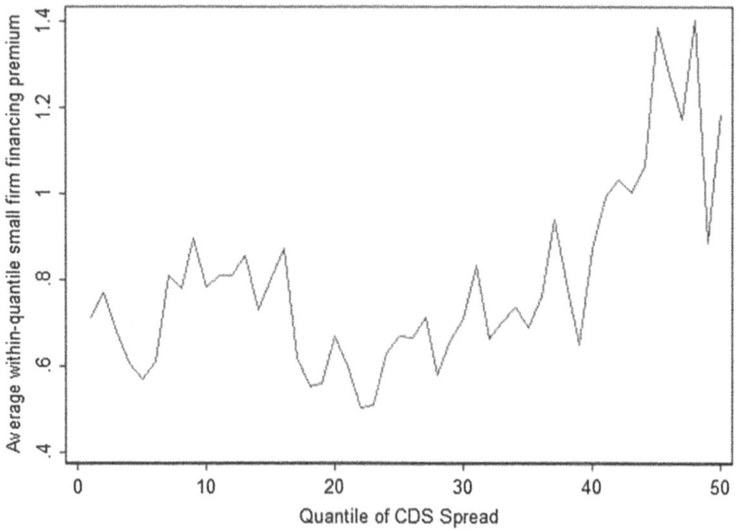

Fig. 5.15 Average SFFP across the distribution of banks' CDS spread

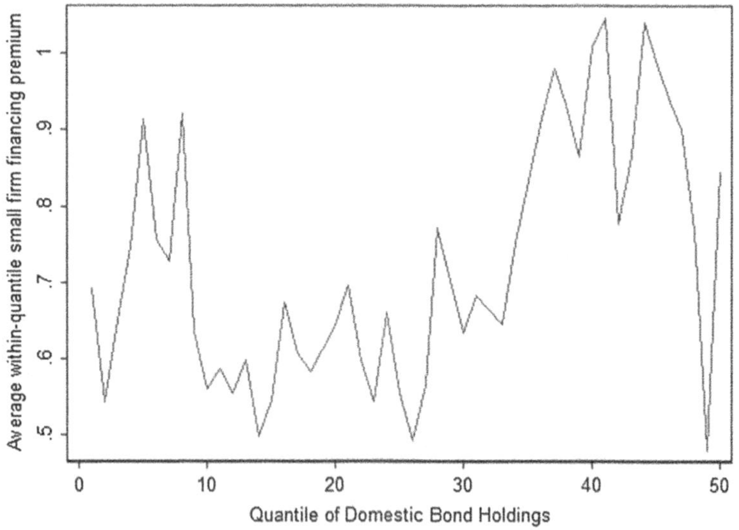

Fig. 5.16 Average SFFP across the distribution of banks' domestic sovereign debt holdings (measured per bank-month as a percentage of total assets)

debt and the SFFP. However, around the median there is a clear pattern of increased holdings of sovereign debt leading to increases in the SFFP, with the effect levelling off above the 80th percentile. This suggests that within this range, the impact of the sovereign debt crisis in stressed economies is prevailing over the 'close-to-risk-free' status of these assets.

5.4 Cross-Country Variation in the Impact of Bank-Level Factors

The above sections have shown that, in the period 2007–2015 in the euro area, there is significant variation in the SFFP across countries, over time, and as a function of unemployment, financial market structure and bank characteristics. We now investigate whether there are differences across countries in the relationship between bank characteristics and the SFFP. To do so, we plot the unconditional linear fitted line for the relationship between the SFFP and a range of bank characteristics within the four largest euro area economies, as well as for the full sample. The analysis unveils many important insights into the way in which banks' stresses and characteristics impact SMEs differentially across jurisdictions.

A large literature suggests that banks' market power leads to diminished access to finance and higher cost of credit for SMEs [see for example Carbó-Valverde et al. (2009) and Ryan et al. (2014)]. The country-specific results of Fig. 5.17 suggest that the economic structure matters crucially for the relationship uncovered in Fig. 5.11: in both Spain and Italy, there is a sharp positive relationship between the SFFP and banks' market power. This may be driven by the relatively lower productivity of SMEs in these economies, combined with their higher reliance on banks for financing. In France, there is a similar relationship, but market share values for an individual bank never surpass 10%, suggesting a different market structure and less scope for sharp increases in the SFFP along this channel in France. In Germany, however banks with more market share are shown to charge a lower premium to SMEs, suggesting an entirely different dynamic is at play relative to the other economies under study. Such a negative relationship is in line with predictions of the 'information

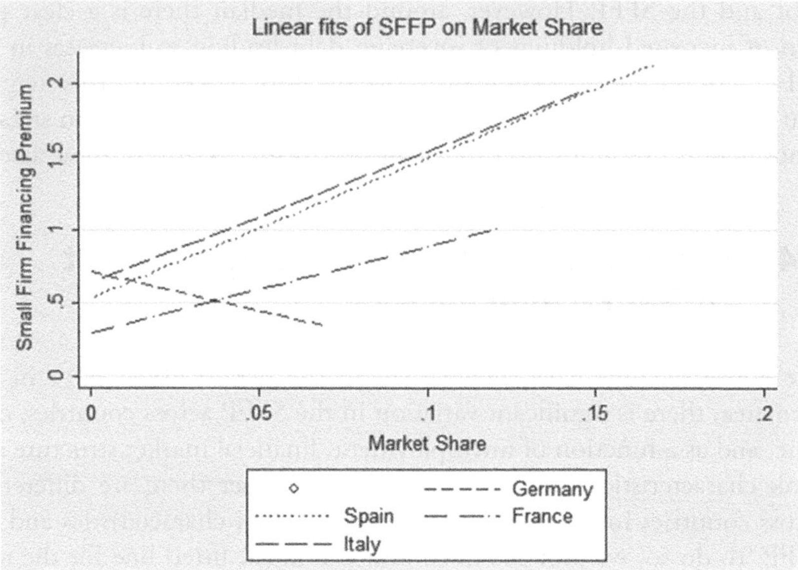

Fig. 5.17 Country-specific relationships: market share

hypothesis' literature (Petersen and Rajan 1994), which proposes that when market share is higher, banks have the scope to invest in their relationships with SMEs and in fact mitigate, rather than exacerbate, credit constraints.

The relationship between SFFP and banks' specialization in SME lending appears much less dependent on the country under study. In each of the four large euro area economies, the simple linear fit appears to imply there are only very weak relationships between specialization and the financing premium (Fig. 5.18).

Figure 5.19 explores the relationship between bank balance sheet stress (measured by the share of the stock of non-performing loans in total assets) and the SFFP. The fitted lines show that the relationship in all four countries is strongly positive. This suggests that where banks suffer balance sheet stress, small firm borrowers will experience a disproportionate funding cost shock. Given that the finding holds within all sampled countries, we can conclude that the relationship is not solely driven by a correlation between NPLs and a deteriorated macroeconomic environment.

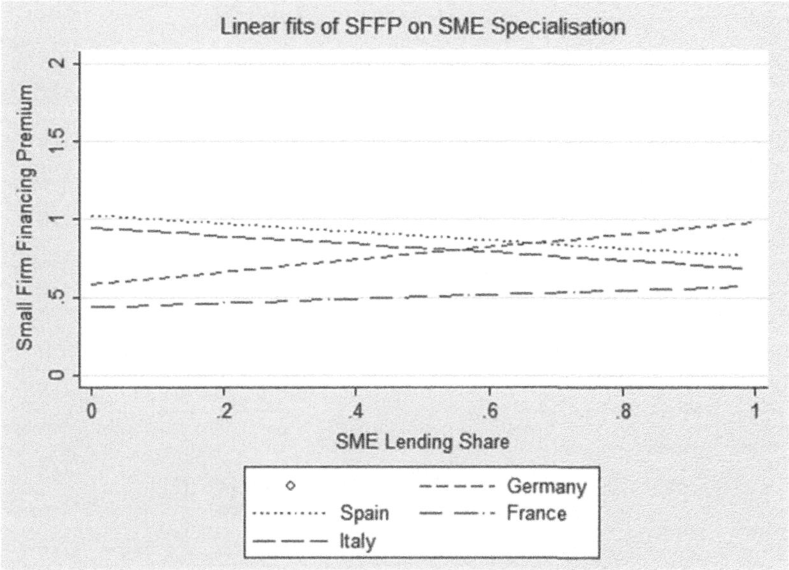

Fig. 5.18 Country-specific relationships: SME specialization

Given that both the NPL ratio and CDS spreads act as proxies for the financial health of banks, it is unsurprising that Fig. 5.20 presents similar findings to those in Fig. 5.19. For France and Germany, considered part of the non-stressed 'core' of the euro area, at low levels of bank CDS (where most banks are found during the sample period), there is no impact of higher CDS feeding through to tighter SME funding conditions; if anything, the relationship runs counterintuitively from higher spreads to lower SFFP. In the euro area stressed economies of Italy and Spain, however, the picture is reversed, with higher bank CDS spreads leading to disproportionately increased funding pressures for SMEs.

Finally, in Fig. 5.21 we plot the relationship between the SFFP and the domestic sovereign bond holdings. In Germany, the large country which has experienced the most benign sovereign market conditions since the onset of the euro area crisis, we see the expected negative relationship, whereby banks with higher holdings of domestic sovereign debt, generally seen as very safe and liquid, are shown to charge lower levels of SFFP.

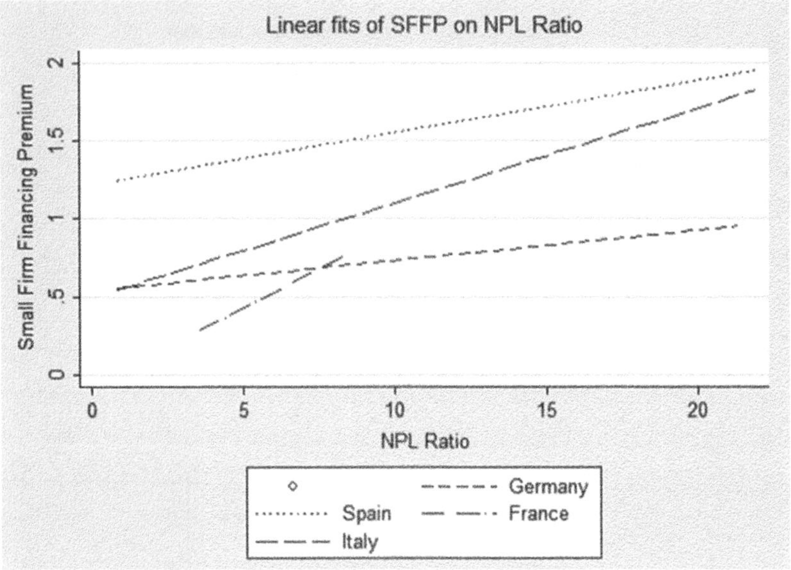

Fig. 5.19 Country-specific relationships: NPL ratio

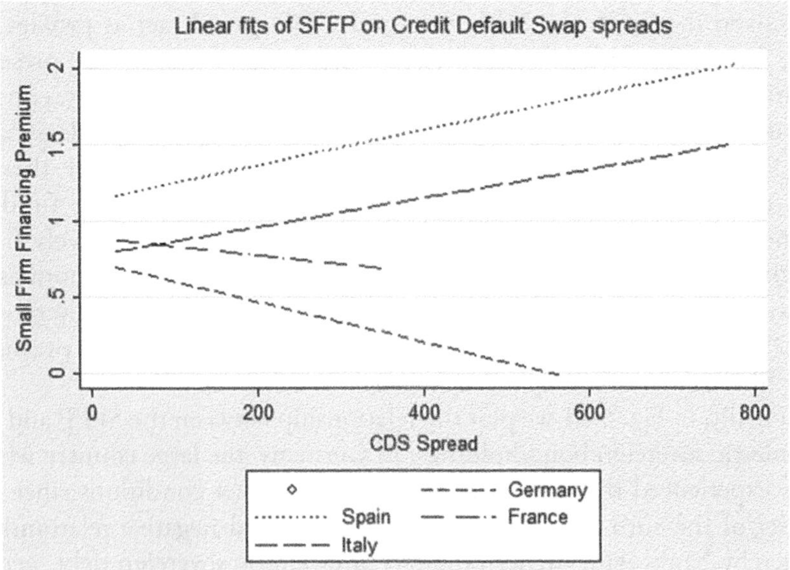

Fig. 5.20 Country-specific relationships: CDS spreads

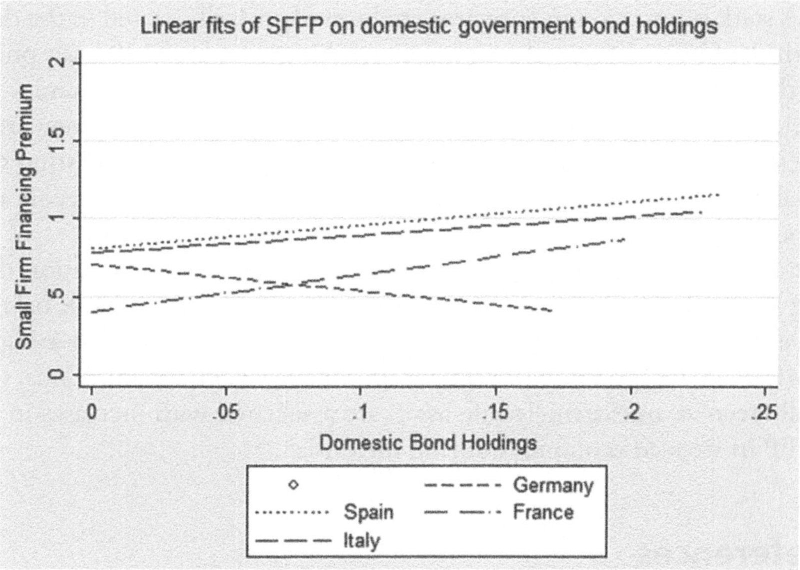

Fig. 5.21 Country-specific relationships: holdings of domestic government bonds

In the other three large countries however, we see the impact of the crisis period, whereby banks with higher holdings of the domestic sovereign are in fact charging higher premiums to SMEs. These patterns again highlight the importance of using bank-level data to examine the heterogeneity underlying euro area and country aggregates.

5.5 Conclusion

Using bank-level panel data, this chapter provides novel evidence on developments in the interest rate differential on loans below and above €1 million [the Small Firm Financing Premium (SFFP)] during the recent euro area crisis. We show that, even in 'normal times' in the euro area credit market in 2007, there were differences in the SFFP across countries. We then highlight the differential evolution of the SFFP across countries, over time and as a function of the characteristics of the domestic economy and the lenders themselves.

A stark bifurcation in euro area credit markets is illustrated in the data, with the SFFP in stressed economies reaching a peak of 120 basis points at the height of the crisis period, while in non-stressed economies the average premium remained at around 50–60 bps. Unemployment rates are shown to be extremely strong correlates of the SFFP, suggesting that smaller firms, more reliant on the domestic economy, can have economic shocks disproportionately exacerbated via the banking system.

We highlight elements of the 'bank lending channel' in operation during the crisis, with higher bank market shares and weaker bank balance sheets, measured by NPL ratios and CDS spreads, leading to a higher SME financing premium. Holdings of domestic government bonds, typically seen as an extremely safe asset, are associated with increases in the SFFP in stressed economies during the crisis.

References

Altman, E., & Sabato, G. (2013). Modeling credit risk for SMEs: Evidence from the us market. In *Managing and measuring risk emerging global standards and regulations after the financial crisis*. Singapore: World Scientific Publishing Co.

Balduzzi, P., Brancati, E., & Schiantarelli, F. (2013). *Financial markets, banks' cost of funding, and firms' decisions: Lessons from two crises* (Boston College working papers in economics 824). Boston College Department of Economics, revised 29 Dec 2014.

Banerjee, A. V., & Duflo, E. (2010). Giving credit where it is due. *Journal of Economic Perspectives, 24*(3), 61–80.

Bernanke, B. S., & Gertler M. (1995). "Inside the Black Box: The Credit Channel of Monetary Policy Transmission," *Journal of Economic Perspectives, Fall, 9*(4), 27–48.

Carbó-Valverde, S., Rodríguez-Fernández, F., & Udell, G. F. (2009). Bank market power and SME financing constraints. *Review of Finance, 13*(2), 309–340.

Dietsch, M., & Petey, J. (2002). The credit risk in SME loans portfolios: Modeling issues, pricing, and capital requirements. *Journal of Banking & Finance, 26*(2–3), 303–322.

Disyatat, P. (2011). The bank lending channel revisited. *Journal of Money Credit and Banking, 43*(4), 711–734.

European Central Bank. (2006, September). *Differences in MFI interest rates across euro area countries* (ECB report).

Gertler, M., & Kiyotaki N. (2011). *Financial Intermediation and Credit Policy in Business Cycle Analysis*, in Friedman B. M., & Woodford M. eds, Handbook of Monetary Economics, Elsevier, New York NY.

Holton, S., & McCann, F. (2016) *Sources of the SME financing premium: Evidence from European banks*. Central Bank of Ireland, mimeo, Dublin

Holton, S., & Rodriguez d'Acri, C. (2015). *Jagged cliffs and stumbling blocks: Interest rate pass-through fragmentation during the Euro area crisis* (Working paper series no. 1850). European Central Bank.

Holton, S., Lawless, M., & McCann, F. (2013). SME financing conditions in Europe: Credit crunch or fundamentals? *National Institute Economic Review, 225*(1), R52–R67.

Holton, S., Lawless, M., & McCann, F. (2014). Firm credit in the euro area: A tale of three crises. *Applied Economics, 46*(2), 190–211.

Mishkin, F. S. (1995). Symposium on the monetary transmission mechanism. *Journal of Economic Perspectives, 9*(4), 3–10.

Organisation for Economic Cooperation and Development. (2009). *The impact of the global crisis on SME and entrepreneurship financing and policy responses*. OECD report, Contribution to the OECD Strategic Response to the Financial and Economic Crisis.

Petersen, M. A., & Rajan, R. G. (1994). The benefits of lending relationships: Evidence from small business data. *Journal of Finance, 49*(1), 3–37.

Rajan, R. G. (1992). Insiders and outsiders: The choice between informed and arm's-length debt. *Journal of Finance, 47*(4), 1367–1400.

Ryan, R. M., O'Toole, C., & McCann, F. (2014). Does bank market power affect SME financing constraints? *Journal of Banking and Finance, 49*(C), 495–505.

Santos, J. A. C. (2011). Bank corporate loan pricing following the subprime crisis. *Review of Financial Studies, 24*(6), 1916–1943.

Santos, C. (2013). *Bank interest rates on new loans to non-financial corporations—One first look at a new set of micro data, Economic Bulletin and Financial Stability Report Articles*. Banco de Portugal: Economics and Research Department.

Saurina, J., & Trucharte, C. (2004). The impact of Basel II on lending to small- and medium-sized firms: A regulatory policy assessment based on Spanish credit register data. *Journal of Financial Services Research, 26*(2), 121–144.

Sharpe, S. A. (1990). Asymmetric information, bank lending, and implicit contracts: A stylized model of customer relationships. *Journal of Finance, 45*(4), 1069–1087.

6

Sovereign and Bank CDS Spreads During the European Debt Crisis: Laying the Foundation for SMEs' Financial Distress

Danilo V. Mascia, Paolo Mattana, Stefania P.S. Rossi, and Roberto D'Aietti

6.1 Introduction and the Literature

A main motivation of the policies adopted during the 2010 European sovereign debt crisis by national governments and the European Central Bank (ECB)—the latter still injecting unprecedented amounts of liquidity into the euro area banking system—was to mitigate concerns that sovereign debt pressures would deteriorate the balance sheets of banks and impair the flow of credit to the real economy. In fact, since 2010, by acquiring enormous amounts of government bonds, aimed to ease tensions in the secondary markets of stressed economies, large banks were alleged to have surrendered to central bank pressures. Given the size of

JEL Classification: G01, G12, G13, G15, G20, D8

D.V. Mascia (✉) • P. Mattana • S.P.S. Rossi • R. D'Aietti
Department of Economics and Business, University of Cagliari, Cagliari, Italy
e-mail: danilo.mascia@unica.it

S.P.S. Rossi (ed.), *Access to Bank Credit and SME Financing*,
Palgrave Macmillan Studies in Banking and Financial Institutions,
DOI 10.1007/978-3-319-41363-1_6

these investments and the consequent increase in risk profiles, banks were then forced to raise equity, thus limiting the supply of credit and increasing the cost of funding borne by borrowers.

Two main branches of the recent financial literature scrutinize these topics. Some studies are more focused on the contagion mechanism between banks and sovereigns. It is worth mentioning that these studies typically recognize the importance of credit default swap (CDS) derivatives as a measure of credit risk (inter alia, Ballester et al. 2016; OECD 2012) and use them to extrapolate the link between sovereign and bank distress.[1] Others are more interested in exploring the way banks transfer stress to borrowers in response to sovereign shocks, namely in terms of reduced lending and/or increased cost of borrowing.

Regarding the former literature, the findings support the notion that bank risk is related to country risk. Alter and Schüler (2012) investigate the relationship between sovereign and bank CDS spreads for certain eurozone countries. Using daily observations from 2007 to 2010, they find a reverse contagion effect according to which the direction of causality was from bank CDS to sovereign CDS spreads before bank bailout policies. However, after public policy interventions, sovereign CDS spreads were important determinants of a bank's risk. Reverse causality—which arose in the pre-bailout period of the sample—was recently confirmed by Fontana and Scheicher (2016). Indeed, they show that sovereign CDS spreads are driven by certain risk factors, among which is the change in banks' CDS spreads. Additionally, Acharya et al. (2014) previously provided empirical evidence of 'two-way feedback' between financial and sovereign credit risk during the recent crisis. De Bruyckere et al. (2013) show the presence of a contagion effect between bank and sovereign CDS

[1] Note that the literature on CDSs and its determinants has recently seen growing attention by researchers given the pivotal role played by bank CDSs during the 2007 global financial crisis (see Angeloni and Wolff 2012; Ejsing and Lemke 2011; Demirguc-Kunt and Huizinga 2011; Acharya et al. 2014; Alter and Beyer 2014; Bosma et al. 2012; Gross and Kok 2013). Of particular interest in the field is the contribution by Annaert et al. (2013). The authors explain changes in banks' CDS spreads through a set of explanatory credit risk variables. The study, inspired by Merton's theoretical credit risk model (Merton 1974), analyzes 31 European banks. The model includes variables linked to CDS liquidity and variables related to the market and the business cycle. The results show how, during the financial crisis, an increase in credit risk significantly raises the CDS spread. An exhaustive and more complete survey of the literature on CDS is in Augustin et al. (2014).

spreads in Europe during 2007–2012 and provide explanations about their determinants. In particular, they describe the intensity of risk spillovers on the basis of bank and sovereign characteristics. They find that, although sovereign debt is the key driving factor of contagion at the country level, a weak capital buffer, a weak funding structure and less traditional banking activities matter at the bank level to increase vulnerability to risk spillovers. Finally, they show that the type of government intervention to manage a contagion is not invariant in reducing spillover intensity. Angelini et al. (2014) analyze the different channels through which sovereign risk affects banking risk and present new evidence on bank-sovereign links. They argue that the key factor underlying the bank-sovereign relationship is the country risk, which affects the economy as a whole. Avino and Cotter (2014) aim to analyze the price discovery process of bank and sovereign CDS spreads in six major European economies. Their findings highlight the concept that sovereign CDSs play a leading role in determining bank CDS spreads in the most distressed economies (i.e., Portugal and Spain), whereas the opposite relation arises for most developed countries (i.e., Germany and Sweden). Overall, the empirical contributions to the literature do not seem to share a common view about the direction of causality of the observed phenomenon.

Regarding the general impact on bank behaviour in response to the euro area sovereign debt crisis, the literature focuses particularly on the effects on bank lending (cf. inter alia, Correa et al. 2012; Ivashina et al. 2012; Popov and Udell 2012; Bofondi et al. 2013; Bedendo and Colla 2015; Adelino and Ferreira 2016; De Marco 2016). Importantly, all of these contributions agree on the evidence that the financial distress that arose during the sovereign debt crisis was transmitted to firms through a shortage in credit supply and an increase in the cost of funding.[2]

[2] Indeed, the propagation mechanism of shocks that may affect the decline in bank lending can have several explanations in the literature (Popov and Van-Horen 2015). Some argue that agency costs (Ueda 2012; Dedola et al. 2013) can be viewed as an explanation for the propagation of shocks that reduce the net worth of financial intermediaries; others include capital requirements (Kollmann et al. 2011; Mendoza and Quadrini 2010) and the monopolistic competition that generates countercyclical price-cost margins (Olivero 2010). Alternatively, information asymmetries between banks and investors can be exacerbated by adverse shocks to banks' net worth, reducing lending to the private real sector.

Our study aims to investigate the extent to which investors' perception about the risk of a country (as proxied by sovereign CDSs) influences the perceived risk of banks (as proxied by bank CDSs). For this purpose, we set up an empirical model that exploits information arising from an unbalanced panel of 24 banks pertaining to seven eurozone countries from 1 January 2010 to 27 May 2014. The observations are daily quotes. Our analysis, closely related to Avino and Cotter (2014), adds to the literature in several directions. More specifically, we exploit the panel dimension of the data. Furthermore, our approach is new in the literature as it faces endogeneity issues by employing dynamic panel techniques. In this regard, the Arellano–Bond estimator is an efficient tool for managing non-consistency problems emerging in the presence of endogeneity.

In detail, we analyze the banks' exposure to the financial and macro dynamics of the countries where they are based. In our model, higher country risk (as perceived by the market) affects banks' CDS price dynamics. The assumption is that, given the intensification of the sovereign debt crisis, the market perception of European banks' credit risk has increased accordingly. The transmission channels of the sovereign debt crisis towards domestic banks are numerous. Typically, banks hold consistent shares of government bonds in their assets (Popov and Van Horen 2015) for both investment reasons and as collateral for repurchase agreements with private counterparts or central banks. Therefore, tension in the secondary markets for government bonds may imply, on the one hand, impairment of bank assets and, on the other hand, an increase in the cost of funding from an increase in the margins of the repurchase agreement.

Our results show that sovereign CDSs played a relevant role during the sovereign debt crisis in Europe. That is, the market perception about a country's credit risk highly affects the evolution of banks' CDSs. Overall, our findings confirm the existence of negative spillovers from 'government stress' to bank risk profile, as measured by CDS price dynamics. This evidence also has important implications for SMEs, as highly documented in the literature (inter alia, Popov and Udell 2012; Bedendo and Colla 2015). In response to sovereign shocks that negatively affect their assets, banks reduce lending to the private sector and increase the cost of borrowing for enterprises. Because SMEs dominate the business landscape in Europe and heavily rely on bank financing, they are particularly affected by banks' financial distress.

The remainder of this chapter is organized as follows. In Sect. 6.2, we present the data and the methodology. In Sect. 6.3, we discuss our empirical results. In Sect. 6.4, we present the main conclusions.

6.2 Data Description and Methodology

6.2.1 CDS Contracts

The CDS is a credit derivative contract created in 1994 in an effort to hedge fixed income investors' credit risk (Kanagaretnama et al. 2016). The CDS market has experienced important growth since then. According to Goldstein et al. (2014), this market now accounts for more than two-thirds of all credit derivatives.

In technical terms, a CDS is an agreement between two counterparties that provides insurance against the default of the so-called underlying entity. In a CDS, the protection buyer regularly pays the protection seller until the occurrence of a credit event (or until the maturity date of the contract if the credit event does not occur). The annualized spread in basis points—usually identified as the CDS spread—represents the premium paid by the protection buyer. The buyer is recompensed for the loss incurred whether the predefined credit event (usually default) on the predefined underlying financial instrument occurs (Da Fonseca and Gottschalk 2014). For instance, if we consider a CDS on a bond, the compensation is calculated as the difference between the par value of the insured bond and its market value after default.

6.2.2 Dependent Variable: Bank CDSs

Our sample is composed of daily observations of five-year bank CDS spreads (data provided by Datastream) related to 24 listed banks chartered in seven euro area countries (Austria, France, Germany, Greece, Italy, Portugal and Spain); see Table 6.1, which contains the names of the banks in our sample.

Table 6.1 List of observed banks

Country		Bank name
Greece	1	Alpha Bank
	2	National Bank of Greece
Italy	3	Banca Monte dei Paschi di Siena
	4	Banca Popolare di Milano
	5	Intesa Sanpaolo
	6	Mediobanca
	7	Unicredit
	8	Unione di Banche Italiane
Portugal	9	Banco Comercial Portugues
	10	Banco Espirito Santo
Spain	11	Banco de Sabadell
	12	Banco Santander
	13	Banco Popular Espanol
	14	Bankinter
	15	Banco Bilbao Vizcaya Argentaria
Germany	16	Commerzbank
	17	Deutsche Bank
	18	IKB Deutsche Industriebank
France	19	BNP Paribas
	20	Credit Agricole
	21	Natixis
	22	Societé Generale
Austria	23	Erste Group Bank
	24	Raiffeisen Bank International

We use five-year CDSs (as in Chiaramonte and Casu 2013) because they represent the largest and most liquid component of the CDS markets (Banerjee et al. 2016; Avino and Cotter 2014). As we are interested in studying the link between bank CDSs and sovereign CDSs during the recent European sovereign debt crisis, we decide to investigate a sample of daily observations from 1 January 2010 (as in Avino and Cotter 2014) to 27 May 2014. The choice of the period is motivated by the fact that the first signals of sovereign stress arose at the beginning of 2010. However, because we also have data on the pre-crisis period (i.e., from 4 March 2008), we are able to show significant differences in the medians of the analyzed CDSs before and after the start of the sovereign debt crisis.

Regarding the criteria adopted when selecting our 24 banks, it is worth noting that we chose only banks for which daily stock prices and CDS spreads were always available (i.e., no missing values). Therefore, we excluded banks that became inactive during the observed period.

Figure 6.1 illustrates the evolution of banks' CDS spreads, expressed in basis points, over time. More specifically, the series represented in the chart is the sample median of the daily observations related to our 24 banks' CDSs. Interestingly, we observe that before 2010 the spreads were mostly lower than a median value of 250 basis points. However, after the first weeks of 2010, our banks' CDS spreads rapidly increased until they peaked at a median value of 700 basis points around the end of 2011. Subsequently, monetary policy announcements by the ECB reduced the pressure in the sovereign bond markets (Corsetti et al. 2014), thus allowing our bank CDS spreads to decline to the average pre-crisis values. Figures A.6.1, A.6.2, A.6.3, A.6.4, A.6.5, A.6.6, and A.6.7 in the Appendix show the specific evolution of the aggregate banks' CDS spreads by country.

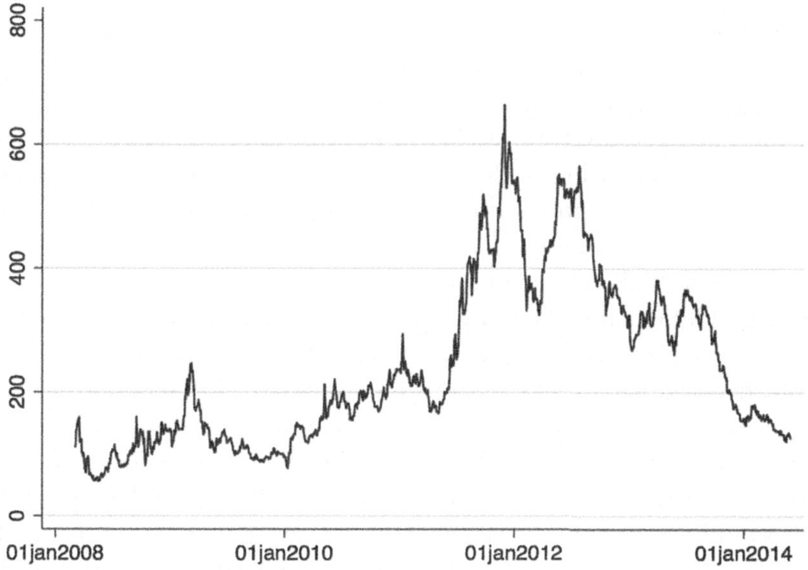

Fig. 6.1 Banks' CDS spreads

6.2.3 Key Variable: Sovereign CDSs

The time series on sovereign CDSs represents the key variable of our analysis. More specifically, we consider CDSs related to the countries in which our observed banks are based. Most of these countries—especially Greece, Italy, Portugal and Spain—experienced important difficulties during the first wave of the financial crisis and, even more, from 2010 onwards because of the European sovereign debt crisis. Therefore, it is interesting to investigate whether bank CDS spreads are influenced by the evolution of the corresponding sovereign swaps.

Figure 6.2 shows the evolution of sovereign CDS spreads over time. The series represented in the chart is the sample median of the daily observations related to our seven countries' CDSs in the sample. Again, we decided to plot the entire period, 2008–2014, to gain a clear picture of the deep surge experienced by sovereign CDS spreads during 2011–2012. More specifically, Fig. 6.2 shows that before 2010 the median sovereign CDS was approximately low and stable—it actually did not go beyond 150 basis points. In contrast, after the beginning of 2010 we document a dramatic increase up to a peak of more than 450 basis points around the end of 2012. The time series then falls to pre-crisis values during the final months of 2013. However, it is worth noting that important heterogeneities arise when we plot each country's CDS series. In particular, the Portuguese CDSs reached a peak of approximately 1500 basis points at the beginning of 2012, whereas German spreads did not even go beyond 80 basis points during the observed period (see Figs. A.6.8, A.6.9, A.6.10, A.6.11A.6.12, A.6.13, and A.6.14 in the Appendix).

Figure 6.3 displays the co-movement of the two series of our banks and sovereign CDSs across the sample period. As previously defined, the bank CDS series represents the aggregate median of the daily observations related to our five-year bank CDS, whereas the sovereign CDS series is the aggregate median of the daily observations pertaining to our five-year sovereign CDS (which refers to the seven countries in which our 24 banks are headquartered). The series show a similar trend. Interestingly, bank CDS spreads are also quite higher than sovereign ones, implying that overall the market perceives that banks are riskier than national governments. Additionally, Fig. 6.3 shows that between 2013 and 2014 CDS spreads declined to pre-sovereign crisis levels. As previously noted, this phenomenon might have

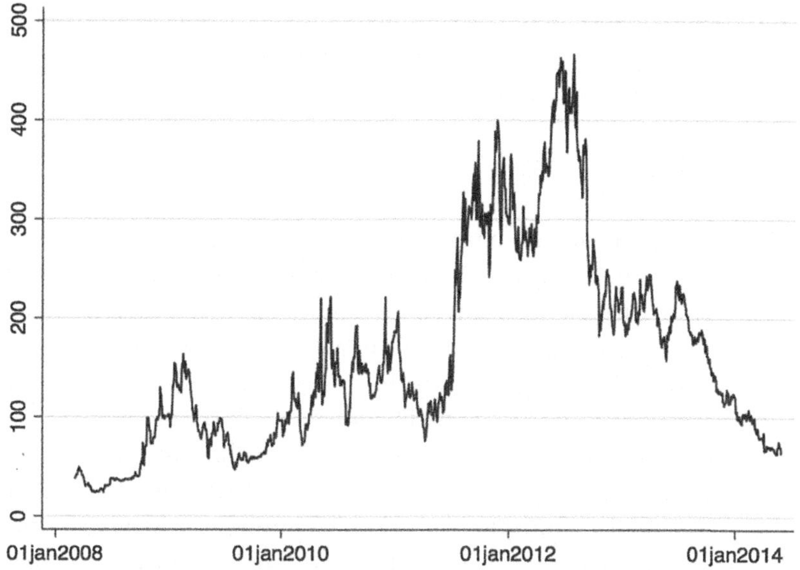

Fig. 6.2 Sovereigns' CDS spreads

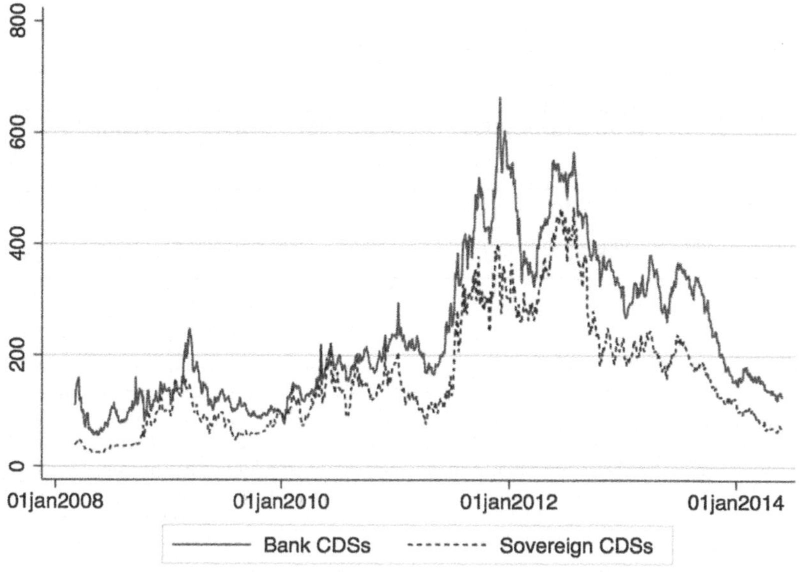

Fig. 6.3 Banks and sovereigns CDSs

been the consequence of the expansionary monetary policies implemented by the ECB rather than the effect of an improvement in macroeconomic conditions related to the most stressed countries in our sample.

6.2.4 Unit Root Test

We decide to perform an augmented Dickey–Fuller panel unit root test to provide evidence of the order of integration of our variables. Testing for the stationarity of our time series is fundamental, realizing that the use of non-stationary data may result in a spurious regression.[3]

The null hypothesis is that a unit root is present (i.e., non-stationarity), whereas stationarity is the alternative hypothesis. Table 6.2 provides the results of the unit root test on our CDS variables for three different periods, namely, the pre-sovereign crisis period (Column 1), the sovereign crisis period[4] (Column 2), and the entire sample period (Column 3). Evidence shows that both bank and sovereign CDSs are stationary throughout the observed period (Column 3). If we restrict our sample to only the observations from the sovereign debt crisis (i.e., from 2010 onwards), the evidence of stationarity is highly (mildly) confirmed for sovereign (banks) CDSs (see Column 2).[5]

Table 6.2 Augmented Dickey–Fuller unit root test

	(1)		(2)		(3)	
	Until 31 Dec 2009		Since 1 Jan 2010		Full sample	
	t-statistic	p-value	t-statistic	p-value	t-statistic	p-value
Bank CDSs	9984.878	0.000	61.872	0.057	66.938	0.037
Sovereign CDSs	2698.372	0.000	92.553	0.000	108.125	0.000

[3] For the sake of clarity, the stationarity of a series might depend on the choice of the length of the period of observation. The majority of papers that found evidence of non-stationarity usually included the period of high uncertainty and stress as the years 2006–2007, which were characterized by a notable increase in CDS premiums and an important destabilization of the financial system. Additionally, the literature often provides support for the hypothesis of non-stationarity of banks' CDSs. Therefore, it is pivotal to test for the possible existence of unit roots in our variables. In fact, if banks' CDSs and sovereign CDSs were integrated in the same order, the analysis of causality could be based on a study of the co-integration of the two series.

[4] Identified as in Avino and Cotter (2014).

[5] Regarding banks' CDSs, indeed, the hypothesis of stationarity is weakly rejected at a 5.7% probability in the restricted version of the sample.

6.2.5 Control Variables and Methodology

The specification of our model is as follows:

$$Y_{i,t} = d\,Y_{i,t-1} + \sum_{g=1}^{G} q_g S_{g,t} + \sum_{k-1}^{K} b_{i,k} X_{i,k,t} + \sum_{g=1}^{G} g_g Z_{g,t} + t_t + e_{i,t} \qquad (6.1)$$

where Y denotes the logarithm of the banks' CDS, S is the (country-invariant) logarithm of the sovereign CDS (as in De Bruyckere et al. 2013), X identifies a bank-specific variable, Z indicates country-invariant controls, τ represents the time dummies, e captures an idiosyncratic error $e \approx$i.i.d.(0, $\sigma^2{}_e$), and subscript i depicts the bank, g the country and t the time.

In particular, X is a measure of the overall performance of the bank, which is proxied by the ratio of the growth rate of the stock market value of each bank to its country's stock market index. Indeed, a positive return of the bank is the result of an increase in stock prices that, in turn, implies a lower perceived probability of default. Therefore, we expect a negative sign for this variable because higher bank performance results in a lower implied probability of default and, thus, a lower likelihood that our bank CDS—as a proxy of bank credit risk—increases (Merton 1974; Galil et al. 2014).

Vector Z includes the five-year euro interest rate swap that we add as a proxy for the risk-free rate, similarly to Annaert et al. (2013), the returns of each country's stock market index and stock market volatility. We expect that our proxy for the risk-free rate have a positive sign. In fact, an increase in the risk-free rate determines a raise in banks' interest expenses that, in turn, might be a source of increasing riskiness, thus affecting the probability of default (Völz and Wedow 2009). The returns of the stock market index are employed as a proxy for the general economic climate. An increase in this variable should signal an improvement in the economic cycle and, thus, a lower probability of default for the banks (Galil et al. 2014). For this reason, we expect a negative coefficient related to this macroeconomic control. Finally, we control for stock market volatility. Greater uncertainty in the market should determine a higher risk premium demanded by investors that, in turn, might lead to a higher probability of default and, consequently, a larger CDS spread (Galil et al. 2014). We proxy volatility using the five-day standard deviation of each

Table 6.3 Descriptive statistics

Variables	Obs.	Mean	Median	St. Dev.	p1	p99
Dependent variable						
Bank CDS (log)	14,910	1.036	0.990	0.749	−0.307	3.114
Key variable						
Sovereign CDS (log)	14,910	0.225	0.320	1.127	−2.071	3.265
Controls						
Bank performance	14,910	0.099	0.099	0.008	0.092	0.107
Risk free	14,910	1.712	1.610	0.688	0.780	3.120
Market index returns	14,910	0.001	0.001	0.015	−0.044	0.040
Market index volatility	14,910	0.136	0.119	0.081	0.030	0.417

country's stock market index returns. Table 6.3 shows the summary statistics of the variables employed in our study.

To estimate Eq. (6.1), we employ an Arellano–Bond dynamic panel data approach. Because of the correlation between the lag of the dependent variable and the idiosyncratic component of the error term, the traditional static (panel data) models are likely to produce biased estimates given the possible existence of endogenous regressors. Therefore, Arellano and Bond (1991) proposed an alternative and more efficient methodology. In particular, they argued that by exploiting the orthogonality condition between lagged values of the dependent variable and the error term, some instrumental variables might be added to control for endogeneity. Therefore, the underlying concept is to employ the past values of the dependent variable and, possibly, the information of some other endogenous regressors as instruments. The lagged values of the other control variables can be employed as instruments as well. We also employ time dummies to capture daily time effects.

6.3 Results

We report the results of our Arellano–Bond model estimates in Table 6.4. In particular, Table 6.4 shows the findings obtained through two options. The first option (Column 1) calls for treating sovereign CDS as an exogenous variable; the second option (Column 2) calls for considering our key variable as endogenous (i.e., we suppose that sovereign CDSs may be somehow influenced by the dependent variable). The latter hypothesis is not inconsequential given that—as previously stated in this chapter—the bank industry and the sovereigns are highly interconnected and may influence each other, especially in the case of financial distress.

More specifically, in the first column, we include—as instrumental variables—five lags (from *t*–3 to *t*–7) for the dependent variable and five lags (from *t*–1 to *t*–5) for the other controls. In the second option, we include the same instruments as in the first column, and we add five lags (from *t*–2 to *t*–6) of the sovereign CDS given the assumed endogeneity previously discussed. The reason behind the choice of excluding the first available lag of our CDS variables as instruments is the existing autocorrelation (that we verified in an unreported test) of such lagged variables

Table 6.4 Impact of sovereign CDSs on bank CDS spreads

	(Sov. CDS exogenous)	(Sov. CDS endogenous)
	(1)	(2)
Sovereign CDS	0.0935***	0.1075***
	(0.0067)	(0.0072)
Y_{t-1}	0.3870***	0.3812***
	(0.0126)	(0.0108)
Bank performance	–0.0891***	–0.1080***
	(0.0334)	(0.0325)
Risk free	0.3276***	0.3307***
	(0.0072)	(0.0952)
Stock index return	0.0068	0.0021
	(0.0254)	(0.0245)
Stock index volatility	0.0266***	0.0218**
	(0.0099)	(0.0094)
Number of observations	14,910	14,910
Number of banks	24	24

*** indicates significance at the 1% level, ** at the 5% level, and * at the 10% level

with the error term, which definitely impedes us from using them as instruments.[6]

The results in Table 6.4 show that our key variable, namely sovereign CDSs, has a positive and highly significant effect on bank CDS spreads. This evidence is in line with our hypothesis on the positive impact that sovereign CDSs had during the sovereign debt crisis in Europe; that is, the market perception about a country's credit risk has a strong effect on the evolution of bank CDSs. For the lagged value of the dependent variable, we note that it is highly determinant in explaining the variations in bank CDSs. In fact, its coefficient displays a magnitude of approximately 0.38, which is significant at the 1% level in both columns. Additionally, the bank-level control and the country-level variables (apart from the market index returns) are significant and show the expected signs.

Given the anomalies shown by the Greek sovereign CDS time series (i.e., lack of data from 23 February 2012, as shown in Fig. A.6.11 in the Appendix), our findings (which we do not report for the sake of brevity) are confirmed if we exclude Greece and its banks from our analysis.

6.4 Conclusions

It is widely acknowledged in the literature that investors' perception of credit risk may be proxied using CDS (inter alia, Ballester et al. 2016). Although the literature on CDSs is voluminous, contributions that evaluate the contagion effect of sovereign debt and bank distress measured using CDS spreads are rather modest because this issue received reasonable attention just after the European sovereign debt crisis. Following this track of the literature, our chapter investigates how countries' probability of default, measured by sovereign CDS spreads, affects the market's perception of a bank's credit risk. More specifically, using daily observations on sovereign and bank CDS spreads from 1 January 2010 to 27 May 2014, as related to 24 banks chartered in seven euro area countries, we provide an appraisal of the contagion effect between the sovereign debt crisis and bank credit risk. Our empirical strategy relies on a dynamic model

[6] Indeed, it is not surprising that daily observations can be correlated with their first lag.

assessed using the Arellano–Bond methodology. The results show that our key variable, namely sovereign CDS, has a positive and highly significant effect on bank CDS spreads. This evidence, which is consistent with our research hypothesis and in line with certain contributions in the literature, corroborates the suggestion of a contagious effect between countries' probability of default and the correspondent bank's perception of credit risk.

More interestingly from our perspective, the implication of this evidence—as highly documented in the literature (inter alia, Popov and Udell 2012; Bedendo and Colla 2015)—indicates that, in response to sovereign shocks, banks transfer the stress to borrowers, thus reducing lending and/or increasing the cost of borrowing for enterprises. In particular, this negative spillover penalizes SMEs, which rely heavily on bank financing.

Acknowledgments Danilo V. Mascia, Paolo Mattana and Stefania P.S. Rossi gratefully acknowledge research grants from the Autonomous Region of Sardinia, *Legge Regionale 2007, N. 7* [Grant Number CRP-59890, year 2012].

6.5 Appendix

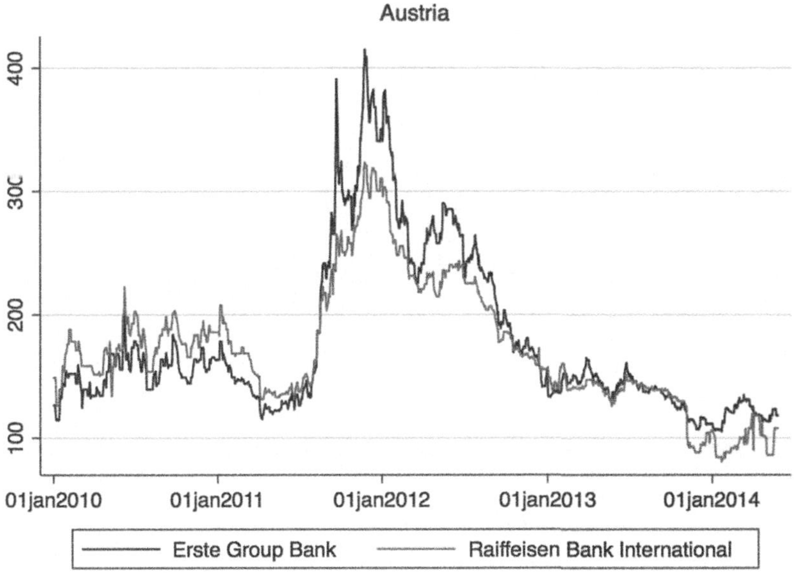

Fig. A.6.1 Austrian banks' CDSs

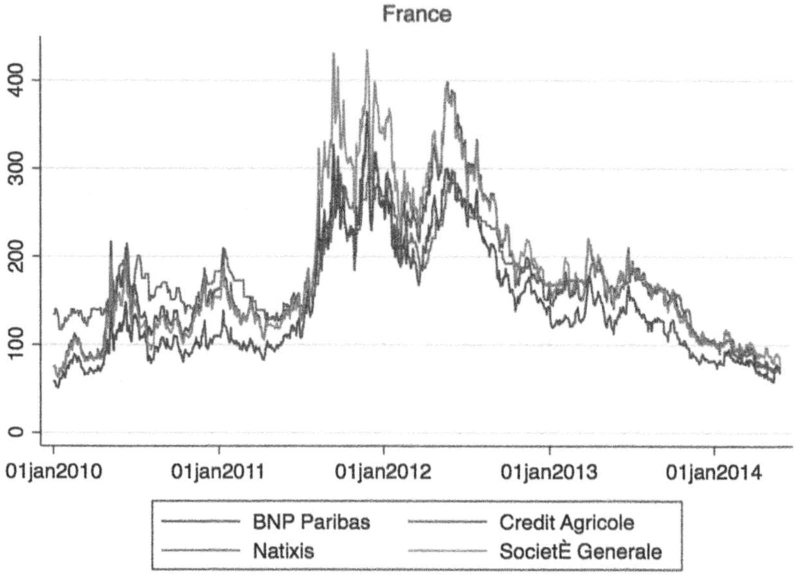

Fig. A.6.2 French banks' CDSs

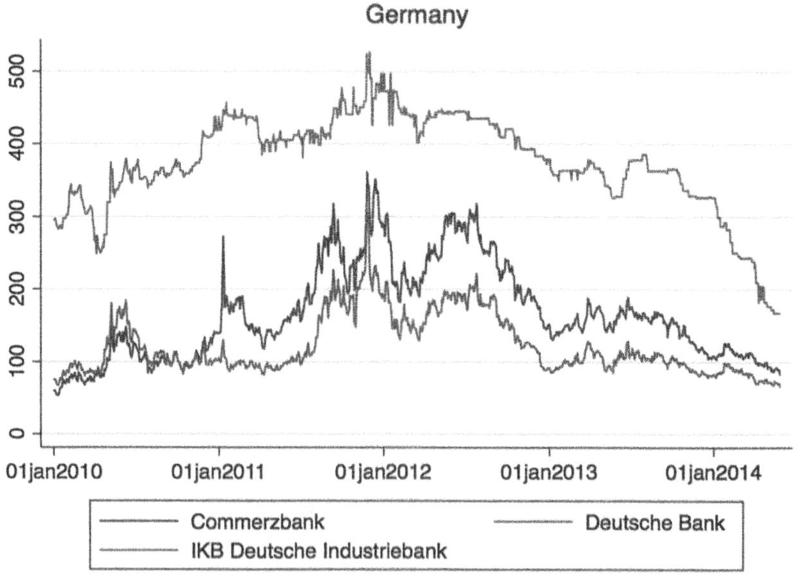

Fig. A.6.3 German banks' CDSs

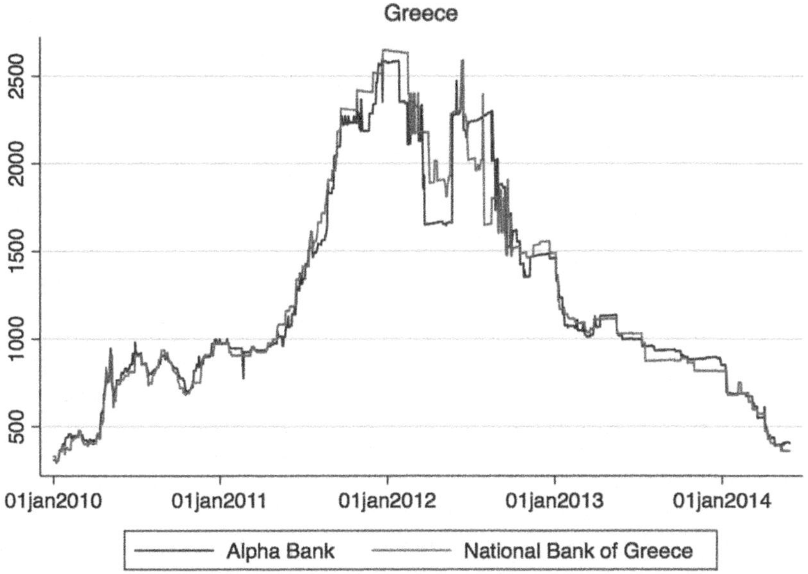

Fig. A.6.4 Greek banks' CDSs

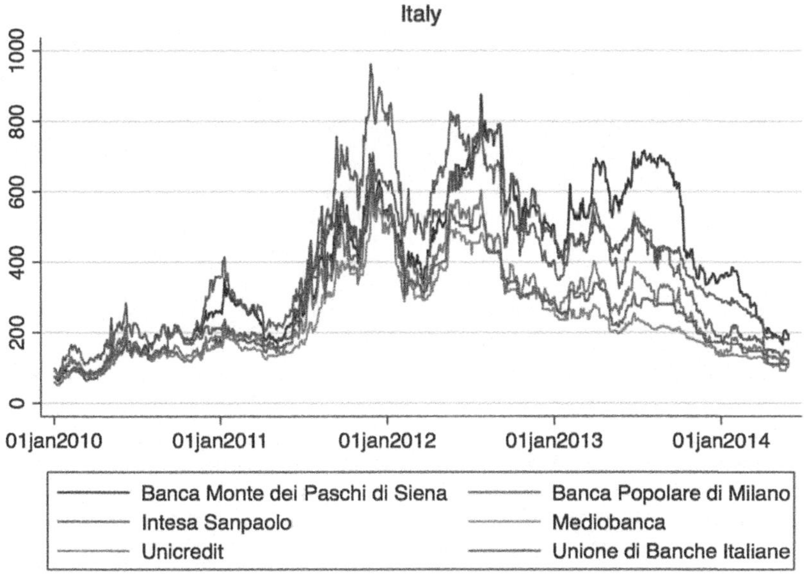

Fig. A.6.5 Italian banks' CDSs

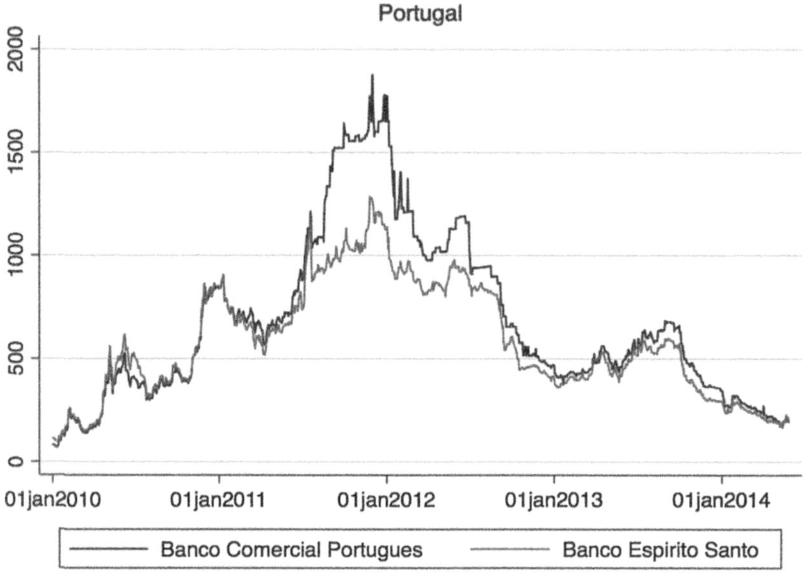

Fig. A.6.6 Portuguese banks' CDSs

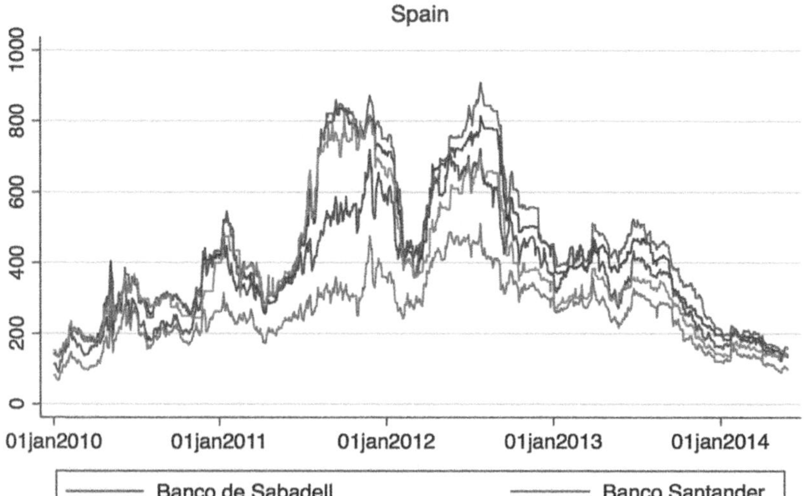

Fig. A.6.7 Spanish banks' CDSs

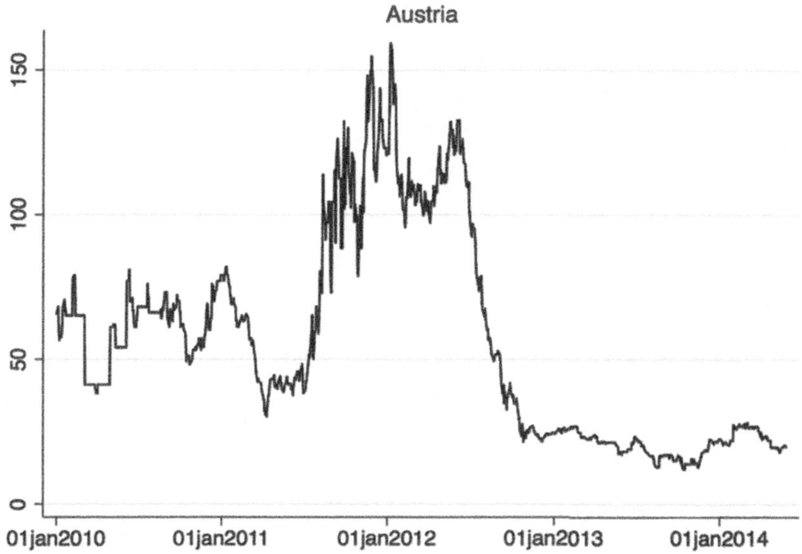

Fig. A.6.8 Sovereign CDS (Austria)

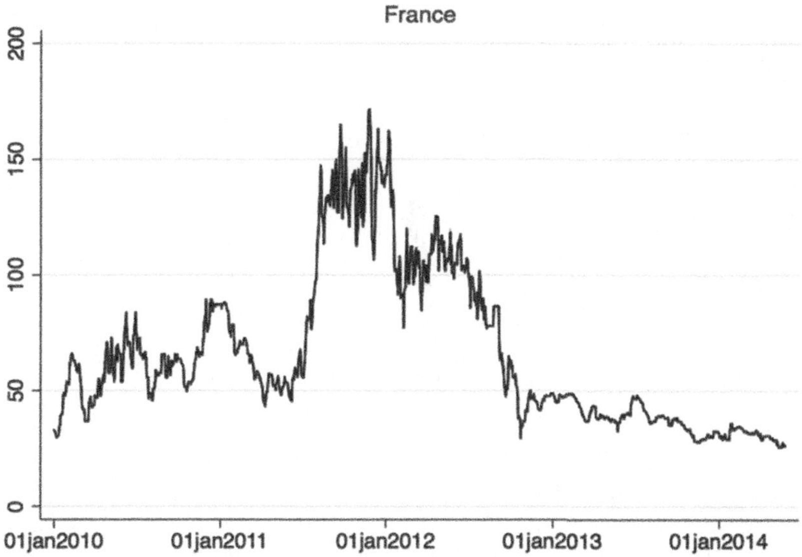

Fig. A.6.9 Sovereign CDS (France)

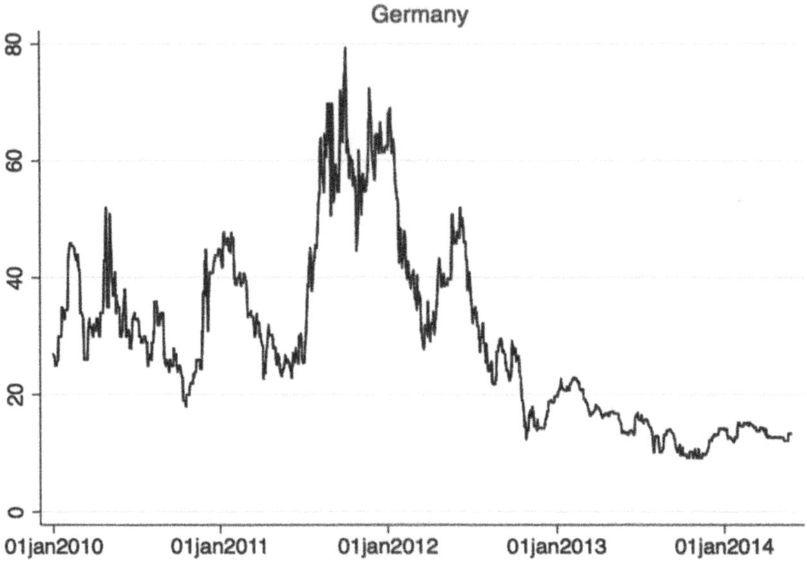

Fig. A.6.10 Sovereign CDS (Germany)

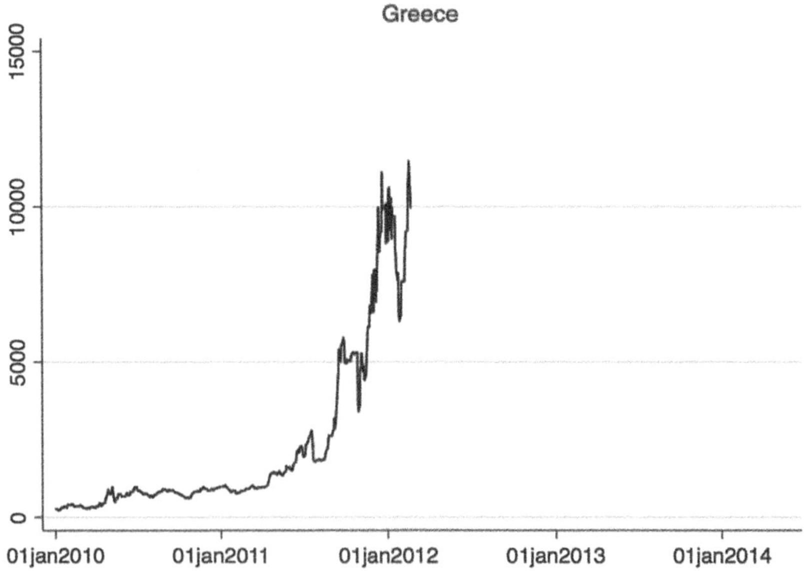

Fig. A.6.11 Sovereign CDS (Greece)

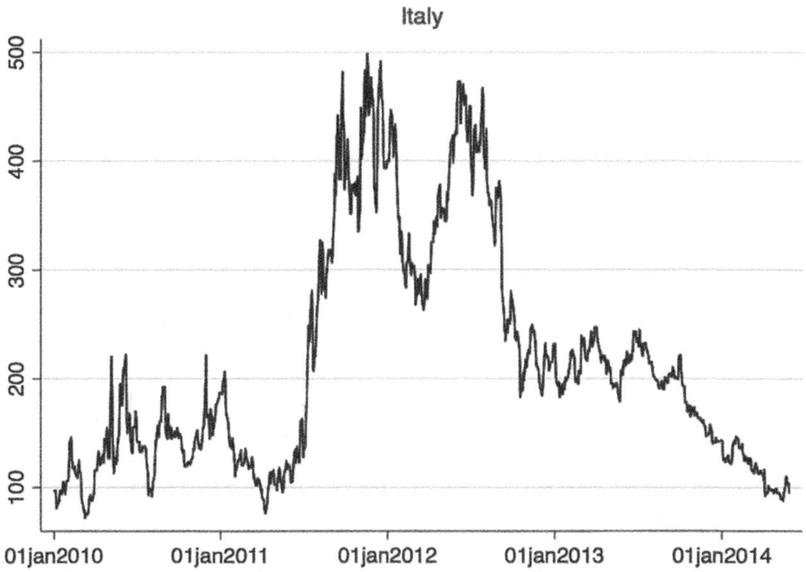

Fig. A.6.12 Sovereign CDS (Italy)

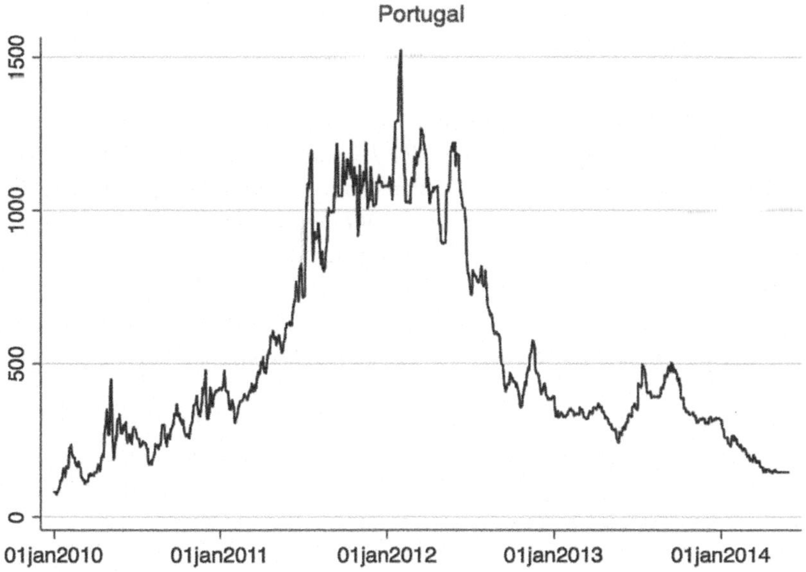

Fig. A.6.13 Sovereign CDS (Portugal)

Fig. A.6.14 Sovereign CDS (Spain)

6.6 References

Acharya, V. V., Drechsler, I., & Schnabl, P. (2014). A pyrrhic victory? Bank bailouts and sovereign credit risk. *The Journal of Finance, 69*, 2689–2739.

Adelino, M., & Ferreira, M. (2016). Bank ratings and lending supply: Evidence from sovereign downgrades. *The Review of Financial Studies, 29*(7), 1709–1746.

Alter, A., & Beyer, A. (2014). The dynamics of spillover effects during the European sovereign debt turmoil. *Journal of Banking & Finance, 42*, 134–153.

Alter, A., & Schüler, Y. (2012). Credit spread interdependencies of European states and banks during the financial crisis. *Journal of Banking & Finance, 36*(12), 3444–3468.

Angelini, P., Grande, G., & Panetta, F. (2014). *The negative feedback loop between banks and sovereigns* (Occasional papers no. 213/January). Bank of Italy.

Angeloni, C., & Wolff, G. (2012). *Are banks affected by their holdings of government debt?* (Bruegel working paper no. 07).

Annaert, J., De Ceuster, M., Van Roy, P., & Vespro, C. (2013). What determines Euro area bank CDS spreads. *Journal of International Money and Finance, 32*, 444–461.

Arellano, M., & Bond, S. (1991). Some tests of specification for panel data: Monte Carlo evidence and an application to employment equations. *Review of Economic Studies, 58*, 277–297.

Augustin, P., Subrahmanyam, M. G., Tang, D. Y., & Wang, S. Q. (2014). Credit default swaps: A survey. *Foundations and Trends in Finance, 9*(1–2), 1–196.

Avino, D., & Cotter, J. (2014). Sovereign and bank CDS spreads: Two sides of the same coin? *Journal of International Financial Markets, Institutions & Money, 32*, 72–85.

Ballester, L., Casu, B., & González-Urteaga, A. (2016). Bank fragility and contagion: Evidence from the bank CDS market. *Journal of Empirical Finance, 38*, 394–416.

Banerjee, A., Hung, C.H.D., & Lo, K. L. (2016). An anatomy of credit risk transfer between sovereign and financials in the Eurozone crisis. *Journal of International Financial Markets, Institutions & Money, 41*, 102–120.

Bedendo, M., & Colla, P. (2015). Sovereign and corporate credit risk: Evidence from the Eurozone. *Journal of Corporate Finance, 33*, 34–52.

Bofondi, M., Carpinelli, L., & Sette, E. (2013). *Credit supply during a sovereign crisis* (Working papers no. 909/April). Bank of Italy.

Bosma, J., Koetter, M., & Wedow, M. (2012). *Credit risk connectivity in the financial industry and stabilization effects of government bailouts* (Discussion paper no. 16). Deutsche Bundesbank.

Chiaramonte, L., & Casu, B. (2013). The determinants of bank CDS spreads: evidence from the financial crisis. *The European Journal of Finance, 19*(9), 861–887.

Correa, R., Sapriza, H., & Zlate, A. (2012). *Liquidity shocks, dollar funding costs, and the bank lending channel during the European sovereign crisis* (Discussion paper no. 1059). Board of Governors of the Federal Reserve System International Finance.

Corsetti, G., Kuester, K., Meier, A., & Müller, G. J. (2014). Sovereign risk and belief-driven fluctuations in the euro area. *Journal of Monetary Economics, 61*, 53–73.

Da Fonseca, J., & Gottschalk, K. (2014). Cross-hedging strategies between CDS spreads and option volatility during crises. *Journal of International Money and Finance, 49*, 386–400.

De Bruyckere, V., Gerhardt, M., Schepens, G., & Vander Vennet, R. (2013). Bank/sovereign risk spillovers in the European debt crisis. *Journal of Banking & Finance, 37*, 4793–4809.

De Marco, F. (2016). *Bank lending and the European sovereign debt crisis.* Unpublished manuscript, Bocconi University.

Dedola, L., Karadi, P., & Lombardo, G. (2013). Global implications of national unconventional policies. *Journal of Monetary Economics, 60*, 66–85.

Demirguc-Kunt, A., & Huizinga, H. (2011). *Do we need big banks? Evidence on performance, strategy and market discipline* (World Bank Policy research working paper no. 5576).

Ejsing, J., & Lemke, W. (2011). The Janus-headed salvation: Sovereign and bank credit risk premia during 2008–2009. *Economics Letters, 110*, 28–31.

Fontana, A., & Scheicher, M. (2016). An analysis of euro area sovereign CDS and their relation with government bonds. *Journal of Banking and Finance, 62*, 126–140.

Galil, K., Shapir, O. M., Amiram, D., & Ben-Zion, U. (2014). The determinants of CDS spreads. *Journal of Banking & Finance, 41*, 271–282.

Goldstein, I., Li, Y., & Yang, L. (2014). Speculation and hedging in segmented markets. *Review of Financial Studies, 27*(3), 881–922.

Gross, M., & Kok, C. (2013). *A mixed-cross-section GVAR for countries and banks*. mimeo.

Ivashina, V., Scharfstein, D., & Stein, J. (2012). *Dollar funding and the lending behaviour of global banks* (NBER working paper no. 18528).

Kanagaretnama, K., Zhang, G., & Zhang, S. B. (2016). CDS pricing and accounting disclosures: Evidence from U.S. bank holding corporations around the recent financial crisis. *Journal of Financial Stability, 22*, 33–44.

Kollmann, R., Enders, Z., & Muller, G. (2011). Global banking and international business cycles. *European Economic Review, 55*, 407–426.

Mendoza, E., & Quadrini, V. (2010). Financial globalization, financial crises, and contagion. *Journal of Monetary Economics, 57*, 24–39.

Merton, R. C. (1974). On the pricing of corporate debt: The risk structure of interest rates. *Journal of Finance, 29*(2), 449–470.

OECD (2012). *OECD sovereign borrowing outlook 2012*. Paris: OECD Publishing.

Olivero, M. (2010). Market power in banking, countercyclical margins, and the international transmission of business cycles. *Journal of International Economics, 80*, 292–301.

Popov, A., & Udell, G. F. (2012). Cross-border banking, credit access, and the financial crisis. *Journal of International Economics, 87*, 147–161.

Popov, A., & Van Horen, N. (2015). Exporting sovereign stress: Evidence from syndicated bank lending during the euro area sovereign debt crisis. *Review of Finance, 19*, 1825–1866.

Ueda, K. (2012). Banking globalization and international business cycles. *Journal of International Economics, 86*, 1–16.

Völz, M., & Wedow, M. (2009, June). *Does banks' size distort market prices? Evidence of too-big-to-fail in the CDS market* (Deutsche Bundesbank discussion paper). Frankfurt.

7

SME Sources of Funding: More Capital or More Debt to Sustain Growth? An Empirical Analysis

Marina Brogi and Valentina Lagasio

7.1 Introduction

Determining factors that affect funding of small and medium-sized enterprises (SMEs) constitute a fascinating and important topic—fascinating because SMEs are not just 'scaled-down' versions of large businesses (European Central Bank 2015a), and because access that SMEs have to bank loans is affected by both supply and demand constraints (Cressy and Olofsson 1997; Abor et al. 2014[1]). This is important because (i) SMEs make up the majority of firms and employ the largest portion

[1] 'The supply constraints refer to those factors that make it difficult for financial institutions like banks to lend (supply loans) to SMEs, including higher levels of informational asymmetries related to SME lending, higher transactional costs, the inherently riskier nature of SMEs and institutional weakness in developing countries that make it more difficult for financial institutions to lend to SMEs.' Abor et al. (2014).

JEL classification: L1, O1, G21

M. Brogi (✉) • V. Lagasio
Faculty of Economics, Sapienza University of Rome, Rome, Italy
e-mail: marina.brogi@uniroma1.it

S.P.S. Rossi (ed.), *Access to Bank Credit and SME Financing*,
Palgrave Macmillan Studies in Banking and Financial Institutions,
DOI 10.1007/978-3-319-41363-1_7

of the labour force in any developed economy, which is particularly true in the euro area,[2] and (ii) they are a key driver of growth because every company starts as a small enterprise whose expansion depends upon the company's ability to continue to invest in profitable projects that will, in turn, reflect its access to funding (European Commission 2015c).

This chapter investigates the evolution in funding sources for an extensive sample of SMEs (as defined by European Union recommendation 2003/361) from the four largest euro area countries (France, Germany, Italy and Spain) during the period from 2006 to 2014. Over 500,000 yearly financial statements were reviewed to determine the contributing factors of bank lending to non-financial firms and especially to SMEs. The aim of this chapter is to understand if the difficulties in accessing bank credit stem from the characteristics of the SMEs applying for financing by applying the reasonable assumption that demand factors, and especially creditworthiness, are relevant determining factors in the financing of SMEs. The results of this chapter provide useful insights at a time when providing funding opportunities for SMEs is an issue at the top of the European economic policy agenda.

This chapter is structured as follows: after briefly describing, in Sect. 7.2, the institutional background and literature related to SME financing, we conduct an empirical analysis of the creditworthiness characteristics of the companies in our sample. Section 7.3 describes sample construction and representativeness, Sect. 7.4 illustrates methodology and variables, Sect. 7.5 presents the empirical investigation and the discussion of results and Sect. 7.6 describes the conclusions reached.

7.2 Backdrop and Relevant Literature

The debate surrounding SME access to funding was fuelled by the financial crisis amid rising concerns regarding the reduction in traditional bank lending, which is particularly important for SMEs (Casey and O'Toole 2014), a group that is largely reliant on bank-related lending to finance

[2] In 2014, SMEs accounted for 99.8% of all enterprises in the non-financial business sector in the EU28 (European Commission 2015b). They also account for 60% of turnover and 70% of employment (European Central Bank 2015a).

their activities (European Banking Authority 2015). As reported by the European Central Bank in its Bank Lending Survey (BLS) (European Central Bank 2016), credit flow has decreased since 2007—having done so especially during the crisis (European Banking Authority 2015). This decrease in lending was a result of both increased restrictiveness in credit standards and conditions applied on loans (European Central Bank, various years) and a lower loan demand by firms (Farinha and Félix 2015). It is also likely that the monetary policy transmission mechanism is different for SMEs compared to large firms because of their greater dependence on bank financing (European Central Bank 2015a; Ferrando et al. 2015).

For the sake of completeness, it must be noted that as of last year BLSs (from early 2015 to 2016) recorded a net easing of credit conditions and an increase in credit demand.

SME access to bank loans is affected by both demand and supply constraints (Cressy and Olofsson 1997; Abor et al. 2014). In regard to supply constraints, the prudential capital framework for banks is designed to reflect the inherent risk of the different types of assets to which banks lend (European Central Bank 2015b). However, the Capital Requirements Regulation introduced in 2014 includes a capital reduction factor for loans to SMEs (the SME Supporting Factor, of 0.7619) to allow credit institutions to provide SMEs with an adequate flow of credit. This factor was designed to free up regulatory capital for use by SMEs and to improve SME lending conditions[3] (European Banking Authority 2015).

From a bank management perspective, SME lending is costly in terms of capital absorption[4]. Moreover, transaction costs in SME lending are higher than what is the case in dealing with large companies due to the former's lack of transparency. Banks create value by overcoming adverse

[3] 'The rationale for the SF is also based on the fact that capital requirements could be one of many factors affecting lending decisions. The capital relief resulting from the application of the SME SF led to an increase of 0.16 percentage point of an average CET1 ratio of 13.1% (weighted). The increase goes up to 0.21 percentage point if we consider only credit RWAs. In absolute terms, the application of the SME SF means that, in total, the minimum required capital has been reduced by approximately EUR 11.7 billion as of the third quarter of 2015' (European Banking Authority 2016).

[4] A lot of SMEs don't get all the financing they ask from banks in Europe [...] It is more costly for SMEs to get a loan from a bank than for bigger companies, especially in countries worst hit by the crisis." European Commission 2015a), Capital Markets Union and SMEs in the EU, 30th September.

selection problems intrinsic to external financing by gathering and evaluating private information to assess a firms' capacity to reimburse their debt (Brogi and Langone 2016). Relationship lending banks may also be capable of exploiting private information in order to evaluate a SME's creditworthiness, thus reducing the risk they face (Petersen and Rajan 1994, 1995; Cole et al. 2004; Fredriksson and Moro 2014). SMEs experience a more severe deterioration during downturns compared to those of larger companies, pointing towards the pro-cyclical nature of SME lending (European Banking Authority 2015).

SMEs are generally riskier than larger firms, with a higher non-performing loans/total loans ratio than large companies (18.6% versus 9.3%) (European Banking Authority 2015), a higher probability of default than larger firms and a lack of information on their credit quality (European Central Bank 2015b). Chai and Bang Dinh (2011) found that after the crisis, lending and credit conditions became more dependent on the level of risk than previously. The spread between rates on loans by firm category increased for younger firms and low-rated firms as a result of a readjustment of credit pricing policies. The level of risk is inversely related to the size of a firm (European Banking Authority 2016; European Central Bank 2015b).

With regard to demand, prior research on firm-level data found that SME accessing finance is more difficult and cost of credit higher than for large firms (Petersen and Rajan 1994; Cole et al. 1996; Schiffer and Weder 2001). Furthermore, these conditions result in constraints to their growth and investment (Schiffer and Weder 2001; Beck et al. 2005, 2008, 2011; Casey and O'Toole 2014). Many studies have found that firm size and leverage are positively related and, specifically, that larger SMEs exhibit higher leverage (Berger and Udell 1995; Chittenden et al. 1996; Michaelas et al. 1999; López-Gracia and Sogorb-Mira 2008).

Our analysis complements existing studies, as it is based on the construction of an extensive dataset of SMEs from the largest euro area countries, which is used to presume lending decisions, which are mirrored in the financial statements of the companies in the sample. More specifically, our research questions are as follows: Can European SMEs support more debt? Does excessive leverage impair company growth? Are there significant across country/regional differences in SME access to finance?

7.3 Sample: Construction and Representativeness

The focus is on lending to SMEs as defined by European Commission recommendation 361/2003:

> '[The] category of micro, small and medium-sized enterprises (SMEs) is made up of enterprises that employ fewer than 250 persons and that have an annual turnover not exceeding EUR 50 million and/or an annual balance sheet total not exceeding EUR 43 million. Within the SME category, a microenterprise is defined as an enterprise that employs fewer than 10 persons and whose annual turnover and/or annual balance sheet total does not exceed EUR 2 million. Within the SME category, a small enterprise is defined as an enterprise that employs fewer than 50 persons and whose annual turnover and/or annual balance sheet total does not exceed EUR 10 million.'[5] (European Commission 2003)

Medium enterprises are the remaining category of SMEs. Large enterprises exceed the number of employees and value of turnover and annual balance sheet total. Data were drawn from the Orbis database by Bureau Van Dijk. The initial extraction was composed of French, German, Italian and Spanish SMEs identified as described above and resulted in a sample of more than 500,000 firms over the 2006–2014 period.

The availability of highly granular financial statement data is crucial for the proposed empirical analysis; therefore, firms without missing values in the variables of interest were excluded from the sample.

Additionally, SMEs within the micro category in the first year of observation (2006) were excluded from the initial sample to limit sample heterogeneity in terms of size and to focus on firms that are perceived as reasonably creditworthy by banks. The final sample is composed of

[5] Note that the European Union Recommendation 361/2003 definition is not perfectly consistent with the Eurostat data quoted in the introduction because Eurostat only considers number of employees. According to the Eurostat definition, micro enterprises are those companies with less than 10 persons employed; small enterprises are those with 10–49 persons employed, medium-sized enterprises are those with 50–249 persons employed, and large enterprises are those with 250 or more persons employed.

58,563 firms from the four largest euro area countries (France, Germany, Italy and Spain) and consists of 527,345 firm-year observations.

There are two potential sources of bias. The first is survivorship bias because the sample excludes companies that no longer exist in 2014. This may lead to overly optimistic results because the sample includes companies successful enough to survive until the end of the period. To minimize this source of bias, we decided to restrict the sample to only small and medium-sized firms in 2006 and to exclude microfirms for which the failure rate is higher (European Central Bank 2015b; Pagano 2001), and so therefore, the survivorship bias would have been more extreme.

The second selection bias may arise from the decision to exclude companies with incomplete data in the Orbis database; this could be another source of bias if the companies that disclose less are the ones with the most problems securing funding.

However, given the nature of the research questions this chapter sets out to answer, namely, if euro area SMEs can support more debt and if excessive leverage impairs growth, it is not likely that these two types of bias will affect the results. Because we are investigating the contribution of the correct financial structure to growth, the survivorship bias may be considered less significant. Because the purpose is to identify the financial structure characteristics of SMEs that grew over the period, focusing on SMEs that have been successful is reasonable.

Table 7.1 shows the sample composition broken down in terms of number of firms, total assets and number of employees. The sample comprises 6736 French small and medium-sized companies, 2049 German SMEs, 31,203 Italian SMEs and 18,575 Spanish SMEs (respectively representing 12%, 3%, 53% and 32% of the total companies in the sample).

In terms of total assets, German companies represent almost 23% of the sample's aggregate, French firms represent approximately 7%, Italian firms represent 50%, and Spanish firms represent 20%. This reflects the fact that German companies are larger and that Germany is the only country that has more medium-sized than small companies in the sample (1579 medium-sized and 470 small, corresponding to 77% and 23% of the German sample, respectively).

Industry breakdown by number of firms is similar across countries (Table 7.2), with the main sectors being 'Wholesale, retail trade' (22.12% full sample, ranging from a minimum of 19.58% in Italy to a maximum

Table 7.1 Sample composition: breakdown by number of firms, total assets and number of employees

	N. of firms				Total assets		N. of employees	
2006	Medium	Small	Total	% of total sample	Total sample	% of total sample	Total sample	% of total sample
France	1537	5199	6736	11.50%	633,755	6.90%	282,724	11.08%
Germany	1579	470	2049	3.50%	2,071,523	22.56%	220,073	8.63%
Italy	8581	22,622	31,203	53.28%	4,609,852	50.19%	1,348,409	52.86%
Spain	3649	14,926	18,575	31.72%	1,868,768	20.35%	699,502	27.42%
Total	15,346	43,217	58,563		9,183,898		2,550,708	

Source: Authors own elaboration

Table 7.2 Sample composition: breakdown of number of firms by industry and country

	France		Germany		Italy		Spain		Total	
Industry	N. of firms	%	N. of firms	%	N. of firms	%	N. of firms	%	N. of firms	%
Chemicals, rubber, plastics, non-metallic products	211	3.13	122	5.95	2507	8.03	1204	6.48	4044	6.91
Construction	1152	17.10	48	2.34	2664	8.54	2569	13.83	6433	10.98
Education, health	196	2.91	78	3.81	899	2.88	474	2.55	1647	2.81
Food, beverages, tobacco	201	2.98	56	2.73	1332	4.27	991	5.34	2580	4.41
Gas, water, electricity	5	0.07	212	10.35	184	0.59	82	0.44	483	0.82
Hotels, restaurants	382	5.67	12	0.59	774	2.48	1011	5.44	2179	3.72
Machinery, equipment, furniture, recycling	406	6.03	236	11.52	4705	15.08	1350	7.27	6697	11.44
Metals, metal products	280	4.16	44	2.15	3058	9.80	1108	5.97	4490	7.67
Other services	1407	20.89	583	28.45	4027	12.91	2135	11.49	8152	13.92
Post, telecommunications	16	0.24	32	1.56	55	0.18	47	0.25	150	0.26

Primary sector	82	1.22	16	0.78	596	1.91	574	3.09	1268	2.17
Public admin, defence	–	0.00	6	0.29	–	0.00	2	0.01	8	0.01
Publishing, printing	137	2.03	46	2.24	496	1.59	380	2.05	1059	1.81
Textiles, wearing apparel, leather	74	1.10	16	0.78	1661	5.32	398	2.14	2149	3.67
Transport	439	6.52	88	4.29	1425	4.57	1077	5.80	3029	5.17
Wholesale, retail trade	1647	24.45	426	20.79	6111	19.58	4772	25.69	12,956	22.12
Wood, cork, paper	101	1.50	28	1.37	709	2.27	401	2.16	1239	2.12
Total	6736		2049		31,203		18,575		58,563	

Source: Authors' own elaboration, highlighted top three industries

of 25.79% in Spain); 'Other services[6]' (13.92% in the full sample, ranging from a minimum of 11.49% in Spain to a maximum of 28.45% in Germany); and 'Machinery, equipment, furniture, recycling' (11.44% in the full sample, from a minimum of 6.03% in France to 15.08% in Italy). These main sectors make up almost half of total firms composing the sample. This enables across-country comparisons to be made.

All companies in the sample were medium-sized or small firms in the first year of observation, although many of them changed their category in the period studied, some decreasing to micro and others growing to large (thus outgrowing the SME categories). Table 7.3 reports changes in categories comparing the first and last year of observation; approximately 11% of sample companies shrank to micro in 2014, and just under 2% had grown to large. A breakdown by country shows that firm size changes in Italy and France are in line with the sample, whilst almost 17% of companies in the German subsample grew to large, and over one-fifth of Spanish companies decreased to micro.

Table 7.3 Companies that changed size: breakdown by country

Country	Large	Medium		Small	Micro
Total			2006		
		15,346		43,217	
		26.20%		*73.80%*	
			2014		
	1269	14,375		34,496	8,423
	2.17%	24.55%		58.90%	14.38%
France			2006		
		1537		5199	
		22.82%		*77.18%*	
			2014		
	131	1506		4349	750
	1.94%	22.36%		64.56%	11.13%
Germany			2006		
		1579		470	
		77.06%		22.94%	
			2014		
	346	1322		360	21
	16.89%	64.52%		17.57%	1.02%

(Continued)

[6] Classified as of NAICS 81 'Other Services (except Public Administration)'. It comprises establishments engaged in providing services not specifically provided for elsewhere in the classification system.

Table 7.3 (Continued)

Country	Large	Medium		Small	Micro
Italy			2006		
		8581		22,622	
		27.50%		72.50%	
			2014		
	565	8350		18,602	3686
	1.81%	26.76%		59.62%	11.81%
Spain			2006		
		3649		14,926	
		19.64%		80.36%	
			2014		
	227	3197		11,185	3966
	1.22%	17.21%		60.22%	21.35%

Source: Authors' own elaboration

7.4 Variables and Methodology

The bank's decision to grant a loan or to expand an existing one is based on the creditworthiness of the applicant, which in turn depends upon the bank's assessment of the company's future prospects and of the soundness of its financial structure. A thorough analysis of the evolution of financial statement aggregates over the nine-year period enables us to assess actual access to finance and short-term loans as experienced by the small and medium-sized companies in the sample. Table 7.4 shows the variables extracted from the Orbis database, and Table 7.5 sets out the margins, key ratios and growth rates used in the creditworthiness analysis conducted in the subsequent sections.

The financial soundness of any firm may be analyzed by examining the maturity mismatch between sources and application of funds. Long-term investing requires long-term financing; ideally, equity financing is the best source of funding for fixed assets because it is a permanent funding source. To remain a going concern any company needs a certain portion of fixed investments. These should be financed by equity because loans—even long-term loans or bonds—must be reimbursed at maturity, and when they come to maturity either the company must find new sources of funds (i.e., it is granted new loans, issues bonds or raises new equity) or

Table 7.4 Variables definition

Variable	Definition
Current liabilities	All current liabilities of the company (loans + creditors + other current liabilities)
Loans	Short-term financial debts to credit institutions (loans and credits) + part of long-term financial debts payable within the year
Creditors	All debts to suppliers and contractors (trade creditors)
Non-current liabilities	All long-term liabilities of the company (long-term financial debts + other long-term liabilities and provisions)
Long-term debt	Long-term financial debt
Shareholders' equity	Total equity (capital + other shareholders' funds)
Total liabilities and shareholder equity	Total shareholder funds and liabilities (Shareholder equity + non-current liabilities + current liabilities)
Current assets	Total amount of current assets (stocks + debtors + other current assets)
Inventories	Total inventories (raw materials + in progress + finished goods)
Turnover	Annual sales net of all discounts and taxes
Taxation	Taxation
Net income	Profit or loss after taxation

Source: Authors' own elaboration from Orbis database

Table 7.5 Variables definition

Variable	Definition
Equity Financing Gap (EFG)	Shareholders' equity – non-current assets
Medium and Long-Term Financing Gap (MLTFG)	Cash and cash equivalents + debtor – current liabilities or (shareholders' equity + long-term liabilities) – (non-current assets + stock)
CAGR turnover	Compounded annual growth rate of turnover
CAGR net income	Compounded annual growth rate of net income
ROA	Net income on total assets
ROI	Net income on non-current assets

Source: Authors' own elaboration

it must reduce its assets. Inability to liquidate part of its assets at adequate prices could lead to default (Brogi 2014).

Therefore, excessive leverage (or insufficient equity) may turn a liquidity problem, the need to reimburse a bond, into a solvency problem if replacement sources of funding are not available and assets are illiquid and difficult to sell without suffering a loss with respect to their book value (which is based on the idea that the company is a going concern). Indeed, when leverage is too high, even if in contractual terms the bank has granted a loan, the position may actually expose it to the risks associated with equity.

If a company's financial structure already reflects excessive maturity mismatch, the bank should turn down the loan request.

Maturity mismatch can be analyzed using two different margins. The Equity Financing Gap (EFG) and the Medium and Long Term Financing Gap (MLTFG) (Fig. 7.1). The EFG is the difference between equity, which is by definition invested in the company indefinitely, and fixed investments.

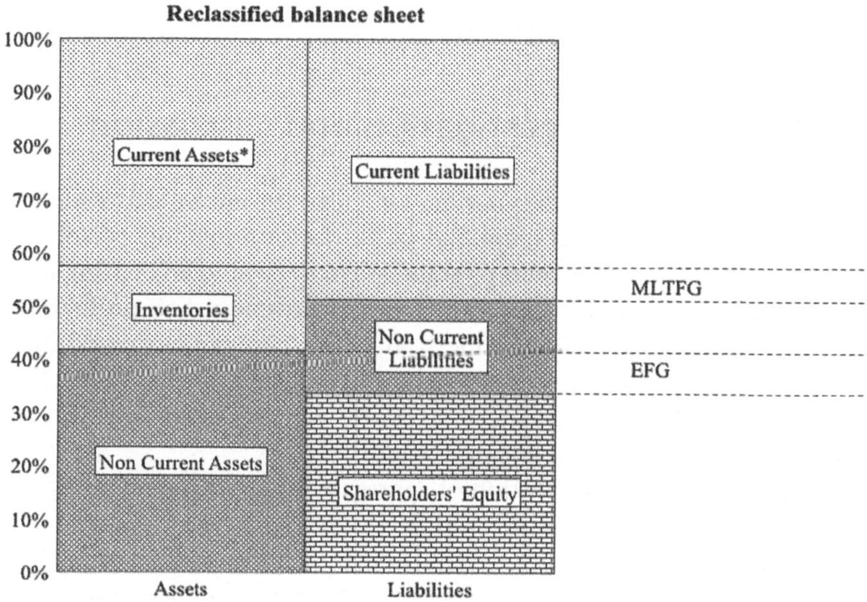

Fig. 7.1 Reclassified balance sheet
(*Source*: Authors' own elaboration, *Current assets is comprehensive of inventories)

When a company has a negative EFG, it presents a mismatch between the sources and the application of funds because part of its long-term investments are already financed by debt. This should lead the bank to turn down a further loan application. Indeed, this margin may be considered an estimate of the firm's capital shortfall, namely, the amount of equity it should raise to limit its maturity mismatch.

The same reasoning applies to the calculation of the MLTFG, which is the difference between long-term funding (i.e., shareholder equity plus non-current liabilities) and fixed assets plus inventories. This reflects the fact that any company must have at least some finished products and some raw materials in order to function.

Again, the MLTFG should be positive because a negative MLTFG means that short-term financing has been used to finance long-term investments or necessary inventory. Moreover, the value of the MLTFG can be considered a proxy of the need to substitute short-term with medium- and long-term financing.

7.5 Empirical Investigation and Discussion

To address the first research question, i.e., 'Can European SMEs support more debt?', we adopt a simplified bank decision-making perspective which entails that the decision to grant a loan or expand an existing facility depends solely on the applicant's creditworthiness, i.e., profitability prospects and its financial soundness. In theory, companies that exhibit a sufficient profitability may service debt, but we presume that in practice, if they have a high-risk financial structure with excessive leverage, the bank will turn down the loan application.

Table 7.6 shows the evolution of aggregate financial statement figures and the margins of firms in the sample.

Considering that the sample is biased by survivorship, it should be noted that in all countries, aggregate total assets of sample companies increased over the period of observation. Likewise, turnover and net income rose over the period.

Table 7.6 Total sample financial statements, margins (in million euros) and ratios (%)

Total sample		2006	2007	2008	2009	2010	2011	2012	2013	2014
N. of firms		58,563	58,563	58,563	58,563	58,563	58,563	58,563	58,563	58,563
Liabilities and Shareholders' Equity	Current Liabilities	409.640	428,322	428,839	409,834	418,748	439,954	450,560	433,291	445,782
	Loans	*83,449*	*96,205*	*103,183*	*93,289*	*95,175*	*102,648*	*99,372*	*97,880*	*100,312*
	Creditors	*144,158*	*156,854*	*146,209*	*136,437*	*148,707*	*154,724*	*148,273*	*146,694*	*146,084*
	Non-current liabilities	144,783	196,591	242,232	246,603	238,787	266,764	243,566	260,946	257,151
	Long-term debt	*97,399*	*132,538*	*159,638*	*164,751*	*182,282*	*183,108*	*160,181*	*179,173*	*159,816*
	Share-holders' equity	283,297	301,087	344,749	361,589	371,457	378,045	385,542	395,299	400,440
	Total liabilities & share-holders' equity	837,720	926,000	1,015,820	1,018,026	1,028,992	1,084,763	1,079,668	1,089,536	1,103,373
Assets	Current assets	487,808	530,000	547,556	538,438	556,743	586,332	579,831	579,078	589,821
	Inventories	*130,264*	*148,602*	*155,345*	*153,848*	*155,053*	*164,629*	*162,649*	*161,299*	*156,653*
	Non-current assets	349,912	396,000	468,264	479,588	472,249	498,431	499,837	510,458	513,552
	Total assets	837,720	926,000	1,015,820	1,018,026	1,028,992	1,084,763	1,079,668	1,089,536	1,103,373

(continued)

Table 7.6 (continued)

Total sample		2006	2007	2008	2009	2010	2011	2012	2013	2014
Income state-ment	Turnover	924,125	986,467	1,024,179	915,220	990,522	1,068,170	1,059,417	1,053,429	1,087,157
	Taxation	15,245	14,523	10,785	6,151	10,417	11,332	10,616	10,530	10,844
	Net income	7,973	33,255	30,312	22,608	26,008	20,833	16,022	16,539	12,949
Margins & ratios	EFG	−66,615	−94,913	−123,515	−117,999	−100,792	−120,386	−114,295	−115,159	−113,112
	EFG/total assets	−7.95%	−10.25%	−12.16%	−11.59%	−9.80%	−11.10%	−10.59%	−10.57%	−10.25%
	MLTFG	−52,096	−46,924	−36,628	−25,244	−17,058	-18,251	−33,378	−15,512	−12,614
	MLTFG/total assets	−6.22%	−5.07%	−3.61%	−2.48%	−1.66%	−1.68%	−3.09%	−1.42%	−1.14%
	ROA	0.95%	3.59%	2.98%	2.22%	2.53%	1.92%	1.48%	1.52%	1.17%
	ROI	41.77%	42.76%	46.10%	47.11%	45.89%	45.95%	46.30%	46.85%	46.54%

Source: Authors' elaboration, data

The EFG is always negative for the aggregate and declines over the period of observation, particularly in the critical years 2008 (from –10.25% to –12.16% of total assets) and 2011 (from –9.80% to –11.10%), resulting in a decrease from the 2006 value (–7.95%) to the 2014 value (–10.25%). The decrease in the margin is the combined effect of a rise in shareholders' equity and a more than proportional increase in non-current assets. Conversely, there is a gradual improvement in the MLTFG, which is negative but increasing, and the MLTFG/total assets ratio registers a marked improvement, although it remains negative overall during the period.

The sample presents a considerable number of SMEs with unbalanced financial structures (23,288 out of 58,563, almost 40% of the sample), with both margins being negative. Conversely, there are 35,275 (60%) firms with an optimal financial structure (both margins being positive).

The absolute value of loans increased from 2006 to 2008, dropped considerably in 2009, returned to almost 2008 levels in 2011, then decreased again in 2012 and increased again to 2014. Considered relative to total assets, short-term loans were stable overall for the period of observation (at approximately 10% of total assets, with a minimum of 8.98% in 2013 and a maximum of 10.39% in 2007).

When taking the entire sample into consideration, it therefore seems that banks did not increase their supply of short-term loans. This is not surprising because the companies in the sample present unbalanced margins, with an aggregate shareholders' equity shortfall of 66.6 billion euros in 2006 (and an average of 107.4 billion euros over the entire period) and a need for further medium to long-term funding of 52.1 billion euros in 2006 down to 12.6 billion euros in 2014. Indeed, aggregate figures underestimate the requirements because surpluses and shortfalls are netted. Considering the sum of shortfalls, the necessary capital injections to balance the EFG would be 135.4 billion euros in 2006 (141.2 billion euros average for the period) and medium to long term lending 58.0 billion euros (32.5 billion euros average for the period). We may conclude that difficulties in expanding credit which emerge from the sample companies reflect creditworthiness concerns deriving from unbalanced

Table 7.7 Sample composition: breakdown by financial structure characteristics

		EFG/Total Assets 2006		
		<	≥0	Total
MLTFG/Total Assets 2006	<	*High-risk* 4114	*Capitalized but illiquid* 3695	7809
	≥0	*Liquid but undercapitalized* 15,479	*Creditworthy* 35,275	50,754
Total		19,593	38,970	58,563

Source: Authors' own elaboration
The EFG is the difference between equity, which is by definition invested in the company indefinitely, and fixed investments. MLTFG is the difference between long-term funding (i.e., shareholder equity plus non-current liabilities) and fixed assets plus inventories

Table 7.8 Sample composition: breakdown by financial structure characteristics and country

		EFG/Total Assets 2006				Total
		<		>=0		
MLTFG/Total Assets 2006	<	407	2,392	1	2,296	7,809
		580	735	58	1,340	
	>=0	1,052	4,198	5,276	9,689	50,754
		440	9,789	971	19,239	
Total		19,593		38,970		58,563

German firms French firms Italian firms Spanish firms

Source: Authors' own elaboration
The EFG is the difference between equity, which is by definition invested in the company indefinitely, and fixed investments. MLTFG is the difference between long-term funding (i.e., shareholder equity plus non-current liabilities) and fixed assets plus inventories

financial structures. On aggregate, these companies need more equity and not more loans.

The importance of financial structure considerations in bank lending decisions is confirmed by analyzing the evolution of loans for sample firms divided into the following four subsamples based on their financial structure characteristics (Tables 7.7 and 7.8):

i) '*Creditworthy companies*' for which both margins are positive (EFG and MLTFG greater than or equal to zero), which were 35,275 (60% of total sample);
ii) '*Capitalized but illiquid companies*' (MLTFG is negative but the EFG is equal to zero or positive), 3695 firms (6.3% of total sample);
iii) '*Liquid but undercapitalized companies*' (MLTFG equal to zero or positive but the EFG is negative), 15,479 companies (26% of total sample);
iv) '*High-risk companies*', the 4114 companies for which both margins were negative (approximately 7% of the sample).

In actual fact, short-term loans considerably increased (+42%) for *creditworthy* companies, which are companies where both margins are positive (Table 7.9), whilst short-term loans granted to *high-risk companies* with unbalanced financial structures decreased, in absolute terms as well as in percentage of total assets. This supports the idea that over the period, banks limited lending to less creditworthy borrowers, but we find no evidence of loan access difficulties for companies that present a sound financial structure (which are the majority of our sample due to our selection process). As a further confirmation of the effectiveness of this simplified decision-making approach based on firm financial structure characteristics, it is worth noting that *high-risk* companies presented a much lower loans/total assets ratio compared to other sample companies (on average approximately 6% over the nine years with respect to approximately 10% for the entire sample).

To analyze the relationship between leverage and growth and answer the second research question, i.e., 'Does excessive leverage impair company growth?', we focus on (i) the growth rates of companies with unbalanced financial structures, and (ii) the financial structure of companies that exhibited positive growth rates for turnover or net income over the nine years.

Companies in our sample showed an aggregate compounded average growth rate of 1.82% for turnover and of 5.54% for net income over the nine years. Conversely, companies with both margins negative showed growth rates of 0.6% and 2.22%, respectively, thus confirming that excessive leverage hampers growth.

Table 7.9 Financial statements, margins (in million euros) and ratios (%): breakdown in subsamples based on financial structure characteristics

		Creditworthy Firms with both margins ≥ 0		*Capitalised but illiquid* Firms with EFG ≥0		*Liquid but undercapitalised* Firms with MLTFG ≥ 0		*High-risk* Firms with both margins <0	
		2006	2014	2006	2014	2006	2014	2006	2014
N. of firms		35,275	35,275	3,695	3,695	15,479	15,479	4,114	4,114
Liabilities & shareholders' equity	Current liabilities	178,754	210,869	24,393	22,529	119,858	139,710	53,289	58,086
	Loans	*31,955*	*45,420*	*6164*	*5820*	*33,017*	*36,637*	*12,255*	*12,205*
	Creditors	*78,140*	*79,150*	*10,717*	*8,347*	*42,833*	*47,056*	*12,254*	*10,333*
	Non-current liabilities	35,187	67,808	4,484	7,188	65,703	68,395	84,611	75,504
	Long-term debt	*14,901*	*30,165*	*3,813*	*4,836*	*38,404*	*40,043*	*69,549*	*51,154*
	Shareholders' equity	136,404	198,476	13,410	18,616	55,185	93,850	55,086	73,700
	Total liabilities & shareholders' equity	350,345	477,153	42,287	48,333	240,746	301,955	192,986	207,290
Assets	Current assets	281,191	340,489	34,370	33,974	123,582	153,048	46,521	54,724
	Inventories	*69,174*	*87,615*	*15,434*	*12,580*	*31,164*	*40,052*	*13,496*	*14,582*
	Non-current assets	69,154	136,664	7,917	14,359	117,164	148,907	146,465	152,566
	Total Assets	350,345	477,153	42,287	48,333	240,746	301,955	192,986	207,290

Income statement	Turnover	511,243	597,213	57,262	57,403	231,492	275,155	95,679	100,949
	Taxation	8,750	6,501	749	130	2,632	2,811	2,934	1,915
	Net income	15,493	12,305	1,702	651	16,438	20,657	9,845	11,993
Margins & ratios	EFG	67,250	61,812	5493	4257	−61,979	−55,057	−91,379	-78,866
	EFG/ total assets	19.20%	12.95%	12.99%	8.81%	−25.74%	−18.23%	−47.35%	-38.05%
	MLTFG	33,263	42,005	−5457	−1135	−27,440	−26,714	−20,264	-17,944
	MLTFG/total assets	9.49%	8.80%	−12.90%	-2.35%	−11.40%	-8.85%	-10.50%	-8.66%
	ROA	18.86%	16.19%	4.02%	1.35%	6.83%	6.84%	5.10%	5.79%
	ROI	95.55%	56.52%	21.50%	4.54%	14.03%	13.87%	6.72%	7.86%

Source: Authors' own elaboration

Table 7.10 Sample companies with positive growth rates of net income and turnover: breakdown by financial structure characteristics

		EFG/total assets 2006			
		<	>	= 0	Total
MLTFG/ total assets 2006	<	4114	1654	2041	7809
	>	10,820	13,740	10,819	35,379
	= 0	4659	2875	7,841	15,375
Total		19,593	18,269	20,701	58,563

		Total	EFG/total assets 2006				MLTFG/total assets 2006				Both			
			< 0		≥ 0		< 0		≥ 0		< 0		≥ 0	
CAGR net income	≥ 0%	27,260	10,068	37%	17,192	63%	3397	12%	23,863	88%	1,865	7%	15,660	57%
	0–25%	19,873	7596	38%	12,277	62%	2651	13%	17,222	87%	1519	8%	11,145	56%
	25–50%	997	454	46%	543	54%	245	25%	752	75%	152	15%	450	45%
	50–75%	137	62	45%	75	55%	34	25%	103	75%	17	12%	58	42%
	75–100%	21	8	38%	13	62%	9	43%	12	57%	5	24%	9	43%
	>100%	6	4	67%	2	33%	5	83%	1	17%	3	50%	–	0%
CAGR turnover	≥ 0%	23,287	8,663	37%	14,624	63%	3500	15%	19,787	85%	1937	8%	13,061	56%
	0–25%	15,002	5,420	36%	9,582	64%	2,487	17%	12,515	83%	1,415	9%	8,510	57%
	25–50%	2,734	1,064	39%	1,670	61%	226	8%	2,508	92%	117	4%	1,561	57%
	50–75%	604	255	42%	349	58%	45	7%	559	93%	21	3%	325	54%
	75–100%	149	59	40%	90	60%	12	8%	137	92%	9	6%	87	58%
	>100%	31	14	45%	17	55%	2	6%	29		–		15	48%
Total		58,563	19,593	33%	38,970	67%	7809	13%	50,754	87%	4114	7%	35,275	60%

Source: Authors' own elaboration

The other connected issue is whether a more balanced financial structure is associated with higher growth rates. Table 7.10 presents two subsets of sample companies, those which achieved positive growth rates in the period for turnover (23,287), and net income (27,260) broken down by financial structure (note that many firms with negative margins and high growth rates have benefited from restructuring and acquisitions). Overall, 57% of companies that registered an increase in net income and 56% of those that increased turnover over the period had balanced financial structures (i.e., both margins are positive).

These results confirm the importance of a sound financial structure and testify that when firms need to finance long-term investments, short-term loans are not the ideal form of funding; actually, banks should advise corporate customers to issue equity or long-term bonds in the primary market. Origination and placement of securities in turn leads banks to intervene on the secondary market, in some cases through proprietary trading (Brogi 2011).

Of course, the institutional setting is also important as:

> 'Firms can choose from a range of external financing instruments, in particular equity, bank loans, debt securities, inter-company loans and trade credit. This provides them with some flexibility in their financing of working capital and investment, although smaller firms are generally more restricted in their financing options.' (European Central Bank 2013)

7.6 Conclusion

This chapter investigates the evolution of financial statement aggregates of a sample of 58,563 euro area small and medium-sized companies over a nine-year period for the purpose of understanding whether these companies can support more debt and if excessive leverage impairs growth.

We adopt a simplified bank decision-making perspective, which entails that the decision to grant a loan or to expand an existing facility depends on the applicant's creditworthiness, i.e., profitability prospects and its financial soundness. In theory, companies that exhibit a sufficient profitability may service debt but we presume that, in practice, if they have a 'risky' financial structure with excessive leverage the bank will turn down their loan application.

If we compare 2014 with 2006, in aggregate terms, the absolute amount of short-term loans granted to companies in the sample did not decrease over the period even though short-term loans grew less than total assets. Many companies in our sample are already highly geared and present an equity financing gap of approximately 140 billion euros average for the nine-year period; it is therefore not surprising that banks did not expand their short-term loans to these borrowers. Moreover, we do find evidence of a credit crunch for companies with an unbalanced financial structure and actually more loans granted to firms with a sound financial structure (creditworthy firms). In sum, euro area firms are undercapitalized though we find evidence that banks lent more to companies that could support more debt.

Regarding the contribution of a sound financial structure to growth, high-risk companies experience lower growth rates of both turnover and net income compared to the total sample. Additionally, companies which expanded turnover or net income in the nine years were mainly creditworthy companies. Our results support the fact that the right type of funding is associated with growth and our empirical evidence confirms that first an investment in more capital followed by more debt can support growth.

There are some across-country differences, but these general results hold for all country subsamples.

These promising results suggest that more refined analyses could be conducted on this sample. In particular, the implications of industry and firm size on financial structure, and of country of origin and industry on profitability, should be further investigated. Additional important research questions related to the issues investigated in this chapter could be as follows: Is the credit crunch due to capital-constrained banks needing to fix their balance sheets or a prudent approach to lending? Can persistently higher sovereign debt premia affect investment by SMEs and ultimately impair growth? Is there evidence that finance constraints impact on firm survival via profitability?

Nevertheless, our analysis sheds light on SME financing by showing that more equity and not more debt is necessary for growth; this confirms that an expansionary monetary policy, even one based on extremely low or negative interest rates, may not lead to more credit for smaller companies if they are already highly geared and that such a policy must be complemented by interventions aimed at improving SME access to equity finance, such as some of the measures contained in the Capital Markets Union initiative.

References

Abor, J. Y., Agbloyor, E. K., & Kuipo, R. (2014). Bank finance and export activities of small and medium enterprises. *Review of Development Finance, 4*(2), 97–103.

Bank of Italy. (2015). *The governor's concluding remarks for 2014*.

Beck, T., & Demirgüç-Kunt, A. (2006). Small and medium–size enterprises: Access to finance as a growth constraint. *Journal of Banking and Finance, 30*, 2931–2943.

Beck, T., Kunt, A., & Maksimovic, V. (2005). Financial and legal constraints to firm growth: Does firm size matter? *Journal of Finance, 60*, 137–177.

Beck, T., Demirgüç-Kunt, A., & Maksimovic, V. (2008). Financing patterns around the world: Are small firms different? *Journal of Financial Economics, 89*, 467–487.

Beck, T., Demirgüç-Kunt, A., & Pería, M. S. M. (2011). Bank financing for SMEs: Evidence across countries and bank ownership types. *Journal of Financial Services Research, 39*(1–2), 35–54.

Berger, A. N., & Udell, G. F. (1995). Relationship lending and the lines of credit in small firm finance. *Journal of Business, 68*(3), 351–381.

Brogi, M. (2011). Capital adequacy, corporate governance and organization in the support of the bank—Firm relationship. In G. Bracchi & D. Masciandaro (Eds.), *XVI Rapporto sul sistema finanziario italiano*. Edibank. Milano, 179–210.

Brogi, M. (2014). Shadow banking, banking union and capital markets union. *Law and Economics Yearly Review, 3*, 383–400.

Brogi, M., & Langone, R. (2016). Bank profitability and capital adequacy in the post-crisis context. In S. P. S. Rossi & R. Malavasi (Eds.), *Financial crisis, bank behaviour and credit crunch*. Switzerland: Springer International Publishing.

Casey, E., & O'Toole, C. M. (2014). Bank lending constraints, trade credit and alternative financing during the financial crisis: Evidence from European SMEs. *Journal of Corporate Finance, 27*, 173–193.

Chai, F., & Bang Dinh, N. (2011). The cost of business credit by firm category. *Quarterly Selection of Articles, 24*, 5–28

Chittenden, F., Hall, G., & Hutchinson, P. (1996). Small firm growth, access to capital markets and financial structure: Review of issues and an empirical investigation. *Small Business Economics, 8*(1), 59–67.

Cole, R. A., Wolken, J. D., & Woodburn, L. R. (1996). Bank and nonbank competition for small business credit: Evidence from the 1987 and 1993 national survey of small business finances. *Federal Reserve Bulletin, 82*, 983–995.

Cole, R. A., Goldberg, L. G., & White, L. J. (2004). Cookie cutter vs. character: The micro structure of small business lending by large and small banks. *Journal of Financial and Quantitative Analysis, 39*, 227–251.

Cressy, R., & Olofsson, C. (1997). European SME financing: An overview. *Small Business Economics, 9*(2), 87–96.

European Banking Authority. (2015). *EBA discussion paper and call for evidence on SMEs and the SME supporting factor.*

European Banking Authority. (2016). *EBA report on SMEs and SME supporting factor.*

European Central Bank. (2013). *Corporate finance and economic activity in the euro area* (Structural Issues Report 151).

European Central Bank. (2015a). *Report on the results of the Survey on the Access to Finance of Enterprises in the euro area—October 2014 to March 2015*. Press release.

European Central Bank. (2015b). *The impact of the CRR and CRD IV on bank financing, Eurosystem response to the DG FISMA consultation paper.*

European Central Bank. (2016). *Bank Lending Survey.*

European Commission. (2015a). *Capital markets and SMEs in the EU.*

European Commission. (2015b). *Annual report on European SMEs 2014/2015.*

European Commission. (2015c). *Green paper: Building a capital markets union.*

European Union. (2003). *Recommendation 2003/361 concerning the definition of micro, small and medium-sized enterprises.*

Farinha, L., & Félix, S. (2015). Credit rationing for Portuguese SMEs. *Finance Research Letters, 14*, 167–177.

Ferrando, A., Popov, A. A., & Udell, G. F. (2015). *Sovereign stress, unconventional monetary policy, and SME access to finance, Working paper series.* Frankfurt: European Central Bank.

Fredriksson, A., & Moro, A. (2014). Bank–SMEs relationships and banks' risk–adjusted profitability. *Journal of Banking and Finance, 41*, 67–77.

López-Gracia, J., & Sogorb-Mira, F. (2008). Testing trade–off and pecking order theories financing SMEs. *Small Business Economics, 31*(2), 117–136.

Michaelas, N., Chittenden, F., & Poutziouris, P. (1999). Financial policy and capital structure choice in UK SMEs: Empirical evidence from company panel data. *Small Business Economics, 12*(2), 113–130.

Myers, S. C., & Majluf, M. S. (1984). Corporate financing and investment decisions when firms have information that investors do not have. *Journal of Financial Economics, 13*(2), 187–221.

Pagano, M. (2001). *Defusing default: Incentives and institutions*. Washington, DC: IDB.

Petersen, M. A., & Rajan, R. G. (1994). Benefits of lending relationships: Evidence from small business data. *Journal of Finance, 49*, 3–37.

Petersen, M. A., & Rajan, R. G. (1995). The effect of credit market competition on lending relationships. *Quarterly Journal of Economics, 110*, 407–443.

Schiffer, M., & Weder, B. (2001). *Firm size and the business environment: Worldwide survey results, Discussion paper, 43*. Washington, DC: International Finance Corporation.

Part II

SME Funding and the Role of Alternative Non-Bank Finance in Italy

8

SME Credit Access After Basel III. Does Size (and Quality) Matter?

Pietro Vozzella and Giampaolo Gabbi

8.1 Introduction

The credit crunch observed in economic systems once the financial crisis began can be defined as a macro-portfolio decision taken by large lenders in many countries.

On one side, part of this phenomenon was actually due to the use of internal ratings-based models and the subsequent procyclical effect. On

JEL Classification: G21, G28, G32

P. Vozzella (✉)
Department of Management and Law, University of Siena, Siena, Italy
e-mail: pietro.vozzella@unisi.it

G. Gabbi
Department of Management and Law, University of Siena and SDA Bocconi School of Management, Milan, Italy

S.P.S. Rossi (ed.), *Access to Bank Credit and SME Financing*,
Palgrave Macmillan Studies in Banking and Financial Institutions,
DOI 10.1007/978-3-319-41363-1_8

the other side, credit availability was affected by the diversification estimate within every credit portfolio.

Our paper is aimed at finding out the concentration risk of the credit portfolios of small and medium enterprises (SMEs) and how regulation could affect lending decisions.

Within credit portfolio frameworks, correlation plays a fundamental role. Asset correlation can be defined for each pair of loans, but the absence of market data pushes banks to aggregate the analysis by groups of companies using a certain rule and to estimate the average asset correlation for each group. This rule is a key factor in estimating asset correlations and is crucial for calculating unexpected losses correctly.

Empirical asset correlations based on external ratings are believed to be critical when applied to loans. Some studies (see. Altman and Saunders 2001) evaluated the impact of internal ratings to estimate the credit risk for different categories of firms. Carey (2000) showed that the success of the internal ratings-based approach depends on the degree to which it considers dissimilarities in portfolio features, such as risk issues, granularity and maturities.

Many involved players (researchers, institutions and central bankers) expressed contradictory views on the Basel Committee proposal. Published in 2001, it suggested that the fair asset correlation value should have been 0.20, regardless of firm size and risk level. Dietsch and Petey (2002) proposed two parametric methods for estimating the credit risk of SMEs, showing that actual capital requirements are significantly lower than those expected when applying the first Basel II release. Lopez (2004), using data from the US, Japan and Europe that was estimated by rating agencies to compute asset correlation, found that firms with a higher default rate were less correlated. He suggested the coefficient range from 0.20 to 0.10 for asset correlation. Nonetheless, significant empirical evidence shows that credit risk based on agency ratings could be critical.

Altman and Saunders (2001) demonstrated that relying on traditional agency ratings may produce cyclically lagging capital requirements, rather than leading ones, and that the risk-based bucketing proposal lacks a sufficient degree of granularity. In keeping with the previous literature (Carling et al. 2002; Dietsch and Petey 2002; Calem and LaCour-Little 2001; Hamerle et al. 2003), they advised employing a risk weighting system that is more similar to the actual loss experience on loans. Some studies evaluated the impact of internal ratings to estimate the credit risk for different categories of firms. In particular, Carey (2000) showed that the success of the internal ratings-based approach depends on the degree to which it considers dissimilarities in portfolio features, such as risk issues, granularity and maturities (Jacobson et al. 2002; Carey and Hrycay 2001).

The discrepancy between loans to large corporations and those made to small and medium enterprises has been the focus of a variety of studies. Some of these studies have focused on the special character of small business lending and the importance of relationship banking for solving information asymmetries. The informative asymmetry puzzle particularly affects SMEs because of the difficulty in estimating their probability defaults (PDs) and fair value (Petersen 2004; Stein 2002) and managing the high frequency of marginal borrowers for small business credits (Berger et al. 2005).

These firms do not usually offer any type of reliable quantitative information because most of them are not obliged to record their numbers on balance sheets. Many studies devise ways to elaborate soft information (Petersen and Rajan 2002).

Other possible risk factors for small business loans are monitoring costs and recovery rates. Many studies confirm that these factors could also be associated with firm size (Degryse and Ongena 2005; Petersen and Rajan 2002; Allen et al. 2004; Schmit 2004; Perli and Nayda 2004).

These contributions from researchers and operators persuaded the Basel Committee to change the assignment of asset correlation based not only on level of risk but also on firm size in its final version. In the Bank Capital Accord (Basel II), the highest asset correlation for corporate exposures will apply to large companies with the lowest probabilities of default and will be raised from 0.2 to 0.24, while the lowest asset correlation applies to small firms with highest PD and will be decreased to 0.12.

Despite these changes, the Basel II Accord final version has been extensively criticized. Dietsch and Petey (2004) analyze observed default probability and asset correlation in French and German SMEs. Their study sampled data from the internal ratings systems of three large credit insurers: Coface in France, Allgemeine Kredit and Creditreform in Germany, and distinguished firms into four classes with turnover thresholds of 1, 7, and 40 million euros. Firms with turnover thresholds over 40 million euros are defined as large firms, and firms with turnover under 40 million euros are considered SMEs. In the analysis of default probabilities in French and German SMEs, the study also took into account the difference in risk classification, in addition to turnover. SME asset correlation coefficient decreases as firm size increases, while the observed asset correlation of large firms is greater than it is for SMEs in different risk classes. In addition, asset correlation among French SMEs shows a decreasing trend, which rises as risk class becomes lower, with the exception of SMEs in the lowest risk class, where asset correlation rises as risk class becomes lower. However, among German SMEs, the relationship between observed asset correlation and risk classification is not significant.

Dietsch and Petey (2004) also find that SMEs are riskier than large businesses and that PDs and asset correlations are not negative, as assumed by Basel II, but positively related to each other. In Taiwan, the results showed by Shen (2005) on the estimation of corporate asset correlation using a generalized factor model indicate that asset correlation is inversely related to firm size, which coincides with the finding of Dietsch and Petey (2004). However, the Shen study did not find a specific relationship between PD and asset correlation.

Although non-financial corporate debt (bond issues and privately issued debt) has become more common in the past 10 to 20 years, bank loans are still the prime source of business finance, especially for small and medium enterprises (SMEs). As a consequence, banks' ex-ante assessment of the riskiness of loan applicants and their resulting decision to grant credit (or not) at some risk-adjusted interest rate, are of great importance for businesses. Bank regulators increasingly lean on the risk assessments made by banks: in the Basel Committee's new capital adequacy rules, the so-called Basel II Accord (Basel Committee 2004), internal risk ratings produced by banks have been given a prominent role. Unlike previous regulation, the rules of Basel II will, for many large and internationally active banks, make the size of the required buffer capital contingent on their own appraisal of ex-ante individual credit risk.

Glennon and Nigro (2003) analyze small businesses' repayment behaviour on Small Business Administration loans and determine that default characteristics can vary widely within the SME segment, depending on the original maturity of the loan.

Our study focuses on micro, small and medium-sized companies and is aimed at examining how the relationships between asset correlation, size and risk during the period 1997–2013 could have affected access to credit for non-financial companies.

The contribution is organized as follows: Sect. 8.2 analyses the regulation for credit risk exposures and portfolios, and how asset correlation affects capital requirements. Section 8.3 describes our sample. Section 8.4 explains the methodology we applied to estimate both default and asset correlations based on endogenous default probabilities. Section 8.5 presents the results, comparing the impact of regulatory asset correlation with empirical asset correlation and the impact for micro, small and medium firms. Section 8.6 presents the study's conclusions.

8.2 Regulation

Certain of the findings of the empirical contribution previously quoted partially affected the final release of the Bank Capital Accord signed in Basel in 2004. In the New Accord, the asset correlation is a function of both the borrower's size and its probability of defaulting. Specifically, asset correlations range from 0.12 to 0.24 and receive the highest value for large corporate exposures to large companies (LC) with the lowest probability of default. Its computation is based on the following equation:

$$\rho(PD)_{LC} = 0.12 \cdot \frac{\left(1-e^{-50 \cdot PD}\right)}{\left(1-e^{-50}\right)} + 0.24 \cdot \left[1 - \frac{\left(1-e^{-50 \cdot PD}\right)}{\left(1-e^{-50}\right)}\right], \quad (8.1)$$

where ρ(PD) ranges between 0.12 and 0.24.

Banks applying the internal rating-based approach (IRB) are allowed to adjust the previous formula for SMEs' exposure (less than 50 million in sales):

$$\rho(PD)_{SME} = 0.12 \cdot \frac{\left(1-e^{-50 \cdot PD}\right)}{\left(1-e^{-50}\right)} + 0.24 \cdot \left[1 - \frac{\left(1-e^{-50 \cdot PD}\right)}{1-e^{-50}}\right] - 0.04\left(1 - \frac{S-5}{45}\right), \quad (8.2)$$

where S denotes sales.

In the case where $S > 50$, the last term will take the value of 0, while for $S < 5$ it takes the value of 0.04. Ignoring the adjustment for the firm's size, the asset correlation equals 0.24 for the lowest PD value and 0.12 for the highest PD value. Additionally, according to the size of the firm, either 0 or 0.04 is subtracted from the value of the asset correlation. For firms with sales ranging between 1 and 5 million euros, the assumed asset correlation is reduced by 0.04, whereas for large companies, i.e., those with sales greater than 50 million euros, there is no reduction of the assumed asset correlation at all. There is a linear relationship between these values.

When the size of corporate exposure is under one million euros, $\rho(\text{PD})$ is bounded within the interval [0.03, 0.16]. The main reason for this differential treatment is that small business loans and retail credits are generally found to be less sensitive to systematic risk. Their risk of default is thought to be largely of an idiosyncratic nature, and as a result PD*s* are assumed to be more weakly correlated than corporate loans. Another reason for the preferential treatment of retail credit lies in a technical assumption by the Basel Committee that maturities are expected to be shorter.

The estimation of asset correlation allows banks to use an internal rating-based approach to determine the regulatory capital (RC) through the following equation:

$$RC = LGD \cdot N\left[N^{-1}(PD) \cdot \sqrt{\frac{1}{1-R}} + N^{-1}(0.999) \cdot \sqrt{\frac{R}{1-R}}\right] - PD \cdot L, \quad (8.3)$$

where R is the average asset correlation, obtained from the Basel asset correlation function, and LGD is the loss given default, which can be defined as the amount which is not recovered by the lender should the borrower fail. We estimated the regulatory capital using expected and empirical asset correlations. For each size class, we estimated the correlation coefficients, ranging from 0.92 to 0.98.

Following Eq. (8.3), the regulatory capital absorbed by the credit risk is based only on unexpected losses. This approach is coherent with the purpose to drive banks using the internal model to design appropriate accruals for expected losses.

This also leads to a reduction of the regulatory capital. One concern that was identified in the committee's prior impact surveys was the potential gap of the capital required between the very different approaches for credit risk since the approval of the first Basel Accord in 1988.

Our study shows that empirical evidence for SMEs are far from adequately represented in regulatory formulae that were approved before the beginning of the financial crisis. Again, the innovations introduced by the Basel Committee in 2009 (Basel III) and the CRDIV (2013/36/EU) and CRR (Regulation EU, No 575/2013), which transposed those proposals within the European regulatory framework, did not change the supervisory formula to calibrate asset correlations. The recent debate to improve internal rating-based models has produced a consultative document (2016) including a number of complementary measures aimed to: (i) reduce the complexity of the regulatory framework and improve comparability; and (ii) address excessive variability in the capital requirements for credit risk. These proposals, in addition to others, provide greater specification of parameter estimation practices to reduce variability in risk-weighted assets (RWA) for portfolios where IRB approaches remain available and do not modify the asset correlation impact.

Our study remains relevant by providing findings that allow policymakers and other agents involved in the credit process to debate the opportunity for making risk-weighted assets and credit unexpected loss more reliable and closely linked to SME features.

8.3 Data

Over the last decade, the role of small and medium enterprises has increased. According to Eurostat data released in 2014, SMEs are approximately 99% of European enterprises and 92% of those are micro-enterprises. Aside from their quantity, the role of SMEs appears to be crucial in contributing to economic growth and employment: more than 90 million Europeans work for SMEs, and 57% of EU wealth depends on them. Between 2000 and 2013, SMEs contributed 86% to the net creation of work positions in the European Union. The average contribution to employment given by SMEs is higher than the value that they add, especially in such industries as manufacturing activities and information and communication services. In fact, it has been observed in some European countries that, due to their intrinsic features, small and medium enterprises have quite a low level of capital intensity and do not stand to benefit from economies of scale or the adoption and development of innovations.

Although SMEs play a relevant role in all EU member states, there are some differences among the various states. Some of these differences can be explained by the importance of particular branches of the national economy or by the institutional and cultural preferences for self-employment and/or family business. The importance of SMEs is particularly high in southern member states, such as Italy, Spain and Portugal. The role of SMEs in the Italian economic context is essential: in addition to representing the main industrial reality of its economy, the growth and development of the country depend on the capability of this segment to contribute to the creation of new jobs, to the development of innovations and, in general, to economic growth.

The Italian financial system is characterized by the centrality of banking intermediation, by the financing model of enterprises, and by the choices of saving allocation of families. According to Survey on the Access to Finance (SAFE) of small and medium-sized enterprises in the euro area (European Central Bank 2014), the financial structure of Italian SMEs is mainly bank-oriented and bank lending channel is more relevant than that of other European countries. More recently, the highest net percentages of SMEs reporting an increase in their need for bank loans were recorded in Greece (30%), Italy (14%) and France (12%). A financial system mainly based on bank loans corresponds to a scarcely developed capital market. The stock market is generally geared towards large enterprises, and in the last decade it has been downsized even more because of short-term adverse trends.

Many empirical studies examine two issues: the relationship between the development of stock markets and economic growth (finance and growth) on the one hand and the comparison of financial structures on the other, referring to bank-oriented systems and market systems (financial structure and growth). Regarding the first issue, empirical facts that were widely collected (King and Levine 1993; Beck et al. 2000) effectively proved the existence of a positive relationship between liquid stock markets and growth. Concerning the second issue, the most recent surveys show how the most developed financial systems have the tendency to part from the bank-oriented structure.

The data used in our analysis was collected from Aida (Bureau van Dijk), a large financial information provider. Our sample contains accounting data for 1.4 million Italian small and medium-sized firms during the years 1997–2013. According to the conventional SMEs definition, we distinguished firms in three size classes of turnover (Table 8.1). Micro-firms (i.e., those with turnover up to 2 million euros) represent 87% of the sample, whereas small firms (those with turnover between 2 and 10 million euros) represent approximately 10%, and medium firms are only 2.5%, with a turnover between 10 and 50 million euros. Our analysis focuses on the Italian sample for SMEs due to the concentration of the small-sized firms and their contribution to the whole GDP. Not surprisingly, their strong link with the banking system funds their financial needs.

The default probability (and, therefore, the rating notch) and the default state associated with each firm are the variables used in our study. In contrast to the other empirical studies previously quoted, the firm's default probability is drawn by our rating system and not from external rating agencies or large banking institutions. Additionally, in our study we refer to unlisted companies, as opposed to firms issuing publicly traded debt, which are usually rated by the large international rating agencies.

In our analysis we refer to default as as dissolution of an Italian company (when the representative declares bankruptcy) applying to the court for the application of the Bankruptcy Act and for liquidation.

Table 8.1 Sample feature (1997–2013)—distribution by size (sales amount in million euros)

Size classes (sales in million euros)	Number of firms	% of total
Up to 2M	1,242,661	87.2
2–10M	146,789	10.3
10–50M	35,352	2.5
Total	1,424,802	100.0

Source: Our elaborations from data drawn by AIDA, Bureau van Dijk

Table 8.2 Risk-size distribution of Italian firms (1997–2013)

Size classes (sales in million of euros)	Risk classes						
	A	B	C	D	E	F	Total
Up to 2M	406,176	156,482	166,700	226,841	154,073	132,389	1,242,661
% in size class	*33.0*	*13.0*	*13.0*	*18.0*	*12.0*	*11.0*	*100*
% of total	*29.0*	*11.0*	*12.0*	*16.0*	*11.0*	*9.0*	*87.0*
2–10M	40,378	25,007	29,213	36,873	9158	6160	146,789
% in size class	*28.0*	*17.0*	*20.0*	*25.0*	*6.0*	*4.0*	*100*
% of total	*3.0*	*2.0*	*2.0*	*3.0*	*1.00*	*0.00*	*10.0*
10–50M	11,847	7575	7647	6030	1355	898	35,352
% in size class	*34.0*	*21.0*	*22.0*	*17.0*	*4.0*	*3.0*	*100*
% of total	*0.01*	*1.00*	*1.00*	*0.00*	*0.00*	*0.00*	*2.0*
Total	458,401	189,064	203,560	269,744	164,586	139,447	1,424,802
% of total	*32.0*	*13.0*	*14.0*	*19.0*	*12.0*	*10.0*	*100*

Source: Authors' elaborations

The risk classes shown in Table 8.2 were built by mapping the ranges of expected default frequencies estimated with our model with the Standard & Poor's (S&P) scale. The A-rated companies are the best, F-rated firms the worst. It is worth highlighting that when we compared the S&P scale with the default frequencies drawn by our model, we found that the best firms of our sample correspond only with a BBB+ rating of S&P. This is why most of the companies fall within the A and B rating notches, while a lower percentage fall within speculative or non-investment grade (i.e., D or below).

8.4 Methodology

In the estimation of credit unexpected losses within portfolio models, the shape of the loss distribution is a crucial issue. The nature of the distribution tails could affect the amount of capital absorbed by the credit risk. Correlation changes observed among credit exposures transfer the risk from the mean to the tail of the loss distribution with a relevant impact on the economic and regulatory capital.

Financial literature (Fitch Ratings 2005; Düllmann et al. 2010) suggests three approaches to estimate asset correlations: (i) equity market-based information (or the equity-based approach), which can be applied only to borrowers or issuers listed in equity markets (Duan et al. 2003); (ii) ratings-based transitions (or the parametric approach), which cannot be easily applied to small firms whose distribution can hardly be defined (Gordy and Heitfield 2002; Kocagil and Liu 2008); and (iii) default-based correlation estimates or the model-free approach (Cassart et al. 2007).

To reduce the downward bias of default-based approaches (Düllmann et al. 2010) and to avoid any parametric assumption on their migration over time, we use data on rating transitions and defaults to explain the univariate and bivariate rating transitions. The cohort approach that we use for computing both the firm-level and joint default probabilities fits well with our sample, where the population of firms and defaults change over time. In order to make results easily construable, after all firms in the sample have been rated, we aggregated the risk classes that constitute the evaluation scale of our model into six grades mapping the S&P scale as shown in Table 8.2. The default state is added.

Because our observation period goes from 1997 to 2013, we created 17 one-year cohorts. The first cohort is constituted by the rated companies at the beginning of our time horizon (1997). We follow them for one year when the new rating is recorded. The defaulted companies during this first year will be deleted and will not be considered in the second cohort. The latter will be composed of sound firms recorded at the end of the first year plus the new rated firms at the beginning of the new year. This procedure will continue over the *t*th *year* (in our case, until 2013). The example in Table 8.3 shows how cohorts are built.

From the example in Table 8.3, we derive that the one-year default probability in the *i*th size or risk class is $\frac{D_{i,t}}{N_{i,t}}$, where $D_{i,t}$ is the number of firms in the *i*th size or risk class defaulted during the *t*th year, and $N_{i,t}$ is the total number of firms in the *i*th size or risk class during *t*th year. This is for each cohort.

Table 8.3 Example of cohort building

Cohort 1: 1997–1998			Cohort 2: 1998–1999		
Firm	Start of the period	End of the period	Firm	Start of the period	End of the period
1	C	B	1	B	A
2	A	A	2	A	B
3	B	C	3	C	B
4	D	C	4	C	C
5	B	B	5	B	A
6	**F**	**DEFAULT**	**6**	**DEFAULT**	**DELETED**
7	A	A	7	A	B
8	B	C	8	C	C
9	C	B	9	B	B
10	**E**	**DEFAULT**	**10**	**DEFAULT**	**DELETED**
11	E	E	11	E	D
12	D	C	12	C	B
13	A	A	13	A	A
14	B	B	14	B	B
⋮	⋮	⋮	⋮	⋮	⋮
50	C	C	50	C	B
			51	**B**	**DEFAULT**
			52	**F**	**DEFAULT**
			53	A	A
			54	E	D
			55	D	D

As in our previous study (Gabbi and Vozzella 2013), we measure default correlation, following the approach developed by De Servigny and Renault (2002). For each cohort we compute the individual (p_i, p_i) and joint default probabilities (p_{ii}), then we aggregate the cohorts to obtain the average default probability (ADP_i) for each size or risk class. First, we aggregate the cohorts to compute the average default probability (ADP_i) for the *i*th size or risk class. Formally:

$$ADP_i = \sum_{i}^{T} \frac{N_{i,t}}{\Sigma_{t=1}^{T} N_{i,t}} \frac{Def_{i,t}}{N_{i,t}}, \tag{8.4}$$

where $\frac{N_{i,t}}{\Sigma_{t=1}^{T} N_{i,t}}$ measures the relative weight of a given cohort.

Once the average default probability (ADP_i) is computed, we need to measure the joint default probability (JDP_{ii}), which measures the likelihood of two firms in a given size or risk class defaulting together and at the same time over a specified time horizon. In our case, we compute the joint default probability for a given year as the ratio between the number of firm pairs in a given size or rating class that moved towards default and the total number of pairs of firms. Formally:

$$JDP_{ii} = \frac{Def_{i,t}}{N_{i,t}} \frac{Def_{i,t}}{N_{i,t}}, \tag{8.5}$$

where $\mathrm{Def}_{i,t}$ indicates the number of firms defaulted in the *i*th starting size or risk class over *t*th year period, and $N_{i,t}$ indicates the total number of firms rated in the *i*th starting size or risk class at the beginning of the *t*th year period.

Because our purpose is to obtain an average default probability over our time horizon (1997–2013), we need to aggregate the default probabilities of each cohort. To that end, we weigh each cohort for the number of firms included in each one over *t* years as follows:

$$\mathrm{AJDP}_{ii} = \sum_{t=1}^{T} \frac{N_{i,t}}{\Sigma_{t=1}^{T} N_{i,t}} \frac{\left(Def_{i,t}\right)^2}{\left(N_{i,t}\right)^2}, \tag{8.6}$$

where $\frac{N_{i,t}}{\Sigma_{t=1}^{T} N_{i,t}}$ is the weight of each cohort in each year.

Finally, the average default probability (ADP_i) and the average joint default probability (AJDP_{ii}) are used as inputs in the default correlation formula as follows (De Servigny and Renault 2002; Bandyopadhyay et al. 2007):

$$\rho_{ii}^{D} = \frac{\mathrm{AJDP}_{ii} - ADP_i ADP_i}{\sqrt{ADP_i(1 - ADP_i\, ADP_i\left(1 - ADP_i\right)}}. \tag{8.7}$$

Once we obtain the default probability (DP_i), the joint default probabilities (JDP_{ii}) and the default correlations $\left(\rho_{ii}^{D}\right)$, we have drawn the asset correlation values (*ACV*) for the *i*th size or risk class over the period 1997–2013 with the bivariate Gaussian copula.

8.5 Results

The empirical process to estimate the asset correlation of Italian micro, small and medium-sized firms by size and risk classes is modelled as follows: (1) computing the probabilities of default by applying a logit approach; (2) estimating the empirical asset correlation coefficients based on a Gaussian copula model and comparing them with the corresponding values of the regulatory framework.

Figure 8.1 shows a monotonic increasing configuration (continuous line) of asset classes, with the minimum value for micro firms and the maximum for the large cluster of our sample. When compared with the empirical asset allocation of Italian small firms we find not only different asset correlation values but also a non-monotonic curve shape. On the right scale of the figure, we show that there is no coherence in terms of dynamics but also, more importantly, none in terms of value.

Empirical correlations (continuous line) appear to be close to zero, which implies a diversification impact higher than that introduced by regulators.

An even more significant difference can be observed when empirical and regulatory asset correlations are compared by risk class (Fig. 8.2). The shape of empirical asset correlation is completely inverted compared with that of regulatory asset correlation, except in the case of the best-rated companies. While the regulatory correlations assume that SMEs' loan portfolios benefit with the lowest values, that is, the best diversification effect. We find correlations ranging from 1% to 5% with the reverse configuration.

From a theoretical point of view, the findings contained in Fig. 8.2 are consistent with the financial accelerator rationalization approach (Bernanke and Gertler 1996). This means that a firm's capacity to borrow essentially depends on the market value of its net worth, especially because lenders suffer with asymmetric information. Therefore, banks require borrowers to reinforce their ability to repay via collateral. When asset prices decline, borrower quality deteriorates. Consequently, firms become unable to roll over their debt with a negative impact on their investment. This creates a vicious cycle financial accelerator.

Part of the first draft of the 2004 Basel Accord argued that the risk-weight curve was too steep and too high. This means that SMEs would

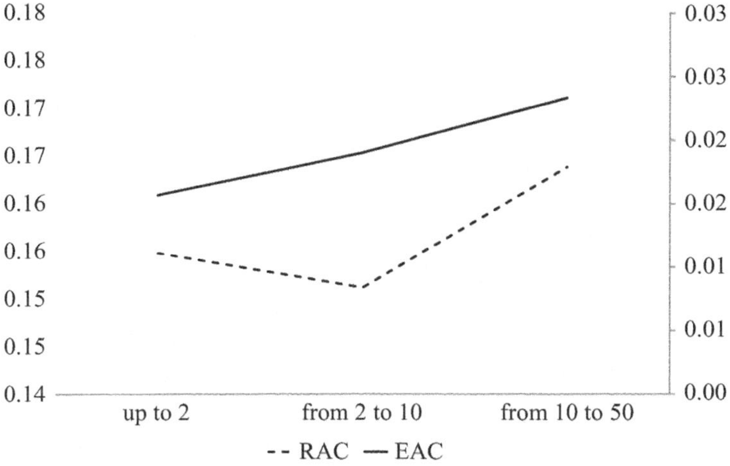

Fig. 8.1 Asset correlation and firm size (1997–2013). Regulatory asset correlation (*Y*-axis, left scale, *dotted line*) by size (*X*-axis) based on the formulas for small business vs. the empirical asset correlation estimated via Gaussian copula model (*Y*-axis, right scale, *continuous line*). For size we used the upper bound of each size class
(*Source*: Our elaborations)

be penalized by very high-risk weights because of their higher default probability with respect to large firms. Consequently, the capital requirement for SMEs would be excessive, which can lead to credit rationing. This process would be exacerbated during recession periods, when default probability increases. To deal with this critique, the last version of the second Basel Accord (2004) introduced a negative relationship between asset correlations and default probabilities. This assumption means that firms with a lower default probability are expected to be more exposed to unexpected macroeconomic changes and systematic risk. In other words, firms with higher default probabilities should be less prone to joint defaults. If so, the negative relationship between default probability and default correlation would be reasonable. This point of view may reflect the intuition that large firms, operating in global markets and characterized, on average, by a better credit quality, are more sensitive to macroeconomic factors, whereas small firms, operating on local markets, are expected to be more sensitive to specific risk factors. Small firms' flexibility to radical

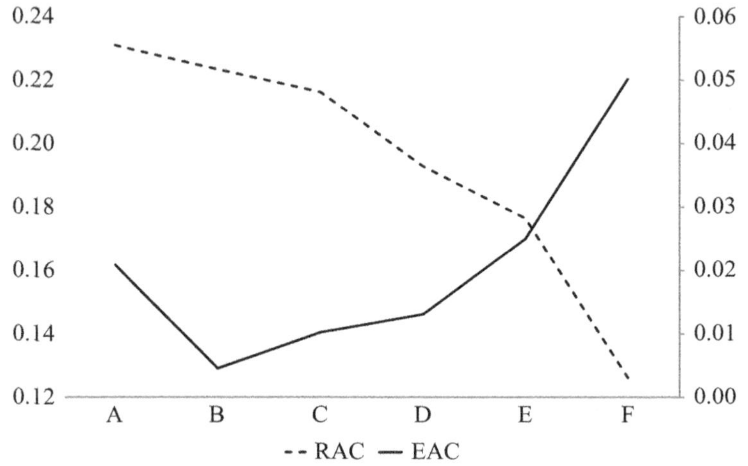

Fig. 8.2 Asset correlation and credit risk (1997–2013). Regulatory asset correlation (*Y*-axis, left scale, *dotted line*) by credit risk (internal rating notch, *X*-axis) based on the formulas for small business vs. the empirical asset correlation estimated via Gaussian copula model (*Y*-axis, right scale, *continuous line*) (*Source*: Our elaborations)

changes and new demands of consumers as described in the literature, at least for some sectors (OECD 2009), cannot compensate for shocks on demand and credit size.

Lopez (2004) confirms that average asset correlation is a decreasing function of the probability of default. His results suggest that firms with a lower credit quality (higher *PD*) are more subject to idiosyncratic risks than to common risk factors and, therefore, are characterized by a lower value of asset correlation. Das et al. (2007) find that firms with better credit ratings (lower *PD*) are more sensitive to systematic risk factors than firms with lower credit quality.

The different pattern between regulatory and empirical asset correlations by rating is confirmed for all the three size clusters of firms we analyzed.

The most relevant specificity can be observed for micro-firms (Fig. 8.3), which are companies with a turnover of under 2 million euros. The U-shaped empirical curve demonstrates that top quality firms diversify a bit less than medium quality ones (those rated C). However, the lower quality firms design an asset correlation behaviour consistent with the general observation commented on in Fig. 8.3.

Companies with turnover above 2 million euros show an empirical pattern that is quite flat for almost all the rating notches, but for the last one (F rating), the correlation estimates jump to an higher value, even though it is slightly lower than the regulatory coefficient (Figs. 8.4 and 8.5).

Implemented in the credit policies, our findings would allow banks to better calibrate capital absorption by size and quality. Within the segment of small and medium firms, the pattern of asset correlations by risk appears to be inverted compared with the regulatory assumption.

Because empirical asset correlations are much lower than regulatory values, at least for Italy, Italian banks could reduce the cost of capital and, consequently, push up the credit supply with real and financial benefits.

Our findings support the revision of the regulatory framework to calibrate the asset correlation coefficients and face the procyclical issue, modelling the weight of small loans in credit portfolios according to the empirical evidence.

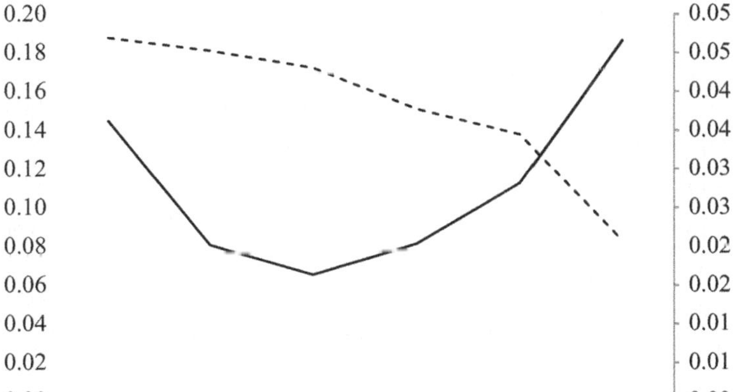

Fig. 8.3 Asset correlation for micro-firms by credit risk (1997–2013). Regulatory asset correlation (*Y*-axis, left scale, *dotted line*) by credit risk (internal rating notch, *X*-axis) based on the formulas for small business vs. the empirical asset correlation estimated via Gaussian copula model (*Y*-axis, right scale, *continuous line*)
(*Source*: Our elaborations)

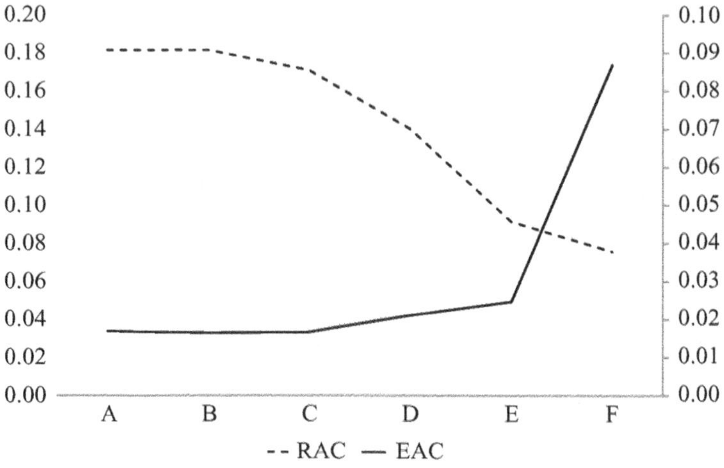

Fig. 8.4 Asset correlation for small firms by credit risk (1997–2013). Regulatory asset correlation (*Y*-axis, left scale, *dotted line*) by credit risk (internal rating notch, *X*-axis) based on the formulas for small business vs. the empirical asset correlation estimated via Gaussian copula model (*Y*-axis, right scale, *continuous line*)
(*Source*: Our elaborations)

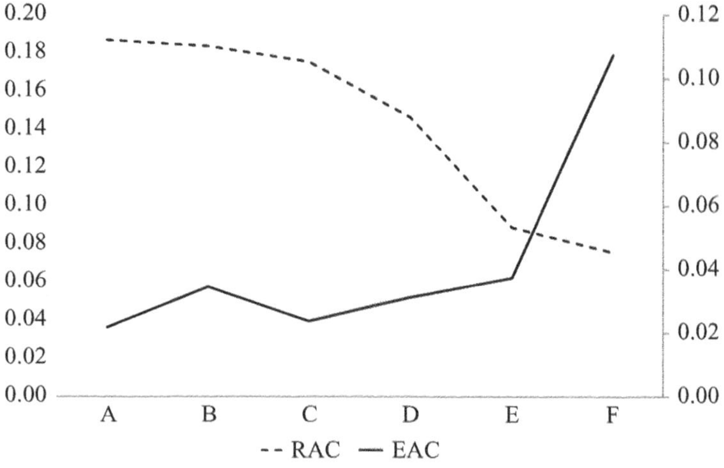

Fig. 8.5 Asset correlation for medium firms by credit risk (1997–2013). Regulatory asset correlation (*Y*-axis, left scale, *dotted line*) by credit risk (internal rating notch, *X*-axis) based on the formulas for small business vs. the empirical asset correlation estimated via Gaussian copula model (*Y*-axis, right scale, *continuous line*)
(*Source*: Our elaborations)

8.6 Conclusions

Our empirical results have important implications for both regulation and management of bank capital. First, the credit availability for small and medium enterprises, at least with the characteristics we can observe in Italy, can be directly and significantly affected by the way portfolio asset correlations are computed. Because there is a regulation that designs how banking capital is computed, financial intermediaries are forced to follow the rule because the capital management process drives the credit policy. When this standard rule is close to the empirical value of correlations, banks' decisions are taken fairly. Otherwise, the credit market can be distorted. More precisely, we observed that the assumptions known as *portfolio invariant* occur when there is only a single systematic risk factor driving correlations across borrowers and when there is no exposure in a portfolio account for more than an arbitrarily small share of total exposure. These assumptions are refuted by the empirical evidence for Italian SMEs. Consequently, the regulatory capital framework overestimates the fair capital absorption for the smallest-sized firms. The impact of this miscalculation is a potential credit crunch due to the incorrect prices that these firms pay, regardless of their rating. This risk is not completely addressed by the countercyclical capital buffer proposed within the Basel III framework because the framework is not designed to consider how asset correlations actually change during cycles for the different firm categories.

Second, Basel regulation requirements considerably underestimate capital need for firms with the highest probabilities of default. This leads to a potential adverse selection process. A correction has been introduced within the Basel III framework, increasing the asset correlation values by 25%, but only among financial institutions. To minimize the identified risks, the regulatory framework should design asset correlations differently than as seen in the Basel II Accord. A calibration by size, default probability and industry would help regulators design a capital adequacy more fitted to retail credit portfolios. Within the segment of small and medium firms, the pattern of asset correlations by risk appears to be inverted when compared with the regulatory assumption. Moreover, a correction for country impact could be taken into consideration.

Our findings support the revision of the regulatory framework to calibrate asset correlation coefficients for each country, modelling the weight of small loans in credit portfolios according to the empirical evidence.

References

Allen, L., DeLong, G., & Saunders, A. (2004). Issues in the credit risk modelling of retail markets. *Journal of Banking and Finance, 28*(4), 727–752.

Altman, E. I., & Saunders, A. (2001). An analysis and critique of the BIS proposal on capital adequacy and ratings. *Journal of Banking and Finance, 25*(1), 25–46.

Bandyopadhyay, A., Tasneem, C., & Asish, S. (2007). Calibrating asset correlation for Indian corporate exposures. Implications for regulatory capital. *The Journal of Risk Finance, 8*(4), 330–348.

Basel Committee. (2004, June). *International convergence of capital measurement and capital standards. A revised framework*. Basel: Basel Committee on Banking Supervision.

Basel Committee. (2016, March). *Reducing variation in credit risk-weighted assets – Constraints on the use of internal model approach, Consultative Document*. Basel: Bank for International Settlements.

Beck, T., Levine, R., & Loayza, N. (2000). Finance and the sources of growth. *Journal of Financial Economics, 58*(1), 261–300.

Berger, N. A., Frame, W. S., & Miller, H. N. (2005). Credit scoring and the availability, price, and risk of small business credit. *Journal of Money, Credit and Banking, 37*(2), 191–222.

Bernanke, B., & Gertler, M. (1996). The financial accelerator and the flight to quality. *Review of Economics and Statistics, 78*(1), 1–15.

Calem, P. S. & LaCour-Little, M. (2001). *Risk-based capital requirements for mortgage loans* (The Federal Reserve Board, Financial and Economics Discussion Series, Working Paper 2001–60).

Carey, M. (2000). *Dimensions of credit risk and their relationship to economic capital requirements* (National Bureau of Economic Research, *Working Paper Series* No. 7629), pp. 1–39.

Carey, M., & Hrycay, M. (2001). Parameterizing Credit Risk models with rating Data. *Journal of Banking and Finance, 25*(1), 197–270.

Carling, K., Jacobson, T., Lindé, J., & Roszbach, K. (2002). *Capital charges under Basel 2: Corporate credit risk modelling and the macroeconomy* (Working Paper Sveriges Riksbank No. 145).

Cassart, D., Castro D., Langendries, R., & Alderweireld, T. (2007). Confidence Set for Asset Correlation, Mimeo.

Das, S. J., Duffie, D., Kapadia, N., & Saita, L. (2007). Common failings: How corporate defaults are correlated. *Journal of Finance, 62*(1), 93–117.

De Servigny, A., & Renault, O. (2002). *Default correlation: Empirical evidence* (Working Paper, Standard and Poor's).

Degryse, H., & Ongena, S. (2005). Distance, lending relationship and competition. *Journal of Finance, 60*(1), 231–266.

Dietsch, M., & Petey, J. (2002). The credit risk in SME loans portfolios: Modelling issues, pricing and capital requirements. *Journal of Banking and Finance, 26*(2), 303–322.

Dietsch, M., & Petey, J. (2004). Should SME exposures be treated as retail or corporate exposures? A comparative analysis of default probabilities and asset correlations in French and German SMEs. *Journal of Banking and Finance, 28*(4), 773–788.

Duan, J. C., Gauthier, G., Simonato, J. G., & Zaanoun, S. (2003). *Estimating Merton's model by maximum likelihood with survivorship consideration* (Working Paper, University of Toronto).

Düllmann, K., Küll, J., & Kunisch, M. (2010). Estimating asset correlations from stock prices or default rates – Which method is superior? *Journal of Economic Dynamics & Control, 34*(11), 2341–2357.

ECB, (2014). *Survey on the access to finance of small and medium-Sized enterprises in the euro area. European Central Bank*. Frankfurt, April.

Fitch Ratings. (2005). *A comparative empirical study of asset correlations*. New York: Mimeo.

Gabbi, G. & Vozzella, P., (2013). Asset Correlation and Bank Capital Adequacy. *European Journal of Finance 19 (1)*, 55 74.

Glennon, D., & Nigro, P. (2003). *An analysis of SBA loan defaults by maturity structure*. Washington, DC: Mimeo.

Gordy, M., & Heitfield, E. (2002). *Estimating default correlations from short panels of credit rating performance data* (Working Paper, Federal Reserve).

Hamerle, A., Liebig, T., & Rösch, D. (2003). *Credit risk factor modeling and the basel 2 IRB approach* (Deutsche Bundesbank Discussion Paper).

Jacobson, T., Lindé J., & Roszbach K. (2002). *Credit risk versus capital requirements under Basel 2: Are SME loans and retail credit really different?* Mimeo

King, R. G., & Levine, R. (1993). Finance, entrepreneurship, and growth: Theory and evidence. *Journal of Monetary Economics, 32*(3), 513–542.

Kocagil, A. E., & Liu, J. (2008). Empirical assessment of asset correlations. In A. Resti (Ed.), *Pillar II in the new basel accord. The challenge of economic capital*. London: Risk Books.

Lopez, J. A. (2004). The empirical relationship between average asset correlation, firm probability of default and asset size. *Journal of Financial Intermediation, 13*(2), 265–283.
OECD. (2009). *The impact of the global crisis on SME and entrepreneurship financing and policy responses*. Paris: OECD.
Perli, R., & Nayda, W. I. (2004). Economic and regulatory capital allocation for revolving retail exposures. *Journal of Banking and Finance, 28*(4), 789–809.
Petersen, M. A. (2004). Information: Hard and soft, Kellogg School of Management, Northwestern University, Mimeo.
Petersen, M., & Rajan, R. (2002). Does distance still matter? The information revolution in small business lending. *Journal of Finance, 57*(6), 2533–2570.
Schmit, M. (2004). Credit risk in the leasing industry. *Journal of Banking and Finance, 28*(4), 811–833.
Shen, T. P. (2005). Empirical study on the effect of new basel accord on SMEs, project report commissioned by Joint Credit Information Center, Mimeo.
Stein, J. (2002). Information production and capital allocation: Decentralized vs. Hiearchical firms. *Journal of Finance, 57*(5), 1891–1921.

9

Credit Supply and Bank Interest Rates in the Italian Regions

Roberto Malavasi and Mauro Aliano

9.1 Introduction

Several analyses have been conducted (inter alia, Mattesini and Messori 2004; Beretta 2004; Gallo and Vannoni 2015) to explain the reasons for the differences in interest rates for loans (spread) in different regions of Italy. The authors find two primary explanations. The first is related to riskier conditions in certain regions due to a system of enterprises characterised by environmental and institutional peculiarity (demand side); the second addresses the structure of the local credit system and characteristics of the banks' business models (supply side).[1]

[1] It is useful to consider, for example, the quality of the credit brokerage that could certainly also be included in the more general environmental effect, as well as other infrastructure useful to realise suitable conditions to facilitate investment and profitability of production activities.

JEL classification: G20, G21, G28

R. Malavasi • M. Aliano (✉)
Department of Economics and Business, University of Cagliari, Cagliari, Italy
e-mail: mauro.aliano@unica.it

S.P.S. Rossi (ed.), *Access to Bank Credit and SME Financing*,
Palgrave Macmillan Studies in Banking and Financial Institutions,
DOI 10.1007/978-3-319-41363-1_9

This chapter will attempt, based on the two explanations presented above, to describe the determinants of the spread in interest rates on loans as well as pricing adequacy measured via the interest rates on loans, regarding the evolution of credit risk as proxied by the non-performing loans ratio, or NPL. Thus, hypotheses can be formulated regarding the direction and magnitude of the analysed phenomena to identify possible advice for policymakers.

The characteristics of loans' demand and supply are analysed to investigate the determinants of the spread in interest rates. The characteristics of demand are captured using two indexes. The first is an index of productive specialisation for each Italian region, representing an adequate proxy of potential economic trends in each geographic area. The second is a measure of the degree of concentration in bank lending by borrower size. These variables should be able to catch both the overall environmental and institutional effects on enterprises' behaviour. Nonetheless, it is worth noting that the second index is also useful to represent the ability of banks to finance new or innovative firms. Furthermore, regarding the supply side, an index of banks' lending specialisation is utilised for each Italian region, capturing the exposure of various economic sectors. The comparison of these three variables should demonstrate the banking system's primary tendencies. Specifically, it should provide information regarding banks' propensity to satisfy the demand for loans coming from the different sectors in each region, based on productive specialisation. Additionally, it might provide information regarding the diversification policies implemented by banks. It seems logical to expect that, in the case of higher, increasing levels of loan concentration by firm size, and particularly if this situation is combined with an important discrepancy between the indexes of productive and banking specialisation, banks' behaviour should be less dynamic in terms of their selection of target companies. Banks in this case would favour the most traditional business activities, thus damaging innovative projects. These behaviours may be motivated by social and political pressures, which intensify in less developed regions, and especially during economic and financial crisis. This in turn leads to an assertion that a lack of lending diversification, for some regions, determines an unsatisfied latent demand.

If the banking system attempts to compensate for the rise in impaired loans via an increase in interest rates, an obvious vicious circle might arise that, in turn, determines increasing levels of non-performing loans. Therefore, to study the adequacy of loan pricing regarding the evolution of credit risk, the following analysis is conducted: namely, the evolution of non-performing loans over total loans (NPL) for the period of 2010–2014, and the dynamics of spreads charged for lending operations by various maturities, are employed to estimate (i) the financial intermediation's overall quality, and (ii) the pricing policies. A vector autoregression model designed to evaluate the interaction between these two variables was also estimated to reinforce analysis results and to aid fully our understanding of the rationale behind this phenomenon.

Section 9.2 describes the data and variables employed in the analyses. Section 9.3 provides results and their implications. Finally, Sect. 9.4 summarises the policy implications.

9.2 Data and Variables

The analysis is based on regional data from the Bank of Italy, ISTAT (Italian National Institute of Statistics) and Prometeia for the period of 2010–2014. An index of productive specialisation is calculated to represent all characteristics of the regional systems and their potential dynamics. Concerning the banking sector, the same specialisation indicator at the regional level is estimated to identify banks' propensity for financing different sectors of the economy. The comparison between these two indexes captures the allocation processes and the financial intermediation's efficiency; thus, this illustrates possible differences among regions. A matrix of added values, demonstrating the value added for each region and sector, such as Agriculture, Manufacturing, Construction and Services, was an origin point used to identify regional production specialisation. Geographical and sectorial specialisation is assessed via the Lo Cascio–Bagarani (LB) index of specialisation, as in the work of Lo Cascio et al. (2012).[2]

[2] Starting from the matrix of the added values, based on data from regional economies firm Prometeia, which shows the value added for each partition area (line) and production sector (column) to capture the geographical and sectorial specialisation, the *LB* specialisation index (Lo Cascio et al. 2012) has been calculated as:

The economic time series, represented by quarterly Gross Domestic Product values, has been derived from the institutional ISTAT website. The data processed was available from the Prometeia regional database, referring to the value added in chained values, with a base year of 2010, to obtain the macroeconomic data used for production specialisation.

A specialisation index was then calculated for bank loans, according to the same regions and sectors used for production, with data provided by the Bank of Italy BDS (*Base Dati Statistica*, Bank of Italy's statistical database).

Starting with the borrowers' size, the Herfindahl-Hirschman concentration index (HHI) was additionally calculated for bank loans[3] in each region. This index represents both a measure of *ex-ante* risk for each regional banking system and a proxy of the funding allocation policy for the most traditional borrowers. Highly concentrated banking systems may signal a weaker process of borrower selection that, in turn, produces

---

$$LB_{i,j} = \frac{q(x)-q(a)}{[1-q(a)]q(x)+[1-q(x)]q(a)},$$

where

$$q(x) = \frac{x_{i,j}}{\sum_i x_{i,j}}$$

$$q(a) = \frac{\sum_j x_{i,j}}{\sum_i x_{i,j}}$$

where $x_{i,j}$ is the value (loans provided in 2012) for the *j*th variable (sector) for the region *i* for $q(x) = q(a)$, $LB_{i,j} = 0$; for $q(x) < q(a)$, $LB_{i,j} < 0$; and for $q(x) > q(a)$, $LB_{i,j} > 0$, $1 \geq LB_{i,j} \geq -1$.

If *LB* presents positive values close to 1, this indicates a specialisation for region *i* in sector *j*. Conversely, negative values close to −1 indicate a despecialisation. The result of calculating the difference between the indicator at time *t* and at time *t* − 1 defines the dynamics of specialisation.

[3] As calculated in the work of Jahn et al. (2013).

higher risk-taking.[4] The regional banking system, with a low concentration, in contrast, diversifies the loan portfolio and can take advantage of the imperfect correlation between performance trends and asset quality for different types of borrowers, thus reducing the overall *ex-ante* risk. Data employed for the calculation of the aforementioned concentration index and data for interest rates on loans and non-performing loans come from the Bank of Italy BDS.

9.3 Results

The analysis results for the levels of productive specialisation, as summarised in Figs. 9.1 and 9.2 (see Figs. A.9.1 and A.9.2 in Appendix A for Construction and Services), clearly illustrates Italy's renowned duality: the south is characterised by specialisation in a primary sector (Agriculture), while the north and the centre are dominated by a strong Manufacturing industry. Another characteristic is the economic stability of the northern region, in contrast to the conditions of increased volatility and the dispersion of production activities that prevail in the south. Comparing this information with that obtained for the specialisation level of bank loans for Agriculture and Manufacturing (see Figs. 9.3 and 9.4)[5] indicates an overall relationship between the two variables. It is possible to observe that for those regions highly specialised in Agriculture, the banking system's response appears delayed and not fully reactive to the dynamics of the real economy. The opposite can be seen in regions characterised by Manufacturing specialisation, where the financial variable proves to be more synchronised with demand from the productive sectors. An automatic link is captured in these contexts between the dynamics of supply and demand for credit, which ensures an almost instantaneous saturation of the latter. These trends are also detectable in the reduction of emergent high levels of sector specialisation: supply always shrinks in proportion to the impulses of demand. The opposite

[4] For example, the excessive concentration in the credit line class is typically attributed to consumer credit (e.g., under 25,000.00 EUR) and exposes its banking sector to trends in household consumption.

[5] See Figs. A.9.3 and A.9.4 in Appendix A for Construction and Services.

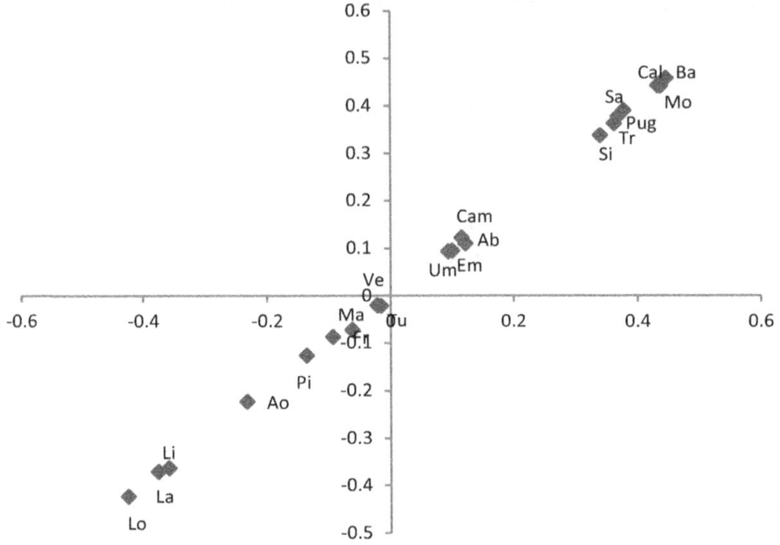

Fig. 9.1 Index of production specialisation in Agriculture, 2010–2014 (the *x*-axis projects the specialisation index in 2010, the *y*-axis reports the same index in 2014; *Ab* Abruzzo, *Ba* Basilicata, *Cal* Calabria, *Cam* Campania, *Em* Emilia-Romagna, *Fr* Friuli Venezia Giulia, *La* Lazio, *Li* Liguria, *Lo* Lombardy, *Ma* Marche, *Mo* Molise, *Pi* Piedmont, *Pug* Apulia, *Sa* Sardinia, *Si* Sicily, *Tu* Tuscany, *Tr* Trentino-Alto Adige/Südtirol, *Um* Umbria, *Ao* Aosta Valley, *Ve* Veneto)

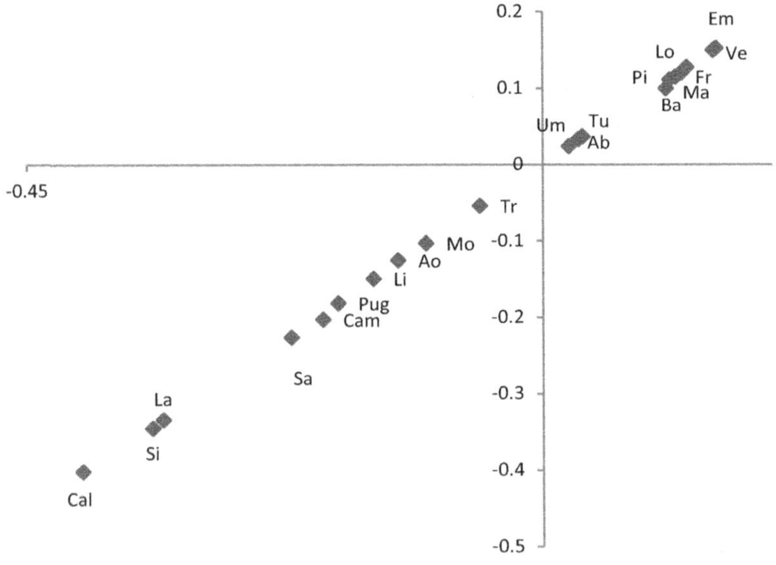

Fig. 9.2 Index of production specialisation in Manufacturing, 2010–2014 (the *x*-axis projects the specialisation index in 2010, the *y*-axis reports the same index in 2014)

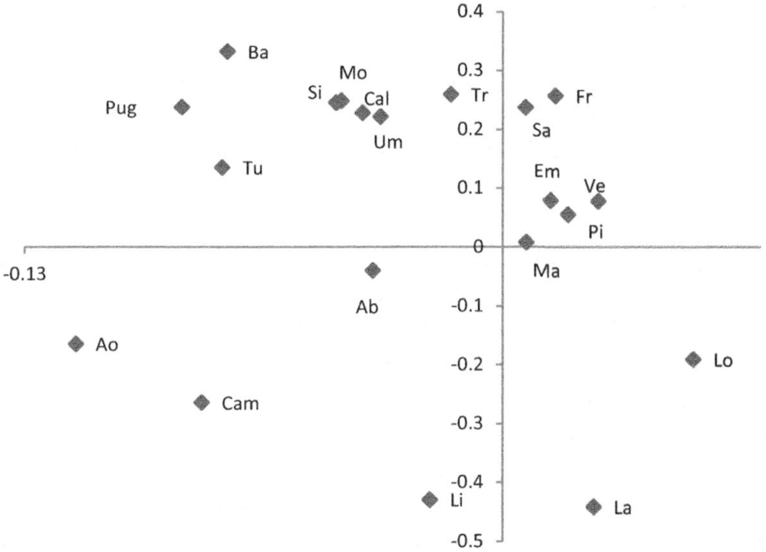

Fig. 9.3 Index of loan specialisation in Agriculture, 2010–2014 (the *x*-axis projects the specialisation index in 2010, the *y*-axis reports the same index in 2014)

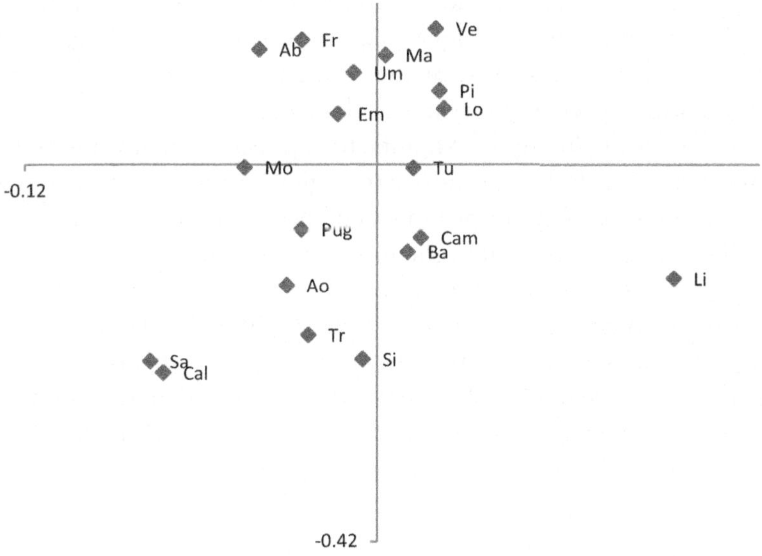

Fig. 9.4 Index of loan specialisation in Manufacturing, 2010–2014 (the *x*-axis projects the specialisation index in 2010, the *y*-axis reports the same index in 2014)

arises in the south, where in the case of even limited reduction in productive specialisation, a strong decrease of credit devoted to the same sector is observed. Regions highly specialised in Services display the same characteristics found in regions with a high specialisation in the primary sector; namely, the supply is delayed compared to the corresponding demand trend. As a non-negligible fact, diversity appears in terms of the dynamics of the Construction sector towards the banking system, while in the south, the supply seems to be higher than the demand, but the trend is opposite in the north. This is because there is increased attention on highly specialised sectors.

A cluster analysis is conducted to support the information provided in the previous charts and to define regional clusters based on the difference between production specialisation and loan specialisation, via Ward's criterion; see also the work of Johnson and Wichern (2007).[6] This analysis results in four clusters, summarised in Table 9.1. The first cluster, represented by the Lazio region, is characterised by a loan specialisation in the Construction sector higher than that of production, while the opposite result is seen for the other sectors. The second cluster indicates levels of specialisation in production for both the Agriculture and Manufacturing sectors higher than those for bank lending. The third cluster, which includes most of the southern regions, indicates degrees of Agriculture specialisation higher than bank lending, in contrast to what occurs in the marginal Manufacturing sector. Finally, in the fourth cluster, which includes the northern regions and part of central Italy, evidence indicates a more pronounced specialisation in bank loans for Manufacturing than for the Agriculture sector, and the opposite emerges in the Service sector. The different response that the credit system manifested in northern and southern Italy regarding the dynamics of production specialisation appears to be relevant and confirms the difficulty intermediaries face to suitably saturate the inputs of demand in territories where the adopted developing model is less defined and stable.

[6] Four clusters were chosen to better explain the results and to isolate the regions with extreme values.

Table 9.1 Cluster analysis the center regions are absorbed in north or south clusters

Regions	Cluster features
Lazio	Significant divergence in Construction (negative) and Services (positive) sectors
Basilicata, Emilia-Romagna, Trentino-Alto Adige/Südtirol	Divergence (positive) in Agriculture and Manufacturing sectors
SOUTH Abruzzo, Calabria, Campania, Liguria, Molise, Apulia, Sardinia, Sicily	Divergence (positive) in the Agriculture and negative in the Manufacturing sector, and relatively low in the Services sector
NORTH Aosta Valley, Friuli Venezia Giulia, Lombardy, Marche, Piedmont, Tuscany, Umbria, Veneto	Divergence (negative) in the Agriculture and Manufacturing sectors, and positive in the Services sector

Cluster analysis was conducted starting with the differences between indexes of production specialisation and loan specialisation. Four clusters were sorted to characterise the best results so as to isolate regions that demonstrated extreme values without losing excessive capability for synthesis.

Results related to the level of concentration of bank lending by borrower size (HHI) are shown in Fig. 9.5.[7] The figure highlights the banking system's different behaviours in two areas: (i) on one side, the southern regions are grouped, where the phenomenon is more intense; (ii) on the other side, the northern and a few central regions have very different characteristics compared to the first area. The hypothesis of a different loan diversification ability is confirmed for the two regional aggregates.

Combining the results of the latter variable, or concentration, with those obtained in the first analysis, or the specialisation in production and loans, at the cluster level, makes clear two different approaches to banking intermediation in terms of credit supply. One is characterised by a more reactive behaviour to demand impulses[8]; the other seems to be more passive and linked to the more traditional and oldest productive sectors.[9]

[7] See Table A.9.1 in Appendix A for more detailed information.

[8] These regions present values below average for the year 2014 with regards to the indicator of loan concentration by borrower size.

[9] The first eight regions with the highest levels of the degree of loan concentration by size, except Basilicata, are included in the second cluster, which represents almost all of the southern regions.

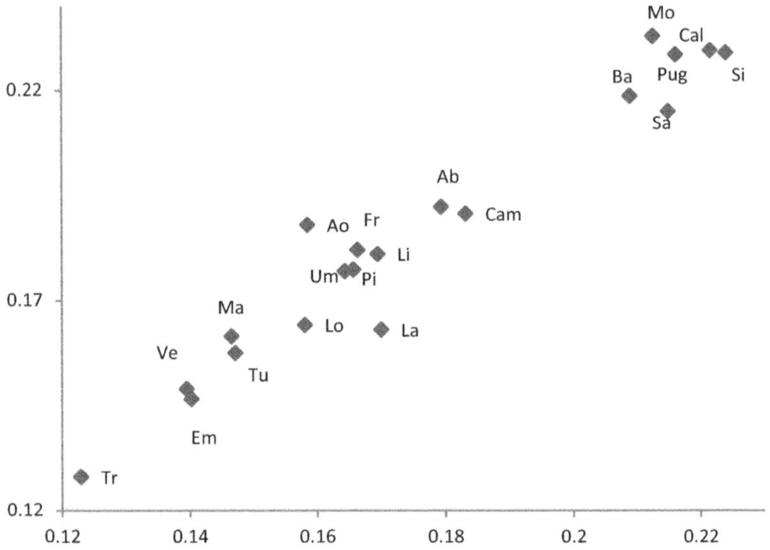

Fig. 9.5 Bank concentration index (by size class), 2010–2014 (the *x*-axis projects the concentration index in 2010, the *y*-axis reports the same index in 2014)

The dynamic of the lending credit quality as assessed by the calculation non-performing loans/total loans, (NPL) is graphically represented in Figs. 9.6 and 9.7.[10] The level of the observed ratio for the period of 2010–2014 can be seen in these figures, for each of the three groups considered (non-financial companies, family businesses and households), for each Italian region. At the regional level, all the groups present similar trends. The comparison between northern and southern regions highlights a substantial difference regarding the trends recorded by non-financial firms. The firms chartered in northern Italy particularly present the lowest levels and weaker NPL growth, whereas the south is characterised in the analysed years by the highest values for the observed ratio. Additionally, the distance separating family businesses is even more evident in the two geographical aggregates.

[10] See Fig. A.9.5 in Appendix A for households.

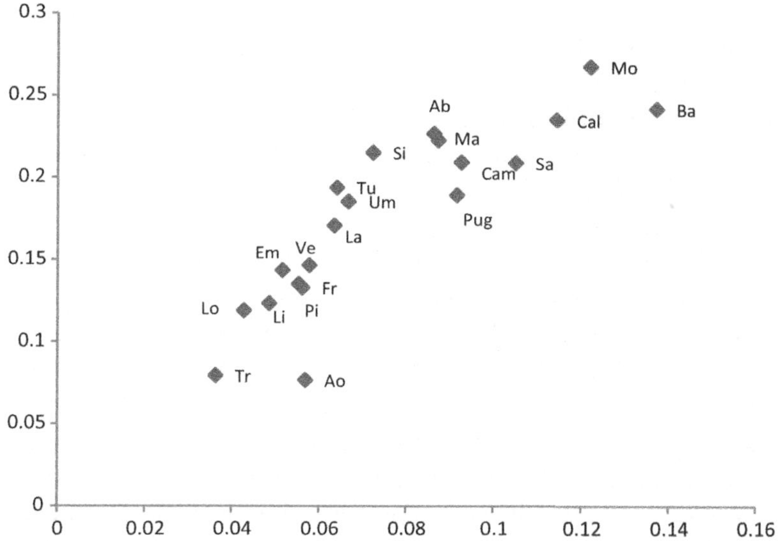

Fig. 9.6 Credit quality for non-financial companies, 2010–2014 (the *x*-axis reports the value of the ratio of non-performing loans to total loans in 2010, the *y*-axis reports the same ratio in 2014)

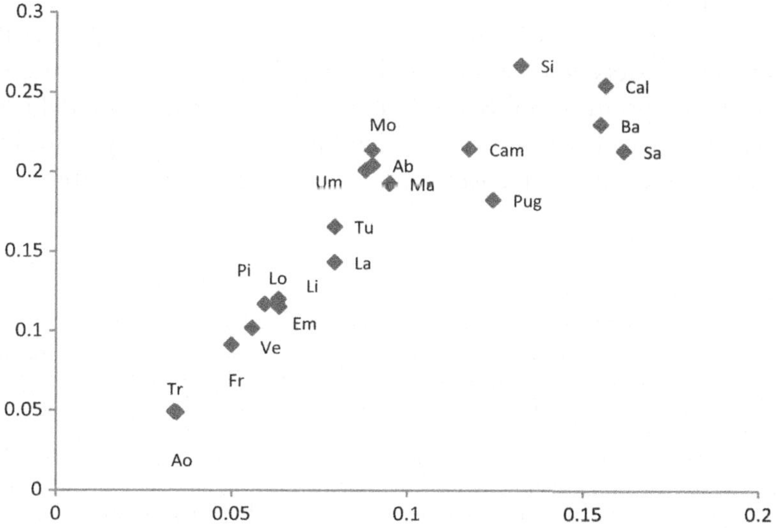

Fig. 9.7 Credit quality for family businesses, 2010–2014 (the *x*-axis reports the value of the ratio of non-performing loans to total loans in 2010, the *y*-axis reports the same ratio in 2014)

Evaluation of pricing policies is conducted through examination of the spreads charged by banks for the various loan maturities. Figures 9.8, 9.9 and 9.10 display the behaviours of spreads for the various regions for the various categories of borrowers and for each maturity: up to 1 year, between 1 and 5 years, and over 5 years.[11] An overall regularity in the results can be noted for all categories, in the sense of a strong, growing difference in the interest rates charged by banks in northern and southern Italy. This difference appears particularly relevant regarding short-term maturities, but becomes even more so for long-term maturities, or those of more than 5 years, and less marked on loans between 1 and 5 years. The strong difference in spreads for the longest maturities between the northern and southern regions is a particular source of concern for the effects on the dynamics of investments, which are already clear,[12] and more specifically regarding the innovative sector.

The structure of the collected data concerning the NPL and the spreads in interest rates for the different loan maturities granted to each category of borrowers allows a further analysis based on information at the panel level. The objective is to verify the effectiveness of pricing policy adopted by banks in the various territories and, therefore, its ability to satisfy credit demand.

A pooled regression with fixed effects[13] is estimated in Appendix B for the various clusters at a regional level in which the dependent variable in a first model specification (Spec. A) is the NPL. Further, a model is then estimated in which the spreads on lending rates according to different maturities (Spec. B) are instead considered as dependent variables.

[11] See Figs. A.9.6 to A.9.11 in Appendix A for households and family businesses.

[12] If the trend of the degree of loan concentration by size of borrowers were used as a proxy of the bargaining power of banks, some useful information could be compared with estimates made on pricing policies adopted by banks at various stages of the relationship. For more on this question, see the work of Parigi (2000).

[13] The decision to construct a regression-pull type with fixed effects relates to the need to assign the peculiarities of origin to a regional banking system and, therefore, a different intercept. Moreover, the specificity of each appears amply justified in light of the results from previous calculations, and particularly the analysis of clusters.

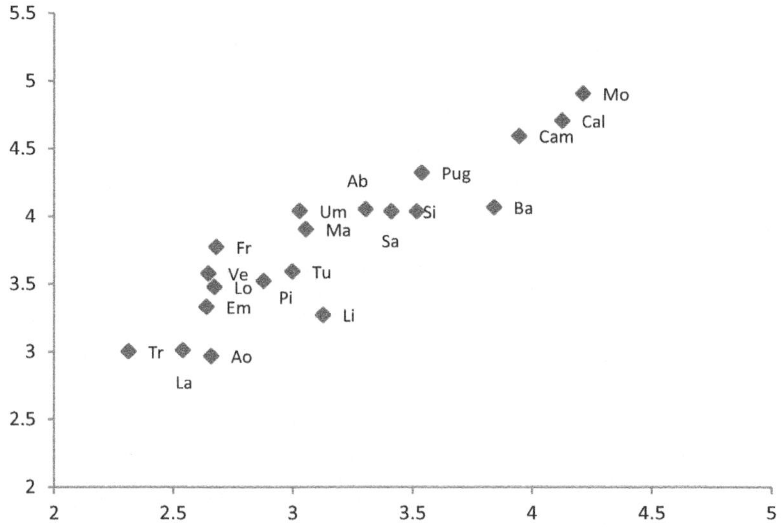

Fig. 9.8 Interest rate spreads with maturity up to 1 year for non-financial companies, 2010–2014 (the *x*-axis reports the value of the interest rate spread in 2010, the *y*-axis reports the same ratio in 2014)

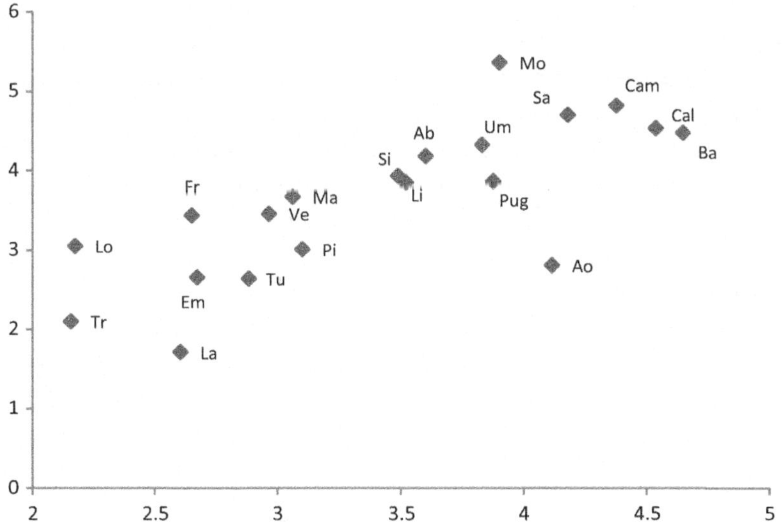

Fig. 9.9 Interest rate spreads with maturity between 1 and 5 years for non-financial companies, 2010–2014 (the *x*-axis reports the value of the interest rate spread in 2010, the *y*-axis reports the same ratio in 2014)

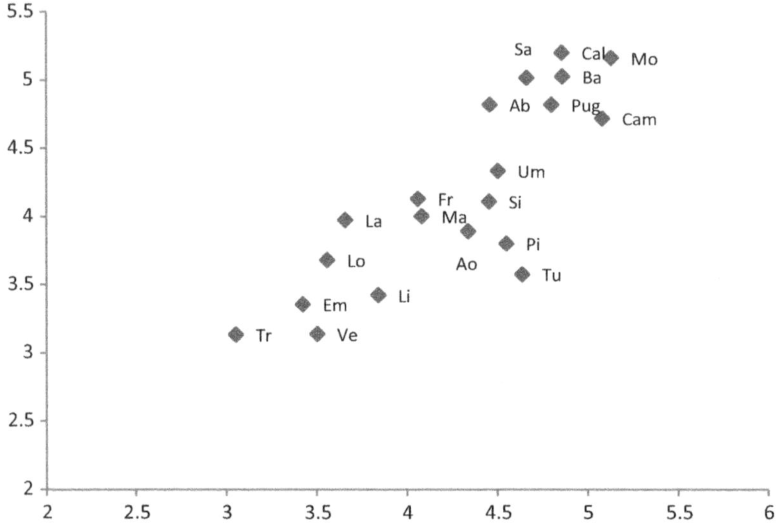

Fig. 9.10 Interest rate spreads with maturity over 5 years for non-financial companies, 2010–2014 (the *x*-axis reports the value of the interest rate spread in 2010, the *y*-axis reports the same ratio in 2014)

The relationship between spreads and credit risk varies in the first model (Spec. A),[14] both for magnitude and sign, according to the different maturities. Specifically, the relationship between the spreads on loans whose maturity is less than 1 year with the NPL ratio is positive and significant only for non-financial companies and family businesses, or generally speaking, the economic units who produce. This indicates a positive effect of spreads on credit risk, especially in the southern regions. This means that in this area an increase of interest rates on lending determines a worsening of credit quality, or an increased level of NPL. The results confirm that when the spreads increase, banks finance riskier firms, implying a worsening in credit quality, especially in southern Italy. The estimated relationship becomes insignificant regarding households for which the phenomenon of adverse selection described above is less clear. The

[14] See Tables B.9.1, B.9.2 and B.9.3 in Appendix B.

result obtained for the northern regions highlights an increase in loan spreads to households coupled with a reduction in NPL; this is also true for non financial firms and for those with 1 and 5 years maturity.

In the second model (Spec. B),[15] the relation of the NPL with the interest spreads presents positive values only for loans expiring within 5 years, in line with the aforementioned. This means that the effect, in terms of higher interest rates caused by the deterioration of credit quality, has an impact only on loans with maturities of less than 5 years. An inverse relationship emerges, in contrast, regarding longer maturities. It is worth noting that the negative relationship between NPL and spreads for longer maturities is more intense for the cluster of northern regions, with the exception of family businesses, which show a greater similarity to non-financial companies.

Finally, a joint analysis of the two specifications (Spec. A and Spec. B) illustrates a high level of interrelation between the variables used. A comparison of the results, in this sense, may represent a similar analysis to one that could emerge from a vector autoregression, or VAR, approach. The comparison between the two specifications allows for an assessment of the reliability of the results and, therefore, the consistency of the relationship. Spec. A is the most reliable in this regard, given that it possesses the highest adjusted R-squared. A superior data fit is particularly observed by splitting the sample according to regional clusters, except for family businesses. Splitting the sample by clusters does not improve the adjusted R-squared for Spec. B, except for households in the northern regions.[16] Spec. A seems to better represent the link between credit quality and spreads; moreover, the clusters by regions contribute to further explain price transmission. Briefly, in a majority of cases in the south, higher spread levels are associated with a growth in NPL. The relationship between the two variables is less significant when considering loans with longer maturity. This might depend on the existence of scarce liquidity

[15] See Tables B.9.4, B.9.5 and B.9.6 in Appendix B.

[16] Regarding the analysis of correlation statistic, see Appendix B, as it is not possible to obtain appropriate information to improve the above proposed interpretative framework.

conditions, which determine an important demand for short-term loans. Concerning banks' behaviours companies' liquidity demand causes an immediate increase in interest rates charged for maturities within 1 year. This in turn determines—with a significant delay—a consequent rise in interest rates for longer maturities.

Considering these results alongside those already described, regarding the concentration of loans by borrowers' size, it seems the south will continue to finance older companies, thereby determining a gradual increase in NPL. The institutional environment appears unstable and degraded in that it does not ensure firms with the necessary conditions to develop innovative and competitive projects. This mechanism, especially for southern regions, excludes the possibility of financing new business ideas and/or new companies in the medium-long term. Additionally, from the banks' perspective, borrower credit risk is particularly high in that even a deep increase in interest rates does not permit complete coverage, thus determining an increase in NPL.

9.4 Conclusions

As evident from the cluster analysis, a comparison among bank loan specialisation, production specialisation indicators and the concentration of loans by size of borrowers indicates the existence of two different typologies of bank behaviours in northern and southern Italy. The north has a pattern of economic growth that is clearer and more stable over time, and the supply of credit is diversified, more proportionate and readily responsive to credit demand. This highlights that banks are more inclined to supply credit to a wider range of borrowers, either in terms of their size or productive sectors. The south has less predictable growth dynamics and a strong productive specialisation in the primary sector; banking intermediation faces a delay in responding to other sectors' demand. More specifically, in the case of an increase in production specialisation, the bank system slowly adapts to demand impulses, thus maintaining a stable composition of borrower typology in a loans portfolio. The decrease in credit supply is more than proportional and immediate in the case of even a modest reduction in the Manufacturing sector's dynamics.

The analysis of the link between NPL and spreads on the one hand confirms the growing distance between northern and southern Italy, and on the other hand indicates that the hypothesis that considers credit quality as the dependent variable, or Spec. A, is more statistically sustainable. Moreover, for the southern regions a positive correlation is found between higher spread and growth in NPL. This evidence confirms banks' difficulty in properly pricing loans according to the institutional environment in which they operate.

Given this, it is suggested that the policymaker undertake the following corrective actions: First, a macroeconomic type is aimed at establishing a credible and stable development model for each of the southern regions, also alleviating these territories from the weights that obstruct enterprises' full competitiveness. Second, a financial type is oriented to improve the ability of the banking system in identifying the projects to be financed. The Universal Bank Model should be revised to do so, provided there is no clear separation between interest income and non-interest income (Bianchi 2015). It could be fundamental in this regard to open the market to new credit intermediaries specialised in evaluating and financing positive net present value projects. The skills of venture capital operators could be exploited, in addition to the expertise of financial intermediaries in traditional lending channels.

The common practice of public central and regional bodies focusing their interventions on the intensification of guarantee schemes, aimed at mitigating credit risk, seems poorly designed to solve the problems widely discussed in this chapter.

9.5 Appendix A

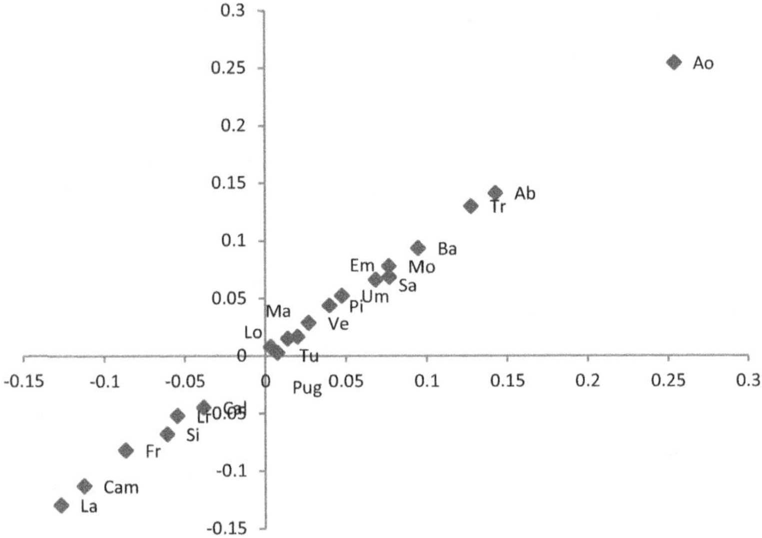

Fig. A.9.1 Index of production specialisation in Construction, 2010–2014 (the *x*-axis projects the specialisation index in 2010, the *y*-axis reports the same index in 2014)

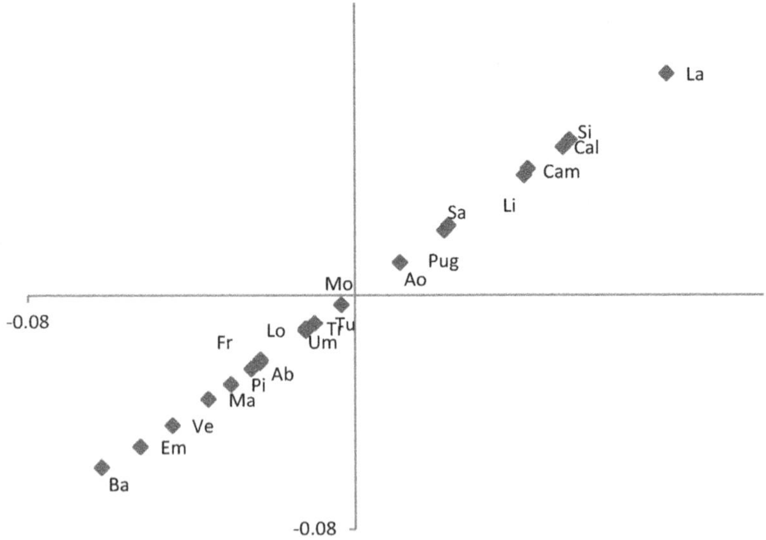

Fig. A.9.2 Index of production specialisation in Services, 2010–2014 (the *x*-axis projects the specialisation index in 2010, the *y*-axis reports the same index in 2014)

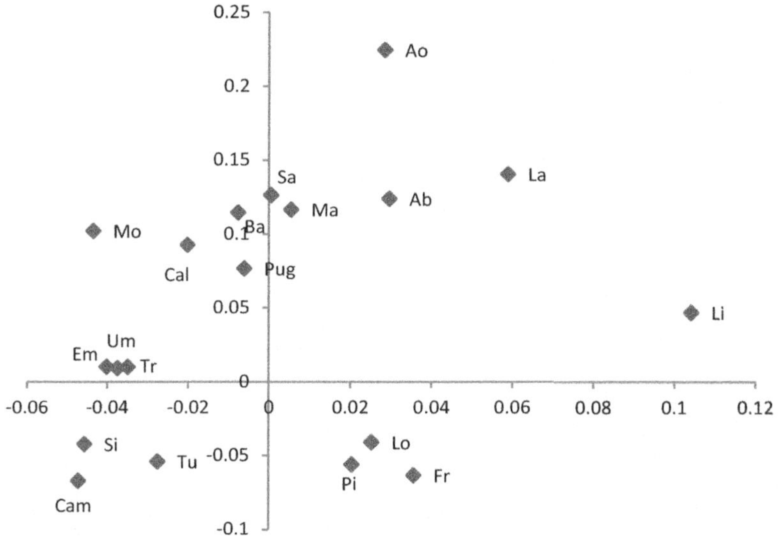

Fig. A.9.3 Index of loan specialisation in Construction, 2010–2014 (the *x*-axis projects the specialisation index in 2010, the *y*-axis reports the same index in 2014)

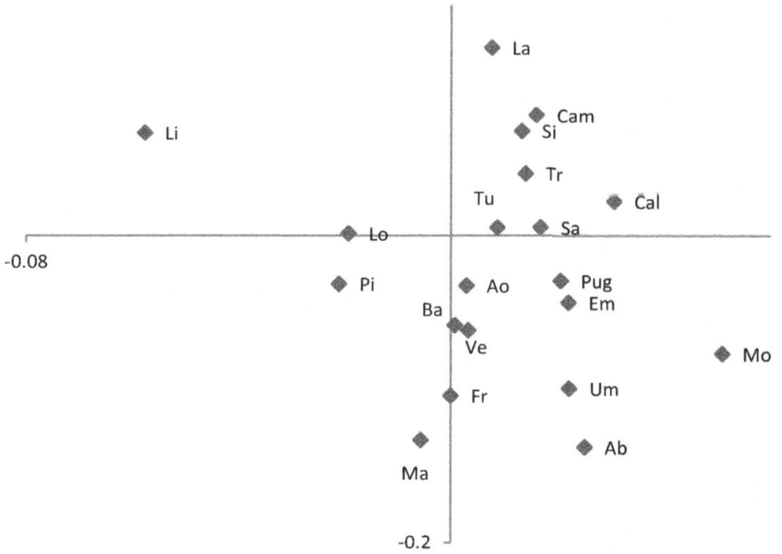

Fig. A.9.4 Index of production specialisation in Services, 2010–2014 (the *x*-axis projects the specialisation index in 2010, the *y*-axis reports the same index in 2014)

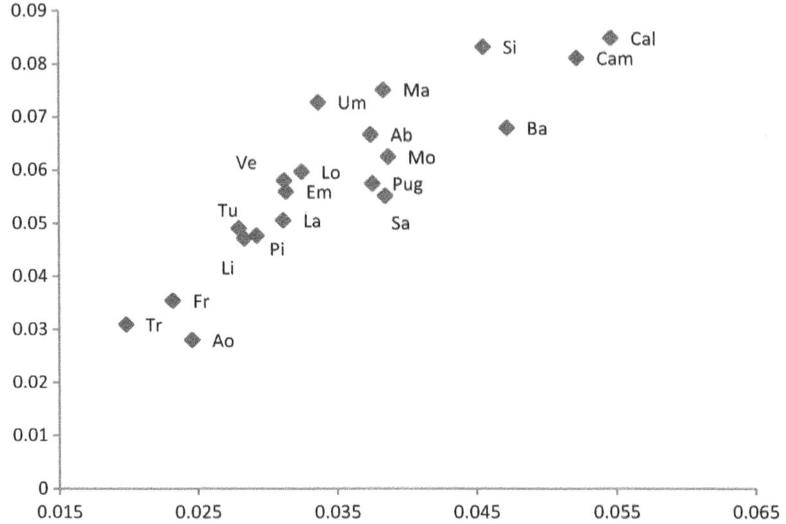

Fig. A.9.5 Credit quality for households, 2010–2014 (the *x*-axis projects the ratio between non-performing loans and total loans in 2010, the *y*-axis reports the same ratio in 2014)

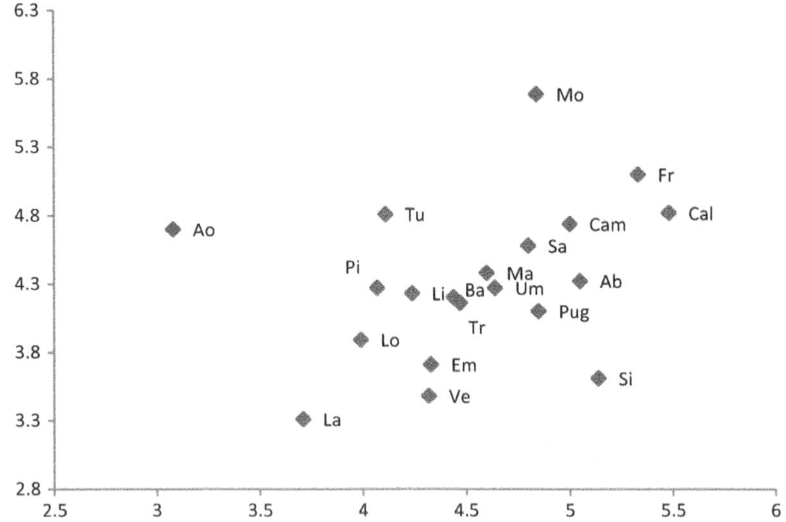

Fig. A.9.6 Interest rate spreads with maturity between 1 and 5 years for households, 2010–2014 (the *x*-axis reports the value of the interest rate spread in 2010, the *y*-axis reports the same ratio in 2014)

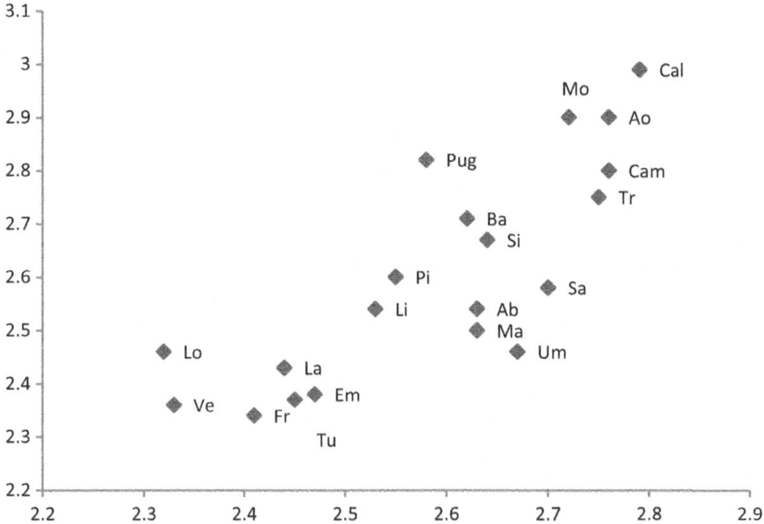

Fig. A.9.7 Interest rate spreads with maturity up to 1 year for households, 2010–2014 (the *x*-axis reports the value of the interest rate spread in 2010, the *y*-axis reports the same ratio in 2014)

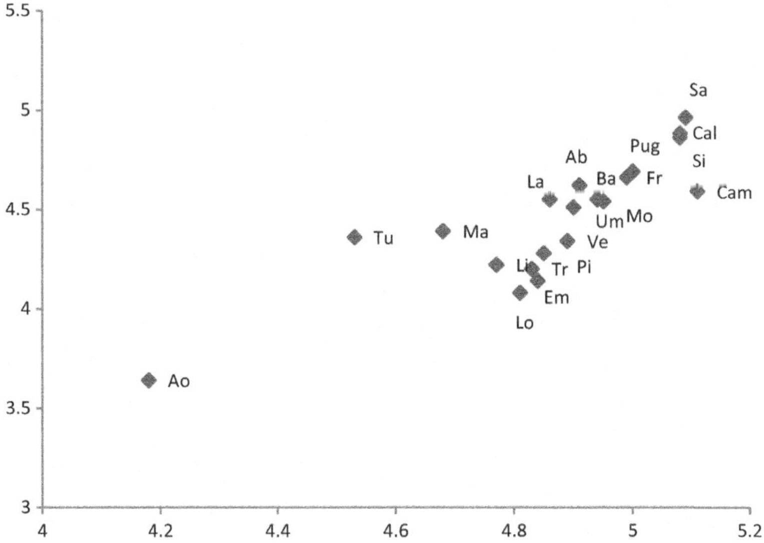

Fig. A.9.8 Interest rate spreads with maturity over 5 years for households, 2010–2014 (the *x*-axis reports the value of the interest rate spread in 2010, the *y*-axis reports the same ratio in 2014)

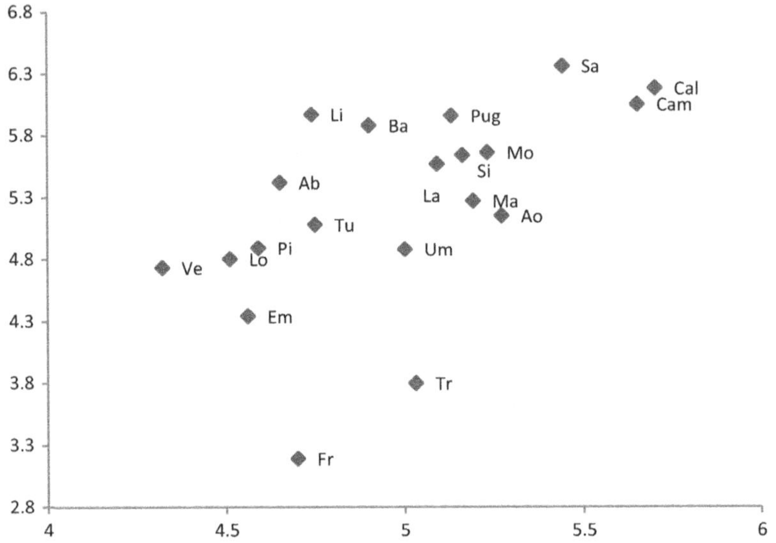

Fig. A.9.9 Interest rate spreads with maturity between 1 and 5 years for family businesses, 2010–2014 (the *x*-axis reports the value of the interest rate spread in 2010, the y-axis reports the same ratio in 2014)

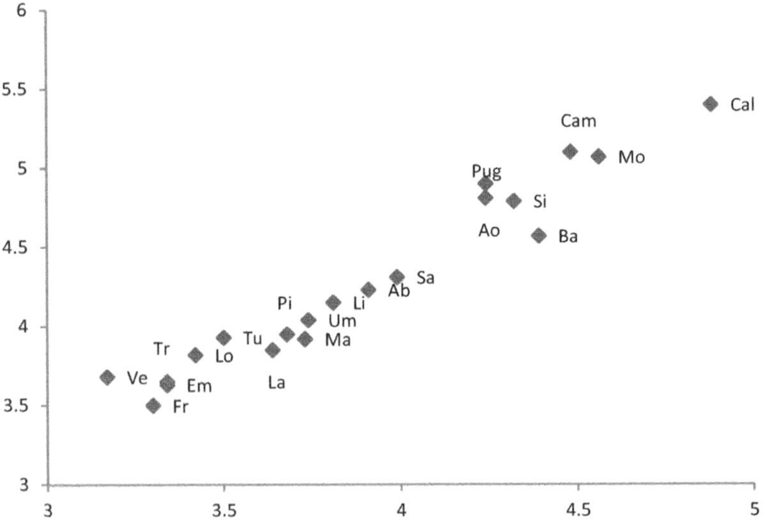

Fig. A.9.10 Interest rate spreads with maturity up to 1 year for family businesses, 2010–2014 (the *x*-axis reports the value of the interest rate spread in 2010, the *y*-axis reports the same ratio in 2014)

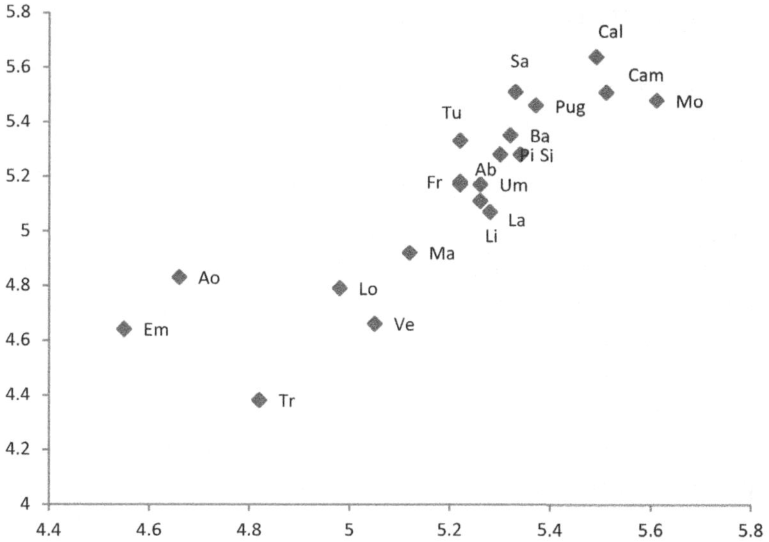

Fig. A.9.11 Interest rate spreads with maturity over 5 years for family businesses, 2010–2014 (the *x*-axis reports the value of the interest rate spread in 2010, the *y*-axis reports the same ratio in 2014)

Table A.9.1 HHI of loans

	2010	2011	2012	2013	2014
Abruzzo	0.179	0.178	0.181	0.188	0.192
Basilicata	0.208	0.207	0.209	0.213	0.218
Calabria	0.221	0.220	0.220	0.223	0.229
Campania	0.183	0.182	0.183	0.186	0.190
Emilia-Romagna	0.140	0.140	0.141	0.144	0.146
Friuli Venezia Giulia	0.166	0.168	0.170	0.175	0.182
Lazio	0.169	0.168	0.168	0.166	0.163
Liguria	0.169	0.169	0.171	0.175	0.181
Lombardy	0.158	0.162	0.168	0.169	0.164
Marche	0.146	0.148	0.151	0.157	0.161
Molise	0.212	0.213	0.218	0.224	0.232
Piedmont	0.165	0.165	0.167	0.171	0.177
Apulia	0.215	0.215	0.217	0.223	0.228
Sardinia	0.214	0.212	0.212	0.215	0.215
Sicily	0.223	0.222	0.223	0.220	0.229
Tuscany	0.147	0.148	0.150	0.152	0.157
Trentino-Alto Adige/Südtirol	0.122	0.124	0.124	0.126	0.128
Umbria	0.164	0.165	0.167	0.171	0.176
Aosta Valley	0.158	0.155	0.155	0.156	0.187
Veneto	0.139	0.140	0.143	0.147	0.148

The table contains the HHI values, calculated on a regional level for 2010–2014. Relatively higher values indicate a greater concentration of loans in the size classes.

9.6 Appendix B: Regression model

The relationship between loan quality and the difference between active and passive interest rates is valid in either direction. On the one hand, the increase in the spread practiced allows (owing to the mechanism of adverse selection) financing only riskier investments that significantly impact the quality of credit; on the other hand, a deterioration in credit quality could increase lending rates compared to passive rates in recovering losses because of the deteriorating quality of loans. It becomes useful, at this point, to investigate the statistical significance and intensity of the relationships in the context of Italian regions.

A first relationship between credit quality and spreads can be specified as (Spec. A), in line with the above definition:

$$q_t = \alpha + \beta_1\left(s_{<1y,t-1}\right) + \beta_2\left(s_{1\_5y,t-1}\right) + \beta_3\left(s_{>5y,t-1}\right), \tag{9.1}$$

where q_t, calculated as the ratio of non-performing loans and total loans, is the quality of loans issued at time t; $s_{<1y,t-1}$ is the spread between lending rates on loans, with a maturity up to 1 year and deposit rates at time $t-1$; $s_{1\_5y,t-1}$ is the spread between lending rates on loans with a maturity between 1 and 5 years and deposit rates at time $t-1$; and $s_{<5y,t-1}$ is the spread between lending rates on loans with a maturity over 5 years and borrowing rates at time $t-1$. The regression coefficients and relative significance indicate the sensitivity of the credit quality to variations in spreads for different maturities and, according to the aforementioned reasoning, this should have a positive coefficient, or an increase in the spread at time $t-1$ should correspond to an increase in credit risk.

The relationship can be reversed, as anticipated, by placing the quality of credit as the independent variable, delayed for a period with respect to the dependent one; the latter is considered according to the maturity of the spread (Spec. B):

$$
\begin{aligned}
s_{<1y,t} &= \alpha + \beta_1 q_{t-1} + \beta_2\left(s_{<1\_5y,t-1}\right) + \beta_3\left(s_{>5y,t-1}\right)\\
s_{1\_5y,t} &= \alpha + \beta_1 q_{t-1} + \beta_2\left(s_{<1y,t-1}\right) + \beta_3\left(s_{>5y,t-1}\right),\\
s_{>5y,t} &= \alpha + \beta_1 q_{t-1} + \beta_2\left(s_{<1y,t-1}\right) + \beta_3\left(s_{1\_5y,t}\right)
\end{aligned}
\tag{9.2}
$$

The expected relationship between q_{t-1} and the spread is positive; namely, a decrease in quality credit (q_{t-1} increases) should determine an increase in the spread, increasing net interest, which offsets the losses associated with increased riskiness.

The dependent variables expressed in Eq. (9.1) and Eq. (9.2) may also be affected by economic situation. In fact, with regard to Eq. (9.1), in favourable economic conditions credit quality should improve, while conversely, in unfavourable economic conditions the credit quality should worsen. With regard to Eq. (9.2), the relationship between economic conditions and spreads for the banks is not known in advance, as on the one hand, banks are inclined to reduce the spread due to improvement in credit quality, and on the other hand, riskier projects in positive economic conditions may prove more profitable. It is useful in light of the aforementioned, and with these specifications, to insert a variable that summarises the economic situation; for this reason, the variable Δy_{t-1} is constructed as the logarithmic difference in GDP.

The level of spread, in addition to the economic situation captured by the GDP, may be influenced by conditions that characterise the financial market, such as the yield on government bonds, which is an opportunity to invest in a business that would be less risky for a bank than lending. If the government bond yield is high, the bank should increase the spread to ensure the same risk-adjusted return. However, by equally adopting investment logic in the financial market for the medium to long term, an increase in government bond returns could lead the bank to reduce the active interest rate to finance less risky assets, offsetting the loss of interest income with higher yields on government bonds. Specifications (9.1) and (9.2) receive another variable for these reasons, which summarises the trend rate for alternative loan investments: the rate of yield for Italian state bonds in 10 years. The following are the results of processing structures for Specs. A and B, sorted by type of borrower.

Table B.9.1 OLS estimates for Spec. A: non-financial companies

	All regions	Northern cluster	Southern cluster
α	0.063*	0.019	0.063***
$s_{<1y,t-1}$	0.060*	0.067*	0.075*
$s_{1\_5y,t-1}$	−0.020*	−0.019*	−0.027*
$s_{>5y,t-1}$	0.005***	0.001	0.005
Delta loans	−0.118***	0.017	0.040
10-year Italy (t − 1)	−0.021*	−0.015*	−0.028*
Δy_{t-1}	−1.271*	−0.841***	−1.144***
Delta NPL (t − 1)	0.041**	0.061***	0.024
Adjusted R-squared	0.899	0.884	0.896
N. of observations	340	146	146

The table contains regression estimates pooled with fixed effects for the regions. The variable Delta loans represents the logarithmic difference of the volume of loans at the time t − 1. The variable Delta NPL is the logarithmic variation of suffering loans at time t − 1. *, ** and *** indicate a significance of coefficients at 99, 95 and 90%, respectively. The dependent variable is the ratio of non-performing loans to total loans in the period of 2010–2014, and expresses loan quality.

Table B.9.2 OLS estimates for Spec. A: households

	All regions	Northern cluster	Southern cluster
α	0.188*	0.161*	0.227*
$s_{<1y,t-1}$	−0.003	−0.006**	0.003
$s_{1\_5y,t-1}$	−0.022*	−0.018*	−0.030*
$s_{>5y,t-1}$	−0.002*	−0.002	−0.003*
Delta loans	−0.296*	−0.438*	−0.336*
10-year Italy (*t* − 1)	−0.003*	−0.003*	−0.004*
Δy_{t-1}	−0.316**	−0.373**	−0.158
Delta NPL (*t* − 1)	0.002	0.018	−0.007
Adjusted R-squared	0.886	0.846	0.891
N. of observations	340	146	146

The table contains the regression estimates pooled with fixed effects for the regions. The variable Delta loans represents the logarithmic difference of the volume of loans at the time *t* − 1. The variable Delta NPL is the logarithmic variation of suffering loans at time *t* − 1. *, ** and *** indicate significance of coefficients at 99, 95 and 90%, respectively. The dependent variable is the ratio of non-performing loans to total loans in the period of 2010–2014, and expresses loan quality

Table B.9.3 OLS estimates for Spec. A: family businesses

	All regions	Northern cluster	Southern cluster
α	−0.027	0.090***	−0.040
$s_{<1y,t-1}$	0.066*	0.030*	0.082*
$s_{1\_5y,t-1}$	−0.015*	−0.012**	−0.020**
$s_{>5y,t-1}$	0.004**	0.004	0.001
Delta Loans	−0.203**	−0.550*	−0.206
10 year Italy (*t* − 1)	−0.015*	−0.016*	0.017*
Δy_{t-1}	−0.531	−0.716	−0.286
Delta NPL (*t* −1)	0.000	0.011	0.011
Adjusted R-squared	0.921	0.872	0.886
No. of observations	340	146	146

The table contains the regression estimates pooled with fixed effects for the regions. The variable Delta Loans represents the logarithmic difference of the volume of loans at the time *t* − 1. The variable Delta NPL is the logarithmic variation of suffering loans, at time *t* − 1. *, **, and *** indicate the significance of coefficients at 99, 95 and 90 %, respectively. The dependent variable is the ratio of non-performing loans to total loans in the period of 2010–2014, and expresses loan quality

Table B.9.4 OLS estimates for Spec. B: non-financial companies

	All regions			Northern cluster			Southern cluster		
	$s_{<1y,t}$	$s_{1\_5y,t}$	$s_{>5y,t}$	$s_{<1y,t}$	$s_{1\_5y,t}$	$s_{>5y,t}$	$s_{<1y,t}$	$s_{1\_5y,t}$	$s_{>5y,t}$
α	2.252*	1.559*	3.297*	1.864*	1.006	2.677*	1.772*	1.942*	3.020*
$s_{<1y,t-1}$	–	0.221***	–	–	0.470	–	–	0.292	–
$s_{1\_5y,t-1}$	0.030	–	0.598*	0.054	–	0.965*	0.107**	–	0.706*
$s_{>5y,t-1}$	0.076*	0.132**	0.018	0.107*	0.092	−0.007	0.109**	0.150***	0.119
Delta loans (t−1)	0.205	1.502	4.518*	−1.375	1.603	5.317**	−0.199	0.949	6.265*
Delta NPL (t−1)	−0.183	0.004	−0.467	−0.265	−0.126	−0.400	−0.154	0.005	−0.130
$q_t - _1$	5.789*	3.243**	−6.242*	7.666*	0.604	−12.443*	5.363*	3.620**	−6.396*
10-year Italy (t−1)	0.043**	0.059	−0.197*	0.011	0.043	−0.210*	0.142*	0.029	−0.262*
Δy_{t-1}	−13.044*	4.110	13.341***	−11.956**	5.802	21.220***	−10.324***	4.783	3.235
Adjusted R-squared	0.930	0.818	0.791	0.786	0.538	0.558	0.919	0.818	0.715
N. of observations	340	340	340	146	146	146	146	146	146

The table contains the regression estimates pooled with fixed effects for the regions. *, ** and *** indicate the significance of coefficients at 99, 95 and 90%, respectively. The dependent variables are indicated in the columns, each of which represents a specific pattern in relation to a certain spread

Table B.9.5 OLS estimates for Spec. B: households

	All regions			Northern cluster			Southern cluster		
	$s_{<1y,t}$	$s_{1\_5y,t}$	$s_{>5y,t}$	$s_{<1y,t}$	$s_{1\_5y,t}$	$s_{>5y,t}$	$s_{<1y,t}$	$s_{1\_5y,t}$	$s_{>5y,t}$
α	3.711*	4.001*	4.829*	5.128*	1.775	4.635*	3.490*	3.798	4.997*
$s_{<1y,t-1}$	–	0.577*	–	–	0.704*	–	–	1.191*	–
$s_{1\_5y,t-1}$	–0.017	–	–0.006	0.019	–	–0.108	–0.000	–	0.009
$s_{>5y,t-1}$	–0.284*	0.031	0.022	–0.574*	0.358	0.078*	–0.267***	0.013	0.024
Delta loans (t–1)	6.921*	–10.442**	–4.586*	8.591*	–14.292	-7.650*	8.328*	–13.441***	–3.019**
Delta NPL (t–1)	0.190	–0.603	0.028	0.405	0.368	0.244	0.010	–1.790	–0.055
q_{t-1}	0.911	–18.845*	–8.444*	–6.666**	–12.370	–10.337*	4.338	–32.173*	–6.566*
10-year Italy (t–1)	0.067*	–0.091***	0.034*	0.052**	–0.104	0.057**	0.074*	–0.180***	0.010
Δy_{t-1}	7.556**	–4.878	12.346*	4.748	–16.731	14.202*	7.920***	12.823	7.071**
Adjusted R-squared	0.599	0.377	0.816	0.664	0.510	0.789	0.471	0.343	0.788
Observations	340	340	340	146	146	146	146	146	146

The table contains the regression estimates pooled with fixed effects for the regions. *, ** and *** indicate the significance of coefficients at 99, 95 and 90%, respectively. The dependent variables are indicated in the columns, each of which represents a specific pattern in relation to a certain spread

Table B.9.6 OLS estimates for Spec. B: family businesses

	All regions			Northern cluster			Southern cluster		
	$S_{<1y,t}$	$S_{1\_5y,t}$	$S_{>5y,t}$	$S_{<1y,t}$	$S_{1\_5y,t}$	$S_{>5y,t}$	$S_{<1y,t}$	$S_{1\_5y,t}$	$S_{>5y,t}$
α	3.788*	2.183**	3.886*	3.933*	1.079	3.432*	3.641*	3.683	4.528*
$S_{<1y,t-1}$	–	0.080	–	–	0.523***	–	–	0.082	–
$S_{1\_5y,t-1}$	−0.023	–	0.250*	0.025	–	0.347**	−0.019	–	0.189**
$S_{>5y,t-1}$	−0.047	0.351**	0.085*	−0.110**	0.213	0.066	−0.038	0.345	0.079*
Delta loans (t−1)	−0.805	1.228	3.408*	−3.932*	7.439***	6.401**	−0.382	−7.407	2.860**
Delta NPL (t−1)	−0.057	−1.104**	−0.151	0.214	−1.145	−0.417	−0.389	−1.160	0.016
$q_t{}_{-1}$	3.964*	5.581*	−1.228***	2.019**	3.849	−0.851	5.611*	2.484	−1.611***
10-year Italy (t−1)	0.074*	0.020	−0.029	0.061*	0.068	−0.011	0.113*	−0.193***	−0.062**
Δy_{t-1}	−6.623**	5.803	5.340	−8.212***	14.049	2.045	−2.069	−5.007	−0.567
Adjusted R-squared	0.937	0.645	0.679	0.871	0.593	0.337	0.912	0.631	0.610
Observations	340	340	340	146	146	146	146	146	146

The table contains the regression estimates pooled with fixed effects for the regions. *, ** and *** indicate the significance of coefficients at 99, 95 and 90 %, respectively. The dependent variables are indicated in the columns, each of which represents a specific pattern in relation to a certain spread

References

Beretta, E. (2004). I divari regionali tra i tassi bancari in Italia. *Banca Impresa Società, 3/2004*, 565–584.

Bianchi, T. (2015). L'economia d'azienda, la disciplina della mia vita accademica e didattica. In L. Guatri (Ed.), *Economia Aziendale. Come era e come è*. Milano: Egea.

Gallo, M. and Vannoni, V. (2015) 'Le determinanti dei tassi di interesse bancari nelle regioni italiane', *Journal of Regional Science*, vol. 14, pag. 67-84.

Jahn, N., Memmel, C., & Pfingsten, A. (2013). *Banks' concentration versus diversification in the loan portfolio: New evidence from Germany* (Discussion paper, Deutsche Bundesbank No 53/2013).

Johnson, R. A., & Wichern, D. W. (2007). *Applied multivariate statistical analysis*. New York: Pearson.

Lo Cascio, M., Bagarani, M., & Zampino, S. (2012). Economic space trajectory through different regional growth models. In M. Bagarani (Ed.), *Il governo delle Regioni e lo sviluppo economico. Limiti e rischi del processo di decentramento comunitari*. Alessandria: Edizioni dell'Orso.

Mattesini, F., & Messori, M. (2004). *L'evoluzione del sistema bancario meridionale: problemi aperti e possibili soluzioni*. Bologna: Il Mulino.

Parigi, B. M. (2000). La concorrenza nel settore bancario: una rassegna della letteratura. In M. Polo (Ed.), *Industria bancaria e concorrenza*. Bologna: Il Mulino.

10
Corporate Bonds for SMEs: A Study of Italian Minibonds

Roberto Malavasi, Giuseppe Riccio, and Mauro Aliano

10.1 Introduction

Since 2012, civil and fiscal laws have been enacted in Italy to align domestic regulations with European ones. In particular, these laws are aimed at easing unlisted firms' collection of funds from capital markets—provided such a possibility was permissible for listed firms only. The target is to provide SMEs with an alternative funding source other than traditional banking channels, thus facing the well-known restrictions characterizing bank credit access. Simultaneously, the Italian stock exchange has established a

---

JEL Codes
G30, G32

R. Malavasi • G. Riccio • M. Aliano (✉)
Department of Economics and Business, University of Cagliari, Cagliari, Italy
e-mail: mauro.aliano@unica.it

S.P.S. Rossi (ed.), *Access to Bank Credit and SME Financing*,
Palgrave Macmillan Studies in Banking and Financial Institutions,
DOI 10.1007/978-3-319-41363-1_10

specific segment of the market called ExtraMot-Pro,[1] which only institutional investors can access.

This chapter aims to verify the qualitative features of minibond issuers as well as the financial and operative characteristics that lead issuers to turn to the minibond market to satisfy their financial needs.

To accomplish this, Sect. 10.2 first considers all issuing firms, to verify size, productivity sector, geographical area and organizational structure. In Sect. 10.3, based on a sample of firms' balance sheet information from 2011 to 2014, we conduct a financial statement analysis for major financial ratios. Section 10.4 presents the results of the analysis. Finally, Sect. 10.5 concludes and draws the policy implications.

10.2 Sample Description

By 30 June 2015, 95 SMEs had listed their minibonds, showing 123 securities traded. This misalignment between the number of firms and the number of minibonds occurred because some of those firms issued minibonds more than once. To be clear, financial firms and bankrupt manufacturers were excluded from the sample. Therefore, the final sample consists of 87 issuers. A majority (73, i.e., 83.9% of the sample) are joint stock companies, but there are also 10 limited liability companies (11.5%), 3 cooperatives (3.4%) and 1 foreign firm. Among the issuers, displayed in Table 10.1, more than half (48, i.e., 55.2% of the sample) belong to international groups; 16 groups (i.e., 18.4% of the sample) work at the domestic level; and the remaining 23 are simple firms.

Table 10.2 illustrates the distribution of firms by turnover, or as it appears in their income statements the year prior to the issuance date. Such a distribution highlights that SMEs, that is, firms with a turnover of up to 50 million euros,[2] cover approximately 46% of our sample, whereas

[1] ExtraMot Pro is the segment designated for the listing of corporate bonds. It is not a market regulated according to the Market in Financial Instruments Directive (MiFID), but it belongs to the Multilateral Trading Facilities (MTF) category, which operates electronically and with limited requisites for admission (e.g., the publication of the last two years' annual reports and the existence of an admission document with essential information).

[2] The European Commission Recommendation 2003/361/CE defines SMEs as those firms with less than 250 employees and a turnover of no higher than 50 million euros or, alternatively, with total assets no higher than 43 million euros.

39.1% of the sample consists of firms with a turnover between 100 and 500 million euros. Specifically, 12 firms had a turnover lower than 10 million euros; additionally, for 5 the turnover was lower than 2 million euros. At first examination, this would lead us to assume that these issuances violate the law, but clearly, those issuers were not asked to comply with the other two requirements: number of employees and total assets.

Table 10.3 displays distribution of firms by size and notes how many of them are listed in the Borsa Italiana (Italian stock exchange), highlighting that only 10 firms, or 11.5% of the sample, were listed in the stock market during the minibond issuance. Other firms (i.e., 14, representing 16% of the sample) had started the process of stock market listing.[3]

Therefore, approximately one-quarter of the issuers were already listed or in the process. A positive correlation is found in both cases between listing and turnover levels, although with some exceptions. Overall, the impact of the regulatory changes adopted since 2012 appears modest, given that only 10.3%, or 9 out of 87, of the unlisted firms have issued more than twice the equity and thus, according to the previous regulation, could not issue minibonds.

Table 10.4 indicates the distribution of firms by industry, according to the classification of economic activities (Ateco 2007) made by the Italian National Institute of Statistics (ISTAT). The highest proportion of firms belongs to the manufacturing industry (29.9% of the sample), followed by the energy sector (13.8%) and information and communications technology (ICT) companies (10.3%); 9.2% of the issuers are then either water providers or garbage managers, or, more specifically, 8 Venetian joint-stock companies, controlled by the state.

A focus on the distribution by size reveals that the highest share of firms in the manufacturing industry is composed of large companies (Table 10.5). In contrast, the SMEs are primarily distributed in other industry sectors.

[3] The Elite Program by Borsa Italiana S.p.A., or the Italian stock exchange, is a platform that provides Italian firms with a variety of services regarding the necessary industrial, financial and organizational knowledge to expand in international markets.

Table 10.6 notes the distribution of firms between listed and unlisted companies. Again, listed firms are primarily from the manufacturing, energy, ICT sectors.

The positive correlation between turnover and the minibond issuance's face value is confirmed in Table 10.7. Issuances larger than 50 million euros belong to the three highest turnover classes. Moreover, one-third of the firms in the sample have issued minibonds for a limited value compared to their turnover (i.e., for less than 10%).

Table 10.8 instead shows that 9 out of 13 firms, which issued minibonds for more than 50 million euros, belong to the manufacturing, trade, professional activities, and entertainment industries.

The declared issuance motivations (Table 10.9) for two-thirds of the issuers concern the needs of growth, either internal or through mergers and acquisitions. Other motivations, such as refinancing existing debt, the sources' diversification and general support of the business, have been proposed by 16 large companies and only 13 SMEs.

Table 10.10 shows issuers' regional distribution. The highest concentration is in Lombardy, which counts 27 firms, or approximately one-third of the sample, followed by Veneto, Emilia-Romagna and Piedmont. More than 80% of the minibond issuers in 2015 were located in northern Italy in 2015, highlighting the rare use of such an instrument by firms in central and southern Italy. Additionally, it is worth noting that SMEs cover 38% of the issuers in northern Italy, as opposed to large firms that represent 62% in the north, 50% in the centre, and 100% in the south.

The strong link between the issuer's size and the value of the issue itself is undeniable: Table 10.11 illustrates that SMEs, compared to large firms, have collected 8.4% of the total funds available (i.e., 400 million euros in absolute value out of 5 billion euros available).

Table 10.12 notes the amount of money raised through minibond issuances by industry. The table demonstrates that the manufacturing industry's supremacy (around 30% of the issuers, as previously observed in Table 10.4) declines to 20% regarding the amount of resources collected via minibonds. Similarly, firms in the energy sector, or approximately 14% of the issuers, have raised only 9% of funds. Firms in the professional and entertainment industry, both counting as 6% of issuers, in contrast have raised approximately 20% and 11% of funds, respectively. Overall, the last two sectors in the manufacturing industry have raised 51.5% of the funds.

The market estimates an issuer's ability to repay debts through a rating provided by the rating agencies. Each agency provides firms with a rating that varies according to their assets' solidity, leverage, profitability, liquidity and expected cash flows, to express the debtor's creditworthiness. The existence of a rating is not necessary for admittance to the ExtraMot-Pro listing segment of the Italian stock exchange. However, a majority of the issuers in this study's sample (46, i.e., approximately 53%) have asked to be assigned a rating, as displayed in Table 10.13; 18 of them have received an investment grade (i.e., not lower than the Better Business Bureau's Standard & Poor's class); 17 have had a speculative grade; and the remaining 11 did not disclose their rating.

The high share of unrated firms, or mostly SMEs, can be justified by the fact that asking for a rating would increase issuance costs, which might lead SMEs to renounce the rating's benefits. On the other hand, SMEs that would like to place minibonds in the market have higher chances to contact interested investors through their banks. These investors may then directly assess potential issuers' solvency as well as their ability to generate money to repay debts.

Table 10.1 Issuers' features

	Total	%	Holding	Operating company
International groups	48	55.17	37	11
National groups	16	18.39	13	3
No groups	23	26.44	–	–
Total	87	100.00		

Source: Elaborations of data from Borsa Italiana

Table 10.2 Distribution of issuers by gross revenues

Slot(euros)	No. of companies	%
≤ 2 million	5	5.75
> 2 million up to 10 million	7	8.05
> 10 million up to 25 million	14	16.09
> 25 million up to 50 million	14	16.09
> 50 million up to 100 million	13	14.94
> 100 million up to 500 million	26	29.89
> 500 million	8	9.20
Total	87	100.00

Source: Elaborations of data from Borsa Italiana

Table 10.3 Distribution of issuers by gross revenues, listed, unlisted and Elite program participants

Slot (euros)	Unlisted		
	No. elite program	Elite program	Listed
≤ 2 million	3	0	1
> 2 million up to 10 million	6	0	2
> 10 million up to 25 million	14	2	0
> 25 million up to 50 million	14	3	1
> 50 million up to 100 million	11	7	1
> 100 million up to 500 million	22	2	4
> 500 million	7	0	1
Total	77	14	10

Source: Elaborations of data from Borsa Italiana

Table 10.4 Distribution of issuers by sector of economic activity (NACE codes)

		No.	%
A	Agriculture, forestry and fishing	2	2.30
B	Mining and quarrying	1	1.15
C	Manufacturing	26	29.89
D	Electricity, gas, steam and air conditioning supply	12	13.79
E	Water supply; sewage; waste management and remediation activities	8	9.20
F	Construction	4	4.60
G	Wholesale and retail trade; repair of motor vehicles and motorcycles	5	5.75
H	Transporting and storage	1	1.15
I	Accommodation and food service activities	2	2.30
J	Information and communication	9	10.34
L	Real estate activities	1	1.15
M	Professional, scientific and technical activities	6	6.90
N	Administrative and support service activities	3	3.45
O	Public administration and defence; compulsory social security	0	0.00
P	Education	0	0.00
Q	Human health and social work activities	2	2.30
R	Arts, entertainment and recreation	5	5.75
S	Other service activities	0	0.00
	Total	87	100.00

Source: Elaborations of data from Borsa Italiana

Table 10.5 Distribution of issuers, SMEs and large company, by Sector of economic activity

		SMEs	%	Large companies	%
A	Agriculture, forestry and fishing	1	2.56	1	2.08
B	Mining and quarrying	0	0.00	1	2.08
C	Manufacturing	4	10.26	22	45.83
D	Electricity, gas, steam and air conditioning supply	8	20.51	4	8.33
E	Water supply; sewage; waste management and remediation activities	7	17.95	1	2.08
F	Construction	2	5.13	2	4.17
G	Wholesale and retail trade; repair of motor vehicles and motorcycles	2	5.13	3	6.25
H	Transporting and storage	0	0.00	1	2.08
I	Accommodation and food service activities	2	5.13	0	0.00
J	Information and communication	4	10.26	5	10.42
K	Financial and insurance activities	0	0.00	0	0.00
L	Real estate activities	1	2.56	0	0.00
M	Professional, scientific and technical activities	4	10.26	2	4.17
N	Administrative and support service activities	1	2.56	2	4.17
O	Public administration and defence; compulsory social security	0	0.00	0	0.00
P	Education	0	0.00	0	0.00
Q	Human health and social work activities	2	5.13	0	0.00
R	Arts, entertainment and recreation	1	2.56	4	8.33
S	Other service activities	0	0.00	0	0.00
	Total	39	100.00	48	100.00

Source: Elaborations of data from Borsa Italiana

Table 10.6 Distribution of issuers, listed and unlisted, by sector of economic activity

		Unlisted	%	Listed	%
A	Agriculture, forestry and fishing	2	2.60	0	0.00
B	Mining and quarrying	1	1.30	0	0.00
C	Manufacturing	24	31.17	2	20.00
D	Electricity, gas, steam and air conditioning supply	9	11.69	3	30.00
E	Water supply; sewage; waste management and remediation activities	8	10.39	0	0.00
F	Construction	3	3.90	1	10.00
G	Wholesale and retail trade; repair of motor vehicles and motorcycles	5	6.49	0	0.00
H	Transporting and storage	1	1.30	0	0.00
I	Accommodation and food service activities	2	2.60	0	0.00
J	Information and communication	6	7.79	3	30.00
L	Real estate activities	1	1.30	0	0.00
M	Professional, scientific and technical activities	5	6.49	1	10.00
N	Administrative and support service activities	3	3.90	0	0.00
O	Public administration and defence; compulsory social security	0	0.00	0	0.00
P	Education	0	0.00	0	0.00
Q	Human health and social work activities	2	2.60	0	0.00
R	Arts, entertainment and recreation	5	6.49	0	0.00
S	Other service activities	0	0.00	0	0.00
	Total	77	100.00	10	100.00

Source: Elaborations of data from Borsa Italiana

Table 10.7 Distribution of issuers by outstanding amount and gross revenues

Proceeds (euros)	Outstanding	
	≤ 50 million	> 50 million
≤ 2 million	5	0
> 2 million up to 10 million	7	0
> 10 million up to 25 million	14	0
> 25 million up to 50 million	15	0
> 50 million up to 100 million	12	1
> 100 million up to 500 million	19	6
> 500 million	2	6
Total	74	13

Source: Elaborations of data from Borsa Italiana

Table 10.8 Distribution of issuers by outstanding amount and sector of economic activity

		≤ 50 million	> 50 million	Total
A	Agriculture, forestry and fishing	2	0	2
B	Mining and quarrying	1	0	1
C	Manufacturing	23	3	26
D	Electricity, gas, steam and air conditioning supply	11	1	12
E	Water supply; sewage; waste management and remediation activities	8	0	8
F	Construction	3	1	4
G	Wholesale and retail trade; repair of motor vehicles and motorcycles	3	2	5
H	Transporting and storage	1	0	1
I	Accommodation and food service activities	2	0	2
J	Information and communication	8	1	9
L	Real estate activities	1	0	1
M	Professional, scientific and technical activities	4	2	6
N	Administrative and support service activities	2	1	3
O	Public administration and defence; compulsory social security	0	0	0
P	Education	0	0	0
Q	Human health and social work activities	2	0	2
R	Arts, entertainment and recreation	3	2	5
S	Other service activities	0	0	0
	Total	74	13	87

Source: Elaborations of data from Borsa Italiana

Table 10.9 Issuance motivations

	Total		SMEs		Large company	
	Obs.	%	Obs.	%	Obs.	%
Internal/external growth	58	66.67	27	67.50	31	65.96
Refinancing debt	12	13.79	1	2.50	11	23.40
Diversification of financing sources	12	13.79	7	17.50	5	10.64
Support operating cycle	5	5.75	5	12.50	0	0.00
Total	87	100.00	40	100.00	47	100.00

Source: Elaborations of data from Borsa Italiana

Table 10.10 Distribution of issuers by region

	Issuers		SMEs/issuers	
	No.	%	SMEs	(in %)
Piedmont	10	11.49	6	
Liguria	1	1.15	1	
Lombardy	27	31.03	10	
Emilia-Romagna	13	14.94	2	
Veneto	16	18.39	7	
Trentino-South Tyrol	5	5.75	2	
Friuli Venezia Giulia	1	1.15	0	
Total North	*73*	*83.90*	*28*	*38.36*
Marche	1	1.15	1	
Tuscany	2	2.30	1	
Umbria	1	1.15	0	
Lazio	4	4.60	2	
Total Centre	*8*	*9.20*	*4*	*50.00*
Campania	1	1.15	1	
Apulia	1	1.15	1	
Basilicata	2	2.30	2	
Sicily	1	1.15	1	
Total South	*5*	*5.75*	*5*	*100.00*
Luxembourg	1	1.15	1	
Total foreign	*1*	*1.15*	*1*	
Total	**87**	**100.00**	**38**	

Source: Elaborations of data from Borsa Italiana

Table 10.11 Distribution of emissions by gross revenue size

Gross revenues (euros)	Outstanding amount	%
≤ 2 million	45,078,000	0.91
> 2 million up to 10 million	22,260,000	0.45
> 10 million up to 25 million	99,200,000	2.01
> 25 million up to 50 million	249,300,000	5.05
> 50 million up to 100 million	301,900,000	6.11
> 100 million up to 500 million	2,407,238,000	48.73
> 500 million	1,815,000,000	36.74
Total	4,939,976,000	100.00

Source: Elaborations of data from Borsa Italiana

Table 10.12 Distribution of emissions by sector of economic activity (NACE code)

		Value (euros)	%
A	Agriculture, forestry and fishing	12,000,000	0.24
B	Mining and quarrying	7,000,000	0.14
C	Manufacturing	1,010,350,000	20.45
D	Electricity, gas, steam and air conditioning supply	428,978,000	8.68
E	Water supply; sewage; waste management and remediation activities	150,000,000	3.04
F	Construction	371,000,000	7.51
G	Wholesale and retail trade; repair of motor vehicles and motorcycles	487,000,000	9.86
H	Transporting and storage	1,500,000	0.03
I	Accommodation and food service activities	3,800,000	0.08
J	Information and communication	474,060,000	9.60
L	Real estate activities	16,800,000	0.34
M	Professional, scientific and technical activities	993,800,000	20.12
N	Administrative and support service activities	429,750,000	8.70
O	Public administration and defence; compulsory social security	0	0.00
P	Education	0	0.00
Q	Human health and social work activities	17,400,000	0.35
R	Arts, entertainment and recreation	536,538,000	10.86
S	Other service activities	0	0.00
	Total	4,939,976,000	100.00

Source: Elaborations of data from Borsa Italiana

Table 10.13 Issuers' rating

	No.	%
No rating	41	47.13
Investment grade	18	20.69
Speculative grade	17	19.54
Rating undisclosed	11	12.64
Total	87	100

Source: Elaborations of data from Borsa Italiana

10.3 Analysis of Performance

Financial firms were dropped from our sample given the peculiarity of their activities and for the sake of increasing the information quality of the analysis throughout this chapter. The remaining 87 firms were then grouped into homogeneous categories according to their financial data. Thus, the following three groups were obtained:

Group 1: If a given firm belongs to a group, then the holding's balance sheet is considered;

Group 2: If a given firm belongs to a holding for which the related balance sheet cannot befound (for instance, because it is not Italian or if the primary shareholder is a state-owned company), then the issuer's balance sheet is considered;

Group 3: If a given firm does not belong to a group, or is a holding itself, then this study relies on the issuer's balance sheet.

Moreover, an additional classification was added, one that groups firms according to their issuance motivation, which leads to the segmentation represented in Table 10.14. Additionally, it was decided the sample be restricted to firms that did not present any missing values throughout the period of 2011–2014; in this way, trends could be examined that characterize the issuing firms for at least two years before the minibond's issuance. Given this criterion, the final sample of 50 firms was achieved, as noted in Table 10.15.

The following ratios are then calculated:

Table 10.14 Distribution of issuers by groups and issuance motivations (financial companies are excluded)

	Group 1	Group 2	Group 3	Total
Investment	17	13	21	51
Diversification of financing sources	5	5	9	19
Investment/diversification	8	5	4	17
Total	30	23	34	87

Source: Elaborations of data from Borsa Italiana

Table 10.15 Sample distribution by groups and issuance motivations

	Group 1	Group 2	Group 3	Total
Investment	5	10	15	30
Diversification of financing sources	3	3	6	12
Investment/diversification	2	2	4	8
Total	10	15	25	50

Source: Elaborations of data from Borsa Italiana

$$ind1 = \frac{\text{borrowings}}{\text{Equity}}$$

This *ind*1 ratio represents the guarantees offered to the external financiers by the firm's equity; therefore, this expresses external investors' risk with the financed company (Pavarani 2006).

The second ratio is:

$$ind2 = \frac{\text{Net debt position}}{\text{Earning before Interest, Taxes and Amortisation (EBITDA)}}$$

The *ind*2 ratio in this case provides information regarding the share of borrowing that can be payable through resources coming from the firms' typical activity. Therefore, this proxies for the time needed to repay these borrowings (Pavarani 2006).

The choice of these two ratios descends from the need to have information regarding firms' financial structure as well as their ability to repay loans via funds originated through typical activities. Nonetheless, the choice of these two ratios is related to a willingness to verify whether they might represent the issuing firms' best performance indicators. More precisely, here the first ratio is < 3, and the second ratio is < 4 (Area Economica di Confindustria Toscana 2013).

The financial structure is further investigated via the following ratio:

$$ind3 = \frac{\text{Short term financial borrowings}}{\text{Long term financial borrowings}}$$

The higher the *ind3* ratio, the higher the firm's financial vulnerability, given that a high *ind3* highlights a closer date for debt renegotiation.

A more traditional ratio is considered after this, one that verifies the coherence between the investments' qualitative characteristics and the quantity of internal funds, the former expressed by fixed assets:

$$ind4 = \frac{\text{Net Fixed Assets}}{\text{Equity}}$$

Again, the higher the *ind4* ratio, the higher the financial vulnerability, given an increasing exposure to external funding as a substitute for the equity.

Regarding the firm's liquidity, the following ratio is analyzed:

$$ind5 = \frac{\text{Liquidity} + \text{Trade receivables}}{\text{Short term loans}}$$

where *ind5* defines the ability to face banks' obligations with liquid resources or immediately liquid ones. Low values for the aforementioned ratio denote a level of criticality for the firm, which could be tolerated in the short run, even if this does not exclude the possibility that, eventually, the firm may not be able to repay the debt.

The firm's economic structure is captured via the return on sales ratio:

$$ind6 = \frac{\text{Operating Income}}{\text{Total Revenues}}$$

The *ind6* ratio represents the leftover proportion of a company's revenue after paying for costs related to the main firm's activity, before finance costs; for example, interests, other revenues or expenses and income tax expenses. The lower the ratio, the higher the firm's criticalities, with specific regard to the structural choices made in terms of the firm's financial profile.

Overall, two fundamental ratios exist for an analysis of the different management conditions: in fact, *ind*2 and *ind*6 represent good proxies for the firms' financial performances. On the other hand, *ind*1 and *ind*3 provide information regarding the preferences between equity and the borrowing of different maturities. Finally, *ind*4 and *ind*5 represent valid proxies of the firm's stability and liquidity.

10.4 Results

The analyses conducted in this section of the chapter are based on data from Aida (Bureau van Dijk) and are integrated with information regarding short- and long-term borrowing, specifically drawn from each firm's annual report across the period of 2011–2014. The sample employed here was previously displayed in Table 10.15.

Hereafter, the results are obtained for the different groupings realized according to the issuers' organizational structure and hence for the type of accounting information used. After this, information is provided emerging from the sample classified according to the issuance motivation. The objective is to provide the reader with different though comparable interpretations, increasing the explanatory power of the business performance under investigation, which seems to justify the use of different analyses from the onset given its patrimonial, financial and economic specificities. Graphics are also used to expedite the ratios' interpretation to observe the evolution across time for each firm. Some descriptive statistics are also provided to assess the aggregate information's overall coherence.

The initial analysis is conducted regarding the first two ratios, *ind*1 and *ind*2, and demonstrates a high variability with regard to the results' distribution, which is explained by the existence of outliers for some firms (see also Figs. A.10.1, A.10.3 and A.10.5 in the Appendix).[4] Interestingly, it is found that the observed ratios for Groups 1 and 3 tend to decrease with time. This suggests a declining effect of borrowing compared to equity. Further, this is consistent, although Group 1 displays a lower ratio than Group 2 and is more similar to the performances of Group 3. Basically,

[4] Graphics related to the indexes of *ind*3, *ind*4, *ind*5 and *ind*6 are available upon request.

holding companies illustrate higher distinctive capitalization abilities. The variability of *ind2* is even stronger, either with time or among firms (see also Figs. A.10.2, A.10.4 and A.10.6 in the Appendix). This is because the ratio might indicate either positive or negative values for both its numerator and denominator. The most important information from *ind2* is that the holding companies (Group 1) are characterized by a higher difficulty in repaying loans through funds raised from the firm's activity.

Regarding the other ratios, the following results are provided:[5]

ind3: Values appear particularly low for all groups considered; this induces a doubt regarding the values' congruence as related to short-term borrowing;

ind4: Values are generally high, constant with time and appear specific for each group; additionally, the median values are lower for Group 1, confirming that holding firms have a higher availability of internal funds;

ind5: Firms belonging to Group 2 demonstrate the highest values, which highlights an important inclination to hold more liquidity than with short-term loans; in contrast, firms belonging to Groups 1 and 3 demonstrate remarkably low values;

ind6: Values for Group 1 are significantly lower than that of other groups, and particularly when compared to Group 2; overall, the results indicate that firms struggle to limit operating costs.

Overall, the primary information arising from this analysis is regarding the heterogeneity characterizing the various groups of issuers and their peculiar internal variability. It is worth noting that in this regard, Group 3 (or firms not belonging to a group) is characterized by less contradictory management conditions, although this group is also characterized by the typical weaknesses affecting Italian firms, in terms of capitalization and difficulties in limiting operating costs (see also Table A.10.1 in the Appendix). Group 1 (holding companies) and Group 2 (holdings for which the related balance sheet could not be found) display conflicting features. While the first group displays the best performances in terms

[5] Graphics associated with such elaborations are available upon request.

of financial construction, although with increased economic difficulties, the second is characterized by a weaker equity compared to liabilities and fixed assets, as well as by a lower level of economic issues. This suggests that being part of a group offers a superior ability to equip with more equity when a firm's size increases, although in an environment characterized by high criticalities with regards to cost control. Overall, it is difficult for the observed firms to capture the unequivocal features of a common best performance model.

Analysis of the results, arising from a grouping of firms according to their issuance motivations (see also Figs. A.10.7, A.10.8, A.10.9, A.10.10, A.10.11 and A.10.12, in the Appendix)[6] provides an observation that the variability of all ratios is more important than that described above for groups created according to the issuing firm's organizational structure. More specifically, firms that decided to issue minibonds to increase their investment opportunities demonstrate a higher share of borrowing compared to equity; longer periods needed to repay loans through internally generated resources; and lower congruence in the coverage of total assets.

Overall, this highlights a framework characterized by higher rigidities, which greatly influences the chance to obtain additional bank funding to support new investments. These findings eventually emphasize the need for firms to use minibonds. This condition might be induced by the same banks that are most likely unwilling to offer further credit to SMEs, and not even at the highest prices possible. On the other hand, those firms that issue minibonds to diversify their funding display a well-balanced financial structure in terms of both their assets' quality and in terms of margins, although their operating costs should be limited. This underlines a more conscious behaviour, most likely guided by a more defined design for the firm's growth. A similar status, although less precise, characterizes those firms that declared both issuance motivations. Nonetheless, this evidence shows that a majority of firms (30 out of 50) declared investment needs as issuance motivation. However, this group gathers different firms (see also Tables A.10.2 and A.10.3 in the Appendix) characterized by complexities in terms of economic, patrimonial and financial conditions, which do not allow for an easy comparison among them. The

[6] The charts related to *ind3– ind6* are available upon request.

previous analysis, conducted for groups assembled according to the type of accounting information utilized, is more stable and significant in this regard. Moreover, the primary concern with a group formed according to the issuance motivation, which gathers very different firms, is that it highlights important criticalities. This means that by assembling firms from groups 1, 2, and 3—each of them characterized by typical economic, patrimonial and financial features—a new group is obtained, which prevails in terms of size compared to the sample analyzed, and whose performances appear particularly contrasting. Therefore, it is fundamental to monitor each specific group over time and capture the overall advantages in funding diversification via minibond issuance. Therefore, we hope to improve our analysis in two years as new accounting information for all the issuers becomes available. Nonetheless, the current analysis is suitable for assessing the diversities of the managerial conditions that have enabled firms to access the minibond market.

10.5 Conclusions

The analysis of the new minibond industry provides some primary considerations regarding the effects of the regulatory changes implemented in 2012 and on the issuers' characteristics. As represented in Table 10.2, the impact of the regulatory changes in the triennium of 2012–2014 was poor, and most of the issuers are ranked as large firms according to the turnover and belong (55.2%) to international groups, sometimes owned by important mutual funds. Moreover, approximately one-third of the firms have issued minibonds for a limited amount compared to the turnover, or less than 10%.

An extreme heterogeneity in the firms' characteristics arises when the issuers' financial conditions are analyzed. It is possible in this situation to discover common features only by grouping firms according to their organizational structure; hence, by the accounting information used. Some prevailing characteristics can be identified in this manner in terms of economic, patrimonial and financial equilibrium, although the width characterizing these sources of firm-level information is not negligible. Moreover, when the number of issuances increases, some sub-aggregations can be conducted by productivity sectors. This would also allow for a comparison of the firms' performances with its own sector averages.

Overall, this analysis leads to the following suggestion for policy-makers: it would be wise to differentiate the controls, by the appointed authority, according to each issuer's different type of organizational structure—either a holding company, single firm or state-owned company. The best-performance ratios could then be more easily defined and applied.

It is also worth noting that a majority (two-thirds) of firms have declared investment needs as issuance motivation. Further, this typically comes from highly leveraged firms, as well as firms that cannot limit their operating costs. This leads to a conclusion that in these cases the idea of issuing minibonds has been directly proposed by the same banks with the objective of decreasing their risk positions toward the issuing firms, as they were most likely overexposed to them. This also highlights that, thus far, both profitable and problematic firms have issued minibonds. In particular, the latter have declared that issuance motivation is linked to investment needs, which would have alternatively been impossible via traditional bank lending channels. The primary concerns in this last case are represented by the unsuccessful realization of planned investments and by the possible, additional, increase in leverage. Therefore, it is fundamental to establish a proper monitoring system. However, this requires potential minibond buyers to be experts in evaluating the issuers' quality and, hence, the risk of the instrument itself, as well as in implementing an adequate portfolio diversification process.

Given the above results, it is worth noting that the rating agencies' role, thus far, has been quite modest. Therefore, it is suggested that authorities not limit their activity to formal control at the time of issuance. Rather, we recommend that controls be extended to after the issuance to verify the manner in which the raised funds are employed. Additionally, rating agencies' responsibilities should increase to avoid an underestimation of risk.

10.6 Appendix

The graphs and tables contained in this section provide information regarding *ind*1 and *ind*2, by issuance motivation and by operating organization (Groups 1, 2 and 3). The graphics and tables related to the indexes *ind*3, *ind*4, *ind*5 and *ind*6 are available upon request.

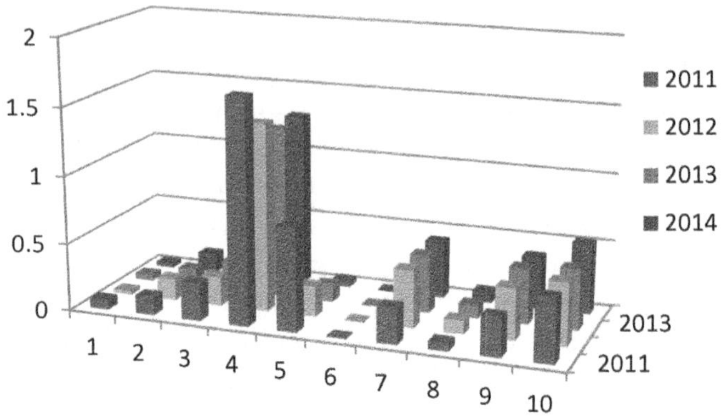

Fig. A.10.1 *ind*1, Group 1 (Elaborations are based on data from Aida—Bureau van Dijk)

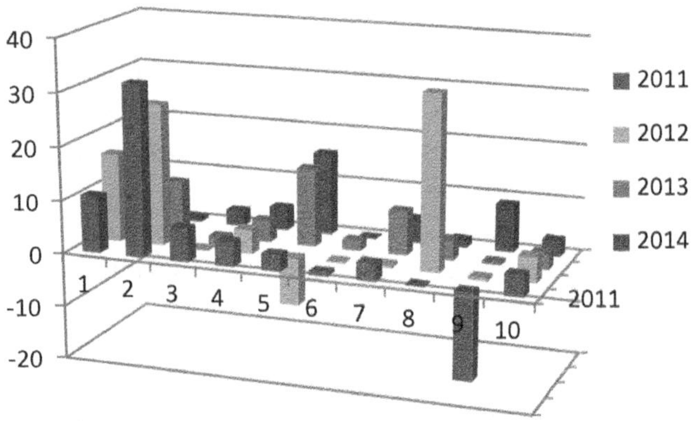

Fig. A.10.2 *ind*2, Group 1 (Elaborations are based on data from Aida—Bureau van Dijk)

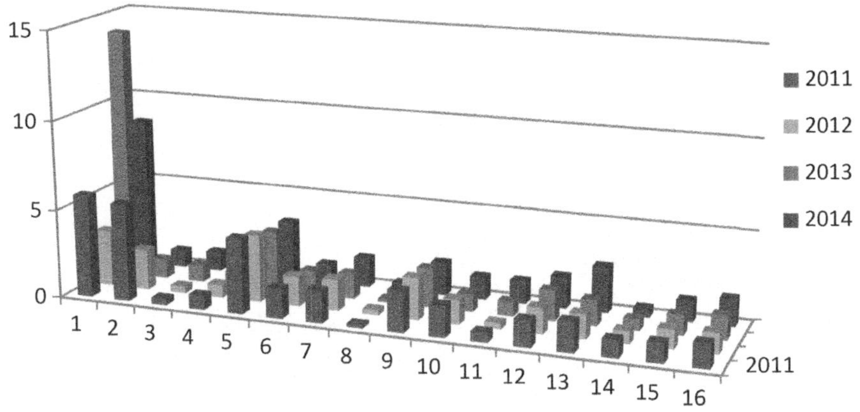

Fig. A.10.3 *ind*1, Group 2 (Elaborations are based on data from Aida—Bureau van Dijk)

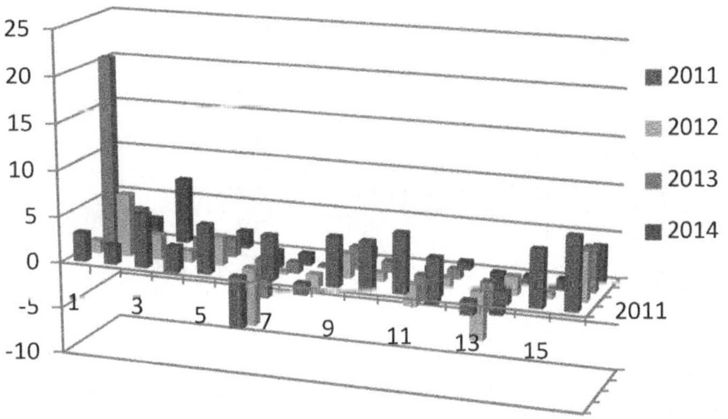

Fig. A.10.4 *ind*2, Group 2 (Elaborations are based on data from Aida—Bureau van Dijk)

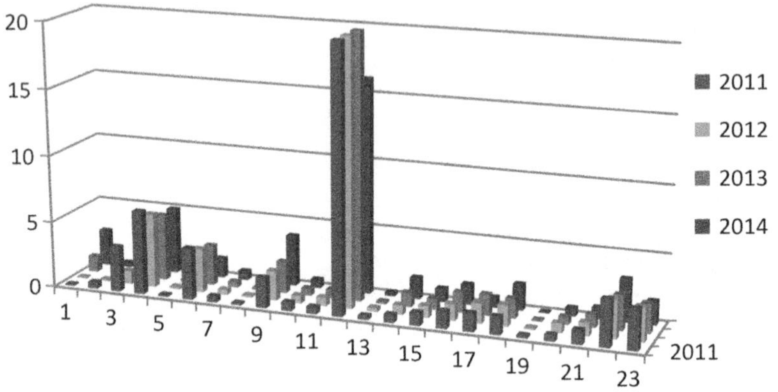

Fig. A.10.5 *ind*1, Group 3 (Elaborations are based on data from Aida—Bureau van Dijk)

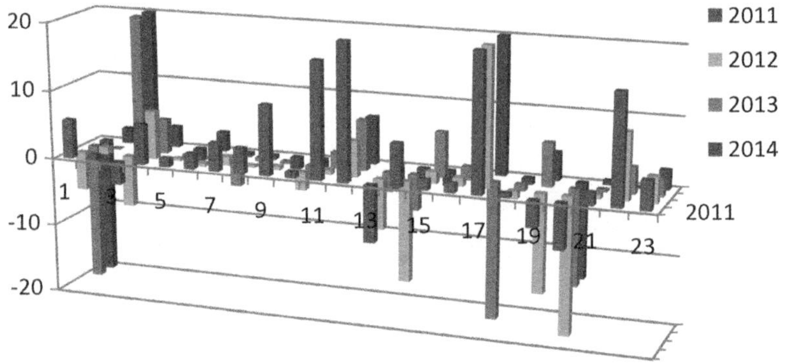

Fig. A.10.6 *ind*2, Group 3 (Elaborations are based on data from Aida—Bureau van Dijk)

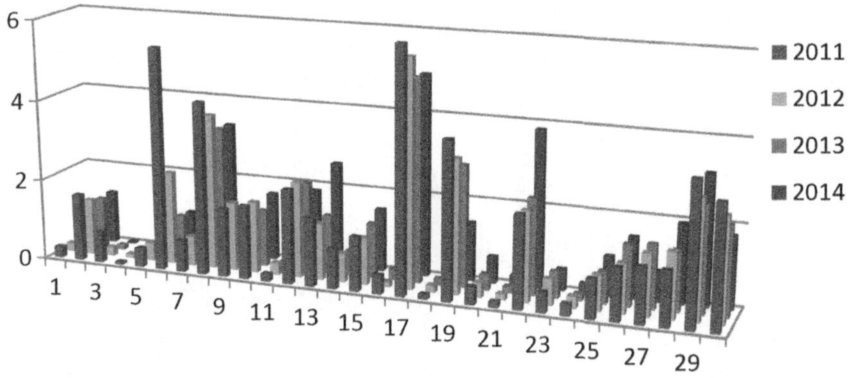

Fig. A.10.7 *Ind*1, motivation: investment (Elaborations are based on data from Aida—Bureau van Dijk)

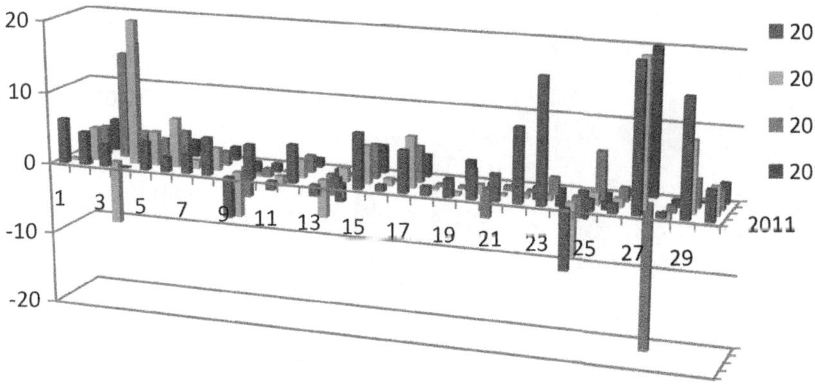

Fig. A.10.8 *Ind*2, motivation: investment (Elaborations are based on data from Aida—Bureau van Dijk)

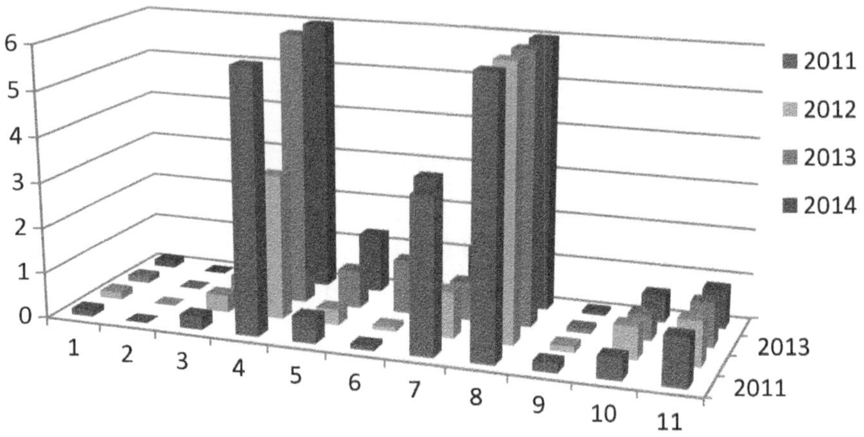

Fig. A.10.9 *Ind*1, motivation: diversification of sources of financing (Elaborations are based on data from Aida—Bureau van Dijk)

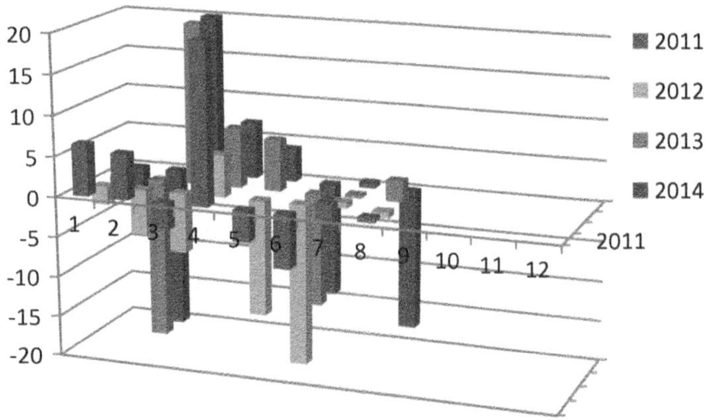

Fig. A.10.10 *Ind*2, motivation: diversification of sources of financing (Elaborations are based on data from Aida—Bureau van Dijk)

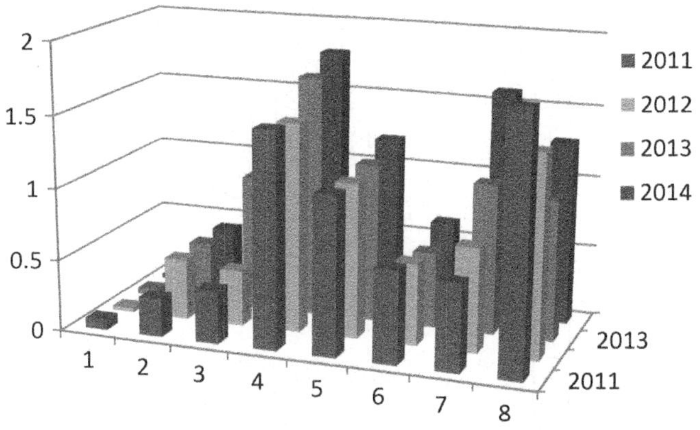

Fig. A.10.11 *Ind*1, motivation: investment/diversification (Elaborations are based on data from Aida—Bureau van Dijk)

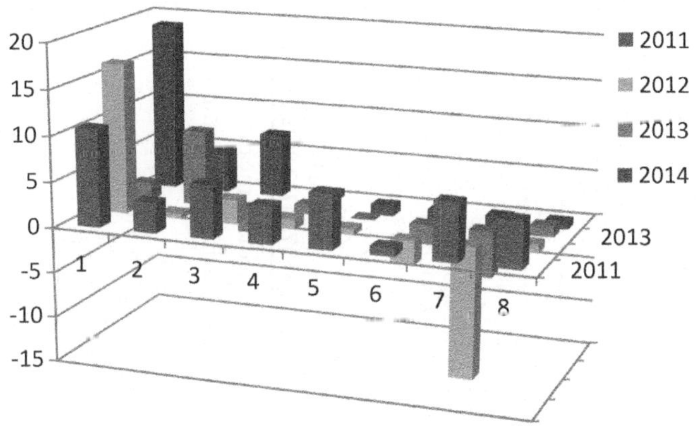

Fig. A.10.12 *Ind*2, motivation: investment/diversification (Elaborations are based on data from Aida—Bureau van Dijk)

Table A.10.1 Descriptive statistics by groups

		Ind1				Ind2				Ind3				Ind4				Ind5				Ind6			
		2011	2012	2013	2014	2011	2012	2013	2014	2011	2012	2013	2014	2011	2012	2013	2014	2011	2012	2013	2014	2011	2012	2013	2014
Group 1	Median	0.27	0.22	0.18	0.23	3.63	2.54	3.37	3.68	0.22	0.22	0.17	0.21	1.17	1.14	1.27	1.25	0.2	0.37	0.42	0.24	0.07	0.05	0.05	0.03
	Mean	0.4	0.34	0.32	0.32	4.85	7.6	4.59	6.03	0.37	1.95	0.96	0.82	1.42	1.35	1.56	1.55	0.62	2.53	1.53	2.63	0	0.09	0.09	0.14
	St. dev	0.5	0.4	0.37	0.38	11.89	13.25	4.93	6.43	0.63	4.48	1.82	1.45	0.65	0.56	0.7	0.69	1.29	3.78	2.87	5.33	0.5	0.39	0.29	0.25
Group 2	Median	1.59	1.4	1.22	1.28	4.45	1.17	0.69	0.34	0.46	0.69	0.67	0.58	1.88	1.81	1.82	1.87	2.1	1.35	2.03	2.29	0.05	0.05	0.06	0.07
	Mean	1.98	1.5	2.08	1.87	3.22	0.76	1.51	0.33	0.67	1.8	2.54	6.09	2.56	2.01	2.56	2.25	5.36	2.03	2.53	3.68	0.13	0.11	2.42	0.24
	St. dev	1.71	1	3.29	1.91	3.5	3.39	5.71	2.87	0.74	3.69	5.8	13.49	2.36	1.34	2.87	1.57	7.68	2.19	2.37	3.07	0.29	0.22	9.45	0.68
Group 3	Median	0.96	0.89	0.95	0.98	2.23	0.56	0.29	−0.55	0.97	1.04	0.94	1.47	1.5	1.33	1.53	1.37	1.32	1.22	1.36	1.44	0.06	0.04	0.05	0.04
	Mean	3.79	2.57	2.12	2.02	21.36	13.92	3.65	34.59	4.49	6.49	3.1	7.6	4.3	3.24	2.81	2.51	7.49	5.01	2.35	3.25	−0.03	−0.02	−0.05	−0.1
	St. dev	11.23	6.39	4.35	3.33	79.52	75.88	75.85	172.17	12.85	19.92	7.38	29.65	11.17	6.08	4.2	3.13	18.39	10.72	3.67	6.7	0.45	0.49	0.48	0.55

Source: The table contains the time series of median, mean, and standard deviation values of the indicators presented in Sect. 10.3. The results are structured by firms' operating organisation (Groups 1, 2 and 3). The elaborations are based on data from Aida—Bureau van Dijk

Table A.10.2 Descriptive statistics by issuance motivations

		Ind1				Ind2				Ind3				Ind4				Ind5				Ind6			
		2011	2012	2013	2014	2011	2012	2013	2014	2011	2012	2013	2014	2011	2012	2013	2014	2011	2012	2013	2014	2011	2012	2013	2014
Investment	Median	1.32	1.19	1.15	0.98	3.39	1.24	1.06	0.72	0.59	0.65	0.73	0.63	1.88	1.69	1.68	1.73	1.21	1.48	1.23	1.56	0.06	0.05	0.06	0.07
	Mean	1.66	1.41	1.27	1.32	16.07	14	−5.06	28.32	1.09	2.07	1.64	2.09	2.38	2.21	2.21	2.14	4.75	3.77	2.61	4	0.05	0.03	1.26	0.06
	St. dev	1.62	1.29	1.15	1.21	69.43	65.82	36.34	150.13	2.17	4.8	4.28	6.35	1.73	1.52	1.37	1.33	10.06	7.71	3.66	6.57	0.46	0.46	6.93	0.71
Diversification	Median	0.47	0.38	0.81	0.84	1.86	−0.57	1.85	0.74	0.14	0.49	1.6	1.52	1.18	1.18	1.28	1.32	0.93	0.56	1.55	0.94	0.05	0.05	0	0.01
of financing	Mean	6.07	3.48	3.67	2.9	6.05	−1.52	27.58	−1.2	6.52	10.76	4.79	14.21	6.65	4.04	4	3.08	9.25	3.83	1.77	2.34	−0.08	0	−0.03	0.02
sources	St. dev	16.27	9.25	7.14	5.03	18.01	1.96	89.61	15.5	13.54	28.33	10.51	42.91	16.21	8.72	6.58	4.43	23.12	10.12	2.15	2.9	0.41	0.24	0.19	0.12
Investment/	Median	0.62	0.65	0.96	1.14	5.49	0.77	0.52	0.03	1.33	1.66	1.67	1.82	1.13	0.99	1.46	1.38	0.87	1.08	1.14	1.99	0.06	0.04	0.05	0.05
diversification	Mean	0.79	0.76	0.85	1	5.31	0.65	0.29	3.1	1.66	2.15	2.48	7.67	1.18	1.17	1.36	1.4	2.52	2.22	1.5	1.76	0.12	0.15	0.13	0.13
	St. dev	0.61	0.51	0.5	0.6	2.83	8.46	3.99	7.17	1.55	2.22	2.57	15.17	0.64	0.63	0.62	0.52	4.61	2.92	1.48	1.18	0.16	0.31	0.18	0.22

Source: The table contains the time series of median, mean, and standard deviation values of the indicators presented in Sect. 10.3. The results are structured by issuance motivation. The elaborations are based on data from Aida—Bureau van Dijk

Table A.10.3 Descriptive statistics: issuance motivation investment by groups

		Ind1				Ind2				Ind3				Ind4				Ind5				Ind6			
		2011	2012	2013	2014	2011	2012	2013	2014	2011	2012	2013	2014	2011	2012	2013	2014	2011	2012	2013	2014	2011	2012	2013	2014
Group 1	Median	0.47	0.23	0.23	0.32	3.94	4.52	3.77	3.03	0.32	0.58	0.18	0.18	1.4	1.54	1.64	1.74	0.41	0.46	0.46	0.26	0.07	0.1	0.07	0.04
	Mean	0.64	0.48	0.43	0.45	3.59	6.52	4.73	5.46	0.63	0.93	1.34	1.09	1.73	1.63	1.87	1.88	1.14	3.16	2.51	4.76	0.14	0.12	0.13	0.11
	St. dev	0.62	0.52	0.48	0.5	2.24	15.51	6	5.73	0.83	0.97	2.42	1.91	0.82	0.69	0.88	0.87	1.74	3.99	3.93	7.2	0.21	0.11	0.16	0.23
Group 2	Median	1.68	1.54	1.33	1.29	2.35	1.58	0.96	0.34	0.46	0.55	0.42	0.43	2.06	1.99	1.82	1.87	2.1	2.1	2.03	3.63	0.05	0.05	0.06	0.08
	Mean	2.06	1.62	1.36	1.48	2.09	0.78	0.67	0.19	0.48	2	2.8	3.91	2.46	1.96	1.96	2	5.1	2.61	2.5	3.89	0.17	0.15	3.86	0.35
	St. dev	1.62	1.02	0.89	0.93	3.98	4.2	2.9	2.41	0.37	4.65	7.3	11.02	2.14	1.41	1.29	1.2	8.51	2.5	2.21	3.26	0.36	0.28	11.95	0.86
Group 3	Median	1.29	1.22	1.47	0.98	3.72	1.02	0.29	−0.55	0.94	0.98	0.82	1.36	1.73	1.68	1.67	1.55	1.32	0.99	0.97	1.37	0.07	0.04	0.06	0.07
	Mean	1.73	1.58	1.48	1.51	29.56	25.3	−12.14	54.69	1.65	2.49	0.96	1.2	2.55	2.58	2.49	2.32	5.71	4.75	2.16	3.83	−0.06	−0.07	−0.1	−0.16
	St. dev	1.76	1.53	1.37	1.44	97.89	92.8	51.08	212.55	2.96	5.74	0.72	0.92	1.69	1.76	1.55	1.57	12.5	10.61	4.1	8.22	0.55	0.6	0.59	0.67

Source: The table contains the time series of median, mean, and standard deviation values of the indicators presented in Sect. 10.3. The results pertain to the firms' group with an issuance motivation of investment, and are structured by firms' operating organization (Groups 1, 2 and 3). The elaborations are based on data from Aida—Bureau van Dijk

References

Area Economica di Confindustria Toscana. (2013). *Linee guida sull'emissione di Minibond*. Toscana: Confindustria.

Pavarani, A. (2006). *L'equilibrio finanziario: criteri e metodologie nella logica di Basilea2*. Milano: McGraw-Hill.

The Commission of the European Communities. (2003). *Commission recommendation of 6 May 2003, concerning the definition of micro, small and medium-sized enterprises,*Official Journal of the European Union, L124/36. http://eur-lex.europa.eu/LexUriServ/LexUriServ.do?uri=OJ:L:2003:124:0036:0041:en:PDF

11

Using Open-End Mutual Fund Resources to Finance SMEs: The Potential Market Share of ELTIFs

Fabrizio Crespi

11.1 Introduction

The Italian financial system has always been considered a bank-oriented system in which the majority of funding for SMEs comes from traditional bank products such as credit lines, commercial credit in the form of receivable discounts, factoring, mortgages and leasing. For other types of financing, such as venture capital and private equity, commercial paper or bond issuing and the public placement of shares is not common for SMEs, even when such tools are available (see Accornero et al. 2015).

The total amount of bank credit for industrial and family businesses accounted for 898,452 million euros in June of 2015 (roughly 55% of the GDP) according to the Statistic Bulletin of the Bank of Italy (Bank of Italy 2015a). Yet, after the government debt crisis of 2011, we witnessed

JEL Classification: G10, G23, G28

F. Crespi (✉)
Department of Economics and Business, University of Cagliari, Cagliari, Italy
e-mail: fabrizio.crespi@unicatt.it

S.P.S. Rossi (ed.), *Access to Bank Credit and SME Financing*,
Palgrave Macmillan Studies in Banking and Financial Institutions,
DOI 10.1007/978-3-319-41363-1_11

a tightening of credit standards and enterprise bank credit access in Italy (especially for SMEs) until at least mid-2015. Better conditions started to appear in the third quarter of last year according to the European Central Bank (ECB 2015).

Similarly, Italian households have generally preferred (at least until now) to invest their savings in bank deposits or bonds issued by financial intermediaries. As a general statistic, the financial wealth of Italian households was estimated by the Bank of Italy at 3897.2 billion euros (238% of the GDP) at the end of 2014 (Bank of Italy 2015b). From 2010 to 2014, the financial wealth of Italian households increased by 8.26%. Of this amount, 714.2 billion euros (18.33%) are invested in bank deposits [521.9 billion euros (or 13.29%) occupy current accounts], and the other 235.6 billion euros (6.05%) are held in bonds issued by banks.

Nevertheless, over the last couple of years, Italian retail investors have been driven by financial intermediaries to intensify their use of asset management products, such as open-end mutual funds and investment trusts (*SICAV*, in Italian terminology). The amount directly invested in mutual funds by Italian households is 376 billion euros (9.65% of the total financial wealth), but it must be noted that mutual funds are also implicitly sold to private investors through insurance products, which amount to 803.8 billion euros (20.63% of the total financial wealth of Italian households).

The reasons for this commercial push can be related to the credit-crunch phenomenon that followed the financial crisis and to the consequent rethinking of business models by several domestic banks. Having yet to address a critical portion of non-performing loans (NPLs)—which for the whole banking system reached an astronomical level of 201.50 billion euros in September of 2015 (10.86% of the total amount of bank credit)—and less prone to amplifying the traditional deposit-credit circuit, domestic banks redirected their focus to advisory and private banking (i.e., less capital-absorbing activities). It should therefore be important to better understand where Italian households' financial resources are invested through asset management products, especially when these products are supplied by Italian investment firms. Indeed, even if more intense international diversification is a primary need for investors typically affected by *home bias*, households may be interested in knowing when their savings are (also) used to finance SMEs operating on the domestic landscape, and government authorities may be interested in redirecting part of these savings to the internal economy.

The aim of our analysis is thus twofold. First, we attempt to estimate how much of the assets controlled by domestic open-end mutual funds are currently invested in Italy (and which types of instruments they are held in). This can give us an approximation of the importance of these investment vehicles as a form of financing for large and small companies. To the best of our knowledge, this topic has never been properly investigated before.

Second, and consequently, we examine opportunities to redirect part of these financial resources, which in the end are largely private investor savings, to the financing of SMEs through the use of European Long-term Investment Funds (ELTIFs), a new investment vehicle introduced by the European Parliament in 2015.

The remainder of this chapter is thus organized as follows. The following section describes the structure and dimensions of the Italian asset management sector to illustrate how the sector has grown overtime, which competition forces are involved in the market, and how assets under management (AUM) are distributed between Italian and foreign investment firms. Section 11.3 introduces the basic rules that govern ELTIFs. Section 11.4 presents a descriptive analysis of investments made via open-end mutual funds supplied by domestic investment firms to estimate the amount of money that is now held in Italy. Finally, considerations are made, in Sect. 11.5, regarding the prospects of a new model of intermediation for the Italian banking sector.

11.2 The Italian Asset Management Sector: Dimensions and Structure

To better determine whether credit to SMEs could be increased using financial resources currently invested in asset management products, we consider it appropriate to describe how the sector has grown in the past and its current dimensions. Moreover, we believe that it is important to understand competitive forces at work in the market and how asset management products are created, sold and bought by final investors. Indeed, asset management products, and open-end mutual funds in particular, have never been considered as tools for the intermediation of financial resources to SMEs; if we wish to explore this possibility, we must determine whether a change in the modus operandi of principal market players is feasible.

The birth of the Italian asset management sector can be traced back to 1983; in that year, a law (n.77/83) introducing open-end mutual funds in domestic legislation was issued by Parliament, and in the following year (1984), the first Italian open-end mutual fund was created by Gestiras. Prior to this, only some foreign investment vehicles had been sold to Italian private investors by financial advisors/tied agents of specialized banks such as Banca Fideuram.

It could thus be argued that Italian households have been acquiring the necessary skills and expertise to invest in these types of products over the last thirty years. In fact, the Italian asset management sector has undergone various phases and difficulties, which can be reported as follows. Until the start of the 1990s, open-end mutual funds (and similarly direct investments in bonds and stocks) were fully outclassed by government bonds, which granted very high returns and which were mistakenly considered risk-free by private investors.[1] However, from 1993 onward a number of events reshaped the landscape: key companies owned by the state were privatized through IPOs reserved for retail investors. Then, a gradual process of harmonization in view of the introduction of the single currency reduced returns granted by government bonds, making it more appealing to invest in diversified open-end mutual funds. Finally, the 'dot.com fever' of the late 1990s (from which Italian retail investors were not immune) favoured the diffusion of equity funds specialized in high-tech companies.

[1] Government bills returned a nominal yield of more than 10%. While inflation was similarly high and public finance was in distress, Italian households considered a government default to be impossible. The situation was partially restored in 1992 through a massive property tax consisting of a forced withdrawal from private bank accounts in favour of the government.

It is thus possible to assert that the Italian asset management sector had reached a satisfying level of maturity by the start of the new millennium: on one hand, a vast array of different products was indeed available for private investors, and the total AUM value exceeded 500 billion euros (roughly 42% of the GDP). On the other hand, the percentage of household wealth invested in mutual funds reached a maximum level of 16%, which it never reached again in subsequent years (Rota 2014).

The first decade of the new millennium was mainly characterized by three key features: first, the strong diffusion of so-called 'open architecture'[2] and the consequent expansion of mutual funds supplied by foreign investment firms; second, the amplified production and sale of 'round-trip' mutual funds (mutual funds created by investment firms domiciled abroad—especially in Ireland and Luxembourg—but entirely owned by a domestic banking group[3]); finally, the financial crisis, with its well-known consequences, was another factor. By the end of 2012, only 31% of the AUM value was invested in domestic mutual funds, 26% was invested in foreign mutual funds and another 43% was invested in round-trip products.

From current features of the sector, it is possible to report the following data. In September of 2015, the total amount of AUM invested in open-end mutual funds [as noted by Assogestioni, the category Association (Assogestioni 2015a)] reached 818,455 million euros, which is approximately the same amount of bank credit dedicated to non-financial institutions as reported above and which is roughly half the domestic GDP estimated at 1,635,384 million euros for the end of 2015. However, only

[2] The open architecture (or multi-brand) approach refers to an opportunity for the sales force of a bank (private bankers, relationship managers and tied agents) to sell mutual funds from different investment firms, and not only those created by the banking group captive investment firm. This is typically achieved through trade agreements made between a bank and numerous domestic and foreign investment firms. The open architecture approach is currently a very common practice in the market.

[3] This practice is still largely used today; it is in effect due to fiscal advantages available to domestic banking groups that have created their own investment firms abroad (until a fiscal revision made in 2012) and due to corresponding advantages available to Italian private investors who have bought these (actually untrue) foreign mutual funds. In any case, the production of mutual funds abroad by Italian banks accompanied by a greater diffusion of mutual funds supplied by foreign investment firms (also in the form of exchange-traded products) has largely extended investment decisions beyond domestic borders. In turn, Italian household money is increasingly conveyed to financial markets by foreign asset managers.

a meagre 27.87% (228,079 million euros) is invested in domestic open-end mutual funds. Italian private investors generally prefer mutual funds specialized in bonds (42.6%); other popular categories include equity funds (21%) and alternative funds (23.5%). Alternative funds (or 'flexible funds' as they are denominated in Italy) can be dedicated 0–100% in bonds or stocks and can use leverage until reaching 200% of fund assets. These products are used to implement sophisticated investment strategies that were originally reserved only for hedge funds.

While Assogestioni reported 231 investment firms, the market is largely concentrated in the hands of large firms. The most important asset management companies are indeed those owned by the two major banking groups: Eurizon and Fideuram (owned by Banca Intesa Group) and Pioneer Investment (owned by Unicredit Group). Next are Generali Investments Europe (Generali Group), Anima Holding (owned jointly by Poste Italiane and BPM group), Mediolanum and Azimut, and other domestic investment firms and global players such as Franklin Templeton, J.P. Morgan, Amundi and Invesco. In regards to open-end mutual funds, Fig. 11.1 shows that the market share of the first five groups accounts for 51%.

To better understand the Italian asset management sector, it is also important to analyze its structure in terms of supply and demand forces. On the supply side, it is possible to distinguish between two main distribution channels: (i) local branches of traditional commercial banks, which mainly distribute open-end mutual funds generated through the captive investment company of the banking group and (ii) private bank/tied agent networks,[4] which are more prone to (also) selling products created by foreign investment firms. Direct investments in mutual funds created by private investors through Internet platforms (even when possible) are rather rare.

---

[4] There are approximately 30,000 operating tied agents. The most influential private banks that use these consultants (who are not employees) are Fideuram, Mediolanum, Fineco, Banca Generali, Azimut, and Allianz Bank. Approximately 66% of mutual funds distributed by tied agents are products domiciled abroad (i.e., round-trip funds or foreign funds). Furthermore, tied agents typically work with affluent and high net worth clients, while the local branches of commercial banks mainly serve retail consumers.

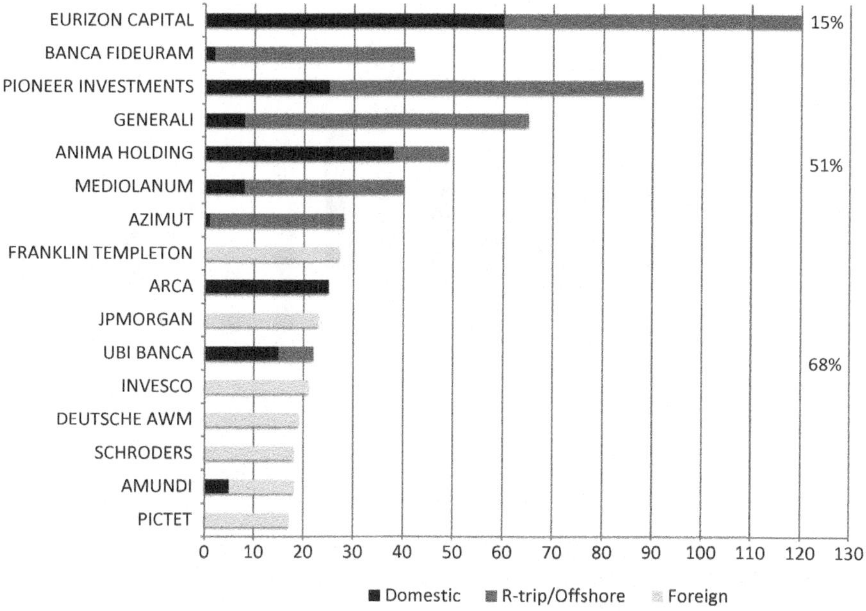

Fig. 11.1 Top 15 groups (open-end funds only) in billions of euros (*Source*: Assogestioni (2015b), *The Italian asset management market. Key Figures*)

In term of dimensions, and considering domestic open-end mutual funds in particular, local branches of commercial banks account for roughly 70% of the amount distributed to private investors. This is a very important feature that must be considered carefully in analyses of the sector. Rather, it is indeed plausible that mutual funds offered through a commercial bank can be influenced by funding requirements imposed by the same bank. In fact, a strong inverse correlation between offering in-house funding products (bonds and deposits) and the commercial push for mutual funds has been proven empirically (Assogestioni 2015b). Especially for the 2010–2014 period (see Fig. 11.2), we have witnessed strong outflows from bonds issued by banks and consequent massive inflows in mutual funds.

The causes of these movements of financial resources can be traced back to difficulties faced in traditional commercial banks during the post-crisis period. It is widely recognized that most Italian banks accumulated

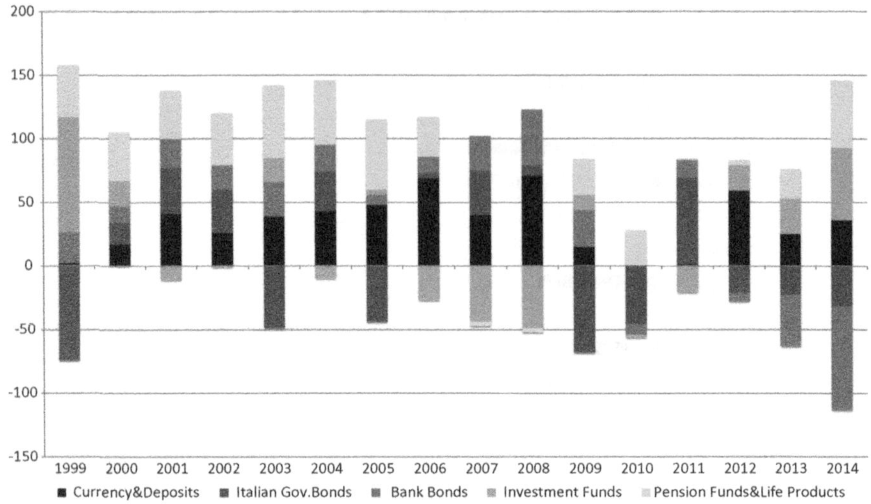

Fig. 11.2 Flows of financial resources into different investment instruments in billions of euros (*Source*: Assogestioni (2015b), *The Italian asset management market. Key Figures*)

considerable NPLs during this phase, and several were forced by authorities (Bank of Italy and ECB) to increase their regulation capital.

This request for additional capital, especially after the introduction of the Capital Requirements Directive (CRD-IV), contributed to a tightening of credit standards required by SMEs in order to access credit and to a diffuse credit crunch phenomenon (Rapacciuolo 2014). On the other hand, commercial banks redirected the investments of private savers into mutual funds; indeed, the placement of asset management products and the availability of advisory services generated commission revenues that effectively boosted profits during a period characterized by very low interest rates. Furthermore, such banking activities do not increase the quantity of risk-weighted assets and consequently require less regulation capital.

From a strategic point of view, this shift towards more intense sales of asset management products accompanied by a decline in traditional intermediation activity (collection of deposits and provision of credits) depicts an interesting change in the business models of several banks.

Yet this change may harm SMEs if, in the long run, it reduces the quantity of household financial resources accessible to finance small companies that are not used to placing their own bonds and stocks in the marketplace. Conversely, if some investments of open-end mutual funds could be redirected for SME financing, a new model of intermediation could be created. To accomplish this, it will likely be necessary to create a new type of asset management product, such as the ELTIFs described in Sect. 11.3.

11.3 ELTIFs: New Instruments for SME Financing

As stated above, open-end mutual funds do not invest significantly in shares or bonds issued by SMEs. In the analysis presented in Sect. 11.4, we show that the majority of investments are directed to government bonds and to shares and bonds issued by large listed companies. To reallocate financial resources to SMEs, focused asset management products are needed. We thus consider it appropriate to introduce to our analysis a thorough description of ELTIF features to better appreciate whether this new asset management product could effectively and efficiently create a new model of intermediation.

On 20 April 2015, the European Council adopted a regulation aimed at increasing the pool of capital available for long-term investment in the EU economy by creating a new fund vehicle. Regulation (UE) 2015/760 was approved on 8 June 2015, and from 9 December 2015 onward it has been in force in the member states. European long-term investment funds are now marketable in the EU.

From a juridical point of view, ELTIFs will be created as EU alternative investment funds (EU AIFs) that are managed by EU alternative investment fund managers (EU AIFMs), who are authorized in accordance with directive 2011/61/EU on AIFMs. ELTIFs can also be divided into different investment compartments, and each compartment is regarded as a separate ELTIF.

ELTIFs offer long-term financing for various infrastructure projects, unlisted companies and listed small and medium-sized enterprises that issue equity or debt instruments for which there are no readily identifiable buyers. By financing such projects, ELTIFs contribute to the financing of the Union's real economy and to the implementation of its policies. Indeed, as the financial crisis has shown, complementing bank financing with a broader variety of financing sources that better mobilize capital markets could help address financing gaps. ELTIFs can play a crucial role in this respect and can also mobilize capital by attracting third-country investors.

By virtue of the asset classes they are allowed to invest in, ELTIFs are expected to provide investors with long-term, stable returns. ELTIFs thus follow a new collective investment framework that allows private investors to invest money in companies and projects that need long-term capital (e.g., infrastructure projects), thereby stimulating employment and economic growth.

ELTIFs will only focus on alternative investments that fall within a defined category of long-term asset classes whose successful development requires long-term investor commitment. These include:

- Equity or quasi-equity instruments that have been issued by a qualifying portfolio undertaking and that have been acquired by the ELTIF from a qualifying portfolio undertaking or from a third party via the secondary market. A qualifying portfolio undertaking is an undertaking which: (i) is not admitted to trading on a regulated market or multilateral trading facility, or which (ii) is admitted to trading on a regulated market or on a multilateral trading facility while at the same time presenting a market capitalization value of no more than 500,000,000 euros;
- Debt instruments issued by a qualifying portfolio undertaking;
- Loans granted by the ELTIF to a qualifying portfolio undertaking with a maturity level of no longer than the life of the ELTIF;
- Units or shares of one or several other ELTIFs, European Venture Capital Funds (EuVECA), and European Social Entrepreneurship Funds (EuSEF) provided that those ELTIFs, EuVECAs and EuSEFs have not themselves invested more than 10% of their capital in ELTIFs;

- Direct or indirect holdings via qualifying portfolio undertakings of individual real assets with a value of at least 10,000,000 euros or its equivalent in the currency in which, and at the time when, the expenditure is incurred.

Essentially, ELTIFs are designed for investing in unlisted companies that require long-term capital such as infrastructure, notably in network industries (e.g., transport and energy) but also in terms of social infrastructure (hospitals, schools and social housing). ELTIFs can also invest in certain small and medium-sized listed enterprises, in real assets that require long-term capital for their development, in intellectual property, in other intangible assets and in EuVECA and EuSEF.

It is thus possible to assert that this new fund vehicle could also be invested in stocks, bonds and other form of credit[5] issued by small companies if they require long-term financing for multi-year project development. ELTIFs are certainly designed to increase non-bank finances available to companies investing in the real economy of the European Union, thus creating a new model of financial resource intermediation that differs from the traditional deposit-credit circuit employed by commercial banks.

Indeed, as we note above, the same commercial banks could see this form of disintermediation as an opportunity: if the deposits of private investors should be partially redirected to ELTIFs investing in SMEs, this could decrease bank credit risk exposure levels as well as the need for regulation capital. Credit risk exposure would be transferred to ELTIFs (and finally to investors), but could be better diversified, as ELTIFs must follow typical rules of diversification established for mutual funds. Banks would eventually lose part of their interest revenue but could increase commission revenues by placing and trading ELTIFs and by providing advice on them.

ELTIFs are subject to additional rules that require them, *inter alia*, to invest at least 70% of their capital in clearly defined categories of eligible

[5] This opportunity for mutual funds to grant loans is not a first of its type under Italian legislation. Indeed, closed-end mutual funds established as alternative investment funds (AIFs) can invest in credit acquired by third parties, in asset-backed securities and in credit granted by the fund itself. This capability has recently been extended to closed-end AIFs established in the European Union.

assets (this limit must be reached within five years after fund creation). Trading in assets other than long-term investments is only permitted for up to a maximum of 30% of their capital. An ELTIF shall invest no more than: (a) 10% of its capital in instruments issued by (or loans granted to) any single qualifying portfolio undertaking; (b) 10% of its capital directly or indirectly in a single real asset; and (c) 10% of its capital in units or shares of any single ELTIF, EuVECA or EuSEF.

The aggregate value of units or shares of ELTIFs, EuvECAs and EuSEFs in an ELTIF portfolio shall not exceed 20% of the value of ELTIF capital. ELTIFs are also conceived of as investment vehicles through which the European Investment Bank (the EIB) Group can channel its European infrastructure or SME financing.

It is important to note that ELTIFs do not generally offer redemption rights before their end of life; technically speaking, they are not open-end mutual funds (i.e., investors cannot have their money back every day as normally prescribed for open-end mutual funds), and this must be clearly disclosed to investors. However, managers can allow investors to get their money back under certain circumstances. In cases where this is allowed, this should be clearly explained to investors before their money is committed.

Moreover, ELTIFs are not prevented from seeking the admission of their units or shares to a regulated market or multilateral trading facility, thus providing investors with opportunities to sell their units or shares before the end of the life of the ELTIF. Indeed, the rules or instruments of ELTIF incorporation should not prevent ELTIF units or shares from being admitted to trading on a regulated market or multilateral trading facility, nor should they prevent investors from freely transferring their units or shares to third parties who wish to purchase those units or shares. This is intended to promote secondary markets as an important venue for retail investors who are buying and selling units or shares of ELTIFs.

Notwithstanding the fact that ELTIFs are not open-end mutual funds, they will target both professional and retail investors in the EU. For this reason, regulations lay down specific rules that help protect retail investors in particular. Fund managers and distributors must ensure that retail investors with portfolios of up to 500,000 euros do not invest aggregate amounts exceeding 10% of their portfolios in ELTIFs, provided that initial amounts invested in one or more ELTIFs are not lower than 10,000€. Moreover, when the lifecycle of an ELTIF exceeds ten years, a fund manager or distributor must issue a written alert that it may not be suitable for retail investors who are unable to sustain such a long-term and illiquid commitment.

In any case, contrary to European Venture Capital Funds (EuVECA) and European Social Entrepreneurship Funds (EuSEF), for which a minimum investment of 100,000 euros is required so that they are targeted at professional investors, ELTIFs could serve as appropriate financial instruments for non-institutional investors. Moreover, ELTIFs could also be included in the assets of other investment products normally bought by retail investors (e.g., funds of funds and insurance products).

11.4 Italian Open-End Mutual Funds Supplied by Italian Investment Firms: A Descriptive Analysis

As noted above, the total amount of open-end mutual fund AUM distributed in Italy is approximately equivalent to the amount of bank credit available to non-financial institutions. To investigate that proportion of these financial resources which is invested in the domestic economy, we created a database of domestic open-end mutual funds (i.e., products domiciled in Italy—and supplied by Italian investment houses—that invest more than 15% of their assets in bonds and stocks issued by domestic companies). The 15% limit was selected after carrying out quantitative simulations. Indeed, if we took mutual funds that invest less than 15% in bonds and stocks issued by Italian companies into account, we would have run the risk of also considering products that only temporarily invest a relatively small amount of money in the domestic economy, and mainly for cash-parking reasons. Our estimate is thus considered an approximation by defect.

Our selection is based upon the following reasoning. As the scope of our analysis is to estimate the potential resources of open-end mutual funds that could be redirected to SME financing and the potential market share of ELTIFs, we consider only those funds which:

(a) Are managed by Italian investment firms that may be interested in investing in Italian SMEs as a commercial strategy (it is indeed plausible to posit, for example, that the expansion of ELTIFs could happen through a focused commercial push directed to sensitize Italian private investors on the need to finance domestic SMEs). For these funds, investment decisions are ultimately made in Italy and could be in some ways 'influenced' by domestic authorities through moral suasion or administrative and fiscal facilitation. This does not mean that foreign investment companies should not be interested in Italian SMEs. Rather, in the case of products domiciled abroad (and this is also true for round-trip funds), the investment process is normally guided by foreign managers, who are typically characterized by an international mindset and who are less sensitive to domestic issues;
(b) Are right now sufficiently invested in Italy. It is in fact obvious that a fund supplied by an Italian investment firm but created to invest in foreign asset classes (e.g., a fund domiciled in Italy but in the American Equity category) will continue to channel Italian household financial resources abroad and will invest only slightly in Italy.

To create our dataset, from the investment firms recorded by Assogestioni, we first selected those mainly owned by Italian shareholders—namely, captive investment firms of primary banking groups or independent investment houses. We then omitted those houses with no funds investing more than 15% of assets in Italy and those for which clear data are not available. We ultimately identified 22 investment firms [or *Società di Gestione del Risparmio* (SGR) as they are called in Italy], which are listed in Table 11.1.

Investment companies listed in our database include principal players of the sector (e.g., Eurizon Capital SGR S.p.A, Pioneer Investment Management SGRpA, Generali Investments Europe S.p.A.). Excluding top foreign investment companies that operate in Italy, we can confirm

Table 11.1 List of Italian investment firms included in our database

AcomeA SGR Spa	Fideuram Investimenti SGR SPA
Agora Investments SGR Spa	Fondaco Sgr
Aletti Gestielle SGR S.p.A.	Generali Investments Europe S.p.A.
Anima Sgr S.p.A	Groupama Asset Management
ARCA SGR S.p.a.	Investitori SGR
Azimut Capital Management SGR S.p.A.	Mediolanum Gestione Fondi SGRp.A.
BancoPosta Fondi S.p.A. SGR	Pioneer Investment Management SGRpA
BCC Risparmio&Previdenza S.G.R.p.a.	Sella Gestioni SGR S.p.A.
Etica SGR SpA	SOPRARNO SGR S.P.A.
Eurizon Capital SGR S.p.A	UBI Pramerica S.p.A.
Euromobiliare Asset Management SGR SpA	Zenit SGR S.p.A.

that the list shown in Table 11.1 almost fully covers the supply side of the market.

We then considered only those open-end mutual funds that invest in Italy consistently. To do so, we used data provided by Morningstar, one of the information providers most commonly used by financial consultants and practitioners. More specifically, we used data reported in the asset allocation section of each fund profile, which lists the number of stocks and bonds owned by a fund, the weights of the first ten positions and the percentage invested in different countries. From this information, which was collected manually by analyzing individual Morningstar data sheets, we were able to determine when a mutual fund invested more than 15% in Italy, and we could analyze types of securities held. Even if we could specifically study only the top ten positions of each fund, it should be noted that these positions normally cover a rather high percentage of assets invested by a fund. In our database, the mean weight of the first ten positions in which funds are invested is roughly 57%. Definitively, our data could be considered a snapshot of the asset allocation of funds on a specific date (September 30, 2015).

We studied 266 funds, and the total AUM related to these funds amounts to roughly 73.58 billion euros.[6] Of course, not all financial

[6]We consider different classes of the same fund (i.e., the class reserved for institutional investors or that reserved for private investors) as different products, as they are assigned different identification numbers (ISINs).

resources of the studied funds are invested in the domestic economy, as a fund that invests more than 15% in Italy can still invest in foreign companies. However, even so, 73.58 billion euros can be considered as a starting point to estimating dimensions of the phenomenon or the amount of financial resources that could be redirected (at least partially) to SME financing and ELTIFs.

Table 11.2 presents summary statistics for our database. The majority of funds (162 or 60.9%) are held in the Macro category bond. More specifically, 46 of these funds are classified by Assogestioni as Bond Government Debt funds (which are also divided into short/medium and long term categories). If we add this number to the number of Cash funds (12), we obtain a total of 58 products characterized by a very low risk profile.

Another important category is flexible funds (55). As among the macro category bonds we also find 47 products that are classified as flexible (even if principally invested in bonds), we find more than 100 products that use innovative (active) strategies of asset allocation. Less surprising, on the other hand, is our identification of few equity funds (27), reflecting Italian investors' limited engagement with the stock exchange and diffuse preference for bonds. Similarly, the median dimension of funds in the macro category bond (266 million euros) is more than double the median dimension of equity funds (118 million euros).

Our specific analysis of the investments made by mutual funds included in our database reveals a total of 5,980 equity instruments and 10,661 bond instruments. In the first ten positions held by each fund (in terms of dimension as reported by Morningstar), we find that domestic instruments (bonds and stocks) amount to 1,809: the financial resources invested in these instruments amount to 28,275 million euros. Of these 1,809 instruments, the vast majority are government bonds (1,155), which amount to a total value of circa 23 billion euros.

It is thus clear that a large proportion of the financial resources of open-end mutual funds included in our database are invested in bonds issued by the government; this means that public debt still drains a fundamental portion of Italian household savings, even when these savings are invested through asset management products. In fact, it should be noted that Italian private investors also buy government bonds on their own. The

Table 11.2 Summary statistics for our database

Macro category	Sub-category (from Assogestioni classification)	N. obs.	N. obs (%)	AUM (value) €ml	AUM (%)	AUM (mean) €ml	AUM (min) €ml	AUM (max) €ml	% First ten posi-tions (mean)
Equity	*Total category*	*27*	*10.2*	*3191.62*	*4.3*	*118.21*	*0.35*	*660.49*	*42.21*
	Equity America	1	0.4	187.97	0.3	187.97	187.97	187.97	28.54
	Equity Euro Area	1	0.4	19.95	0.0	19.95	19.95	19.95	51.88
	Equity Europe	3	1.1	78.00	0.1	26.00	0.35	73.04	31.19
	Equity International	2	0.8	39.56	0.1	19.78	2.93	36.63	21.94
	Equity Italy	19	7.1	2677.54	3.6	140.92	1.31	660.49	44.72
	Equity Pacific	1	0.4	188.60	0.3	188.60	188.60	188.60	72.03
Bal-anced	*Total category*	*10*	*3.8*	*1836.88*	*2.5*	*183.69*	*0.01*	*684.13*	*58.65*
	Balanced	1	0.4	86.98	0.1	86.98	86.98	86.98	56.59
	Balanced Equity	3	1.1	108.67	0.1	36.22	0.01	107.21	67.65
	Balanced Bond	6	2.3	1,641.23	2.2	273.54	0.01	684.13	54.49
Flex-ible	*Total category*	*55*	*20.7*	*20,710.57*	*28.1*	*390.77*	*0.15*	*6581.00*	*54.76*
Cash		12	4.5	4757.41	6.5	396.45	0.01	1,255.85	73.09

(*continued*)

Table 11.2 (continued)

Macro category	Sub-category (from Assogestioni classification)	N. obs.	N. obs (%)	AUM (value) €ml	AUM (%)	AUM (mean) €ml	AUM (min) €ml	AUM (max) €ml	% First ten posi-tions (mean)
Bond	*Total category*	*162*	*60.9*	*43,090.73*	*58.6*	*265.99*	*0.01*	*4909.39*	*58.91*
	Bond other specialization	31	11.7	4620.14	6.3	149.04	0.01	537.60	57.29
	Bond government debt medium/ long term (US dollar)	1	0.4	15.24	0.0	15.24	15.24	15.24	86.70
	Bond euro corporate investment grade	2	0.8	263.27	0.4	131.64	122.81	140.46	17.27
	Bond government debt short-term euro	32	12.0	9750.49	13.3	304.70	0.01	2470.20	63.54
	Bond government debt medium/ long term (euro)	12	4.5	2123.16	2.9	176.93	0.35	841.92	57.38
	Bond flexible	47	17.7	7824.18	10.6	166.47	6.35	1,019.76	59.01
	Bond government debt international	1	0.4	133.57	0.2	133.57	133.57	133.57	53.77
	Bond Italy	7	2.6	1657.06	2.3	236.72	0.01	532.36	77.54
	Bond mixed	29	10.9	16,703.62	22.7	575.99	7.11	4,909.39	53.52
Totals		**266**	**100**	**73,587.21**	**100.0**	**278.74**	**0.01**	**6581.00**	**56.98**

last estimate made by Bank of Italy shows that roughly 171.7 billion euros of household financial wealth (or 4.41% of the total wealth) is directly invested in government bonds. Other debt instruments held by bond funds are mainly debt instruments issued by banks and primary listed companies; bonds issued by small cap companies are virtually absent.

On the other hand, if we look at equity instruments that appear in the first ten positions of the asset allocation of mutual funds analyzed, we find 182 open positions, resulting in a total of roughly 1.7 billion euros. Yet, by examining the data shown in Table 11.3, one can appreciate a very high level of concentration: the first 15 companies, which include the most important blue chips listed on the Italian Stock Exchange (and also some positions in futures on the FTSEMIB, the principal index of the domestic market), cover roughly 90% of the total amount invested. Other positions are mainly held in shares issued by financial institutions, while shares of small cap companies rarely appear.

Ultimately, the asset allocation of equity mutual funds is rather similar to the composition of principal benchmarks of the market, and it is completely biased towards large cap companies; interestingly, we found only one equity fund specialized in SMEs (Eurizon Azioni PMI Italia).

In sum, we can draw the following observations. The total AUM of open-end mutual funds that we considered in our database is 73.58 billion euros, accounting for only 9% of the financial resources invested by all open-end mutual funds across Italy (818,455 billion euros). On one hand, this means a large proportion of Italian household money is channelled abroad. This is not surprising if we consider dimensions of the Italian financial market, the fact that the industrial structure of the domestic economy is mainly composed of unlisted small and medium companies, and the obvious diversification logics of mutual funds.

On the other hand, dimensions of these financial resources are not trivial. As a comparison, the total number of credits of less than 250,000 euros provided by banks and other credit intermediaries (which can approximate SME financing) reached roughly 412 billion euros in June of 2015 according to Bank of Italy data (Bank of Italy 2015a). Financial resources invested in the funds examined thus account for roughly 18% of this value. Moreover, one must remember that the AUM of domestic

Table 11.3 Companies observable in the first ten positions of equity funds studied

Ranking	Companies	N. obs	Value invested (ml)	Cumulated	Cumulated (%)
1	Eni SpA	15	258.84	258.84	15.1
2	UniCredit SpA	15	188.38	447.22	26.0
3	Assicurazioni Generali	15	168.90	616.12	35.9
4	Intesa Sanpaolo	9	165.17	781.29	45.5
5	ENEL SPA	14	164.51	945.80	55.1
6	Ftse/Mib Idx Fut Sep15	6	126.92	1072.71	62.4
7	Atlantia	12	93.45	1166.16	67.9
8	Mediobanca	4	66.50	1232.66	71.8
9	Snam SpA	9	64.61	1297.27	75.5
10	Intesa Sanpaolo Risp	6	55.42	1352.69	78.7
11	Luxottica Group SpA	7	54.34	1407.03	81.9
12	Fiat Chrysler Automobiles NV	9	49.50	1456.53	84.8
13	Tod'S	5	46.69	1503.23	87.5
14	Telecom Italia SpA	5	37.30	1540.53	89.7
15	Italcementi SpA	4	21.25	1561.78	90.9
16	Finmeccanica SpA	1	15.71	1577.48	91.8
17	Telecom Italia SpA Risp	4	14.68	1592.16	92.7
18	Prysmian	1	14.63	1606.79	93.5
19	Interpump Group	3	11.81	1618.60	94.2
20	Brembo	3	10.38	1628.98	94.8
21	Banca Popolare di Sondrio	2	7.49	1636.47	95.3
22	Recordati	1	7.39	1643.85	95.7
23	Banca Generali	1	6.68	1650.53	96.1
24	Credito Valtellinese	2	6.53	1657.06	96.5
25	Anima Holding S.p.A.	1	6.52	1663.58	96.8
26	EI Towers SpA	2	6.43	1670.01	97.2
27	Banca Popolare di Milano	1	5.90	1675.91	97.6
28	FinecoBank S.p.A	2	5.73	1681.64	97.9
29	Marr SPA	2	5.30	1686.94	98.2
30	Hera SpA	1	5.30	1692.25	98.5
31	Industria Macchine Automatiche	2	5.27	1697.52	98.8
32	Amplifon	2	4.59	1702.11	99.1
33	Reply SPA	2	4.16	1706.27	99.3

(*continued*)

Table 11.3 (continued)

Ranking	Companies	N. obs	Value invested (ml)	Cumulated	Cumulated (%)
34	Esprinet	2	3.04	1709.31	99.5
35	Engineering	2	2.99	1712.31	99.7
36	Banco Popolare	2	1.24	1713.54	99.7
37	Banca Carige	2	1.18	1714.73	99.8
38	Banca Pop Emilia Romagna	1	0.79	1715.52	99.9
39	Mediaset	1	0.70	1716.22	99.9
40	Banco Desio Brianza	1	0.47	1716.68	99.9
41	Unipol Gruppo Finanziario Spa	1	0.42	1717.11	100.0
42	A2A SpA	1	0.40	1717.51	100.0
43	Aeffe	1	0.37	1717.88	100.0
	Total	**182**	**1717.88**		

open-end mutual funds chiefly invested in Italy could be greatly increased if other 'Italy focused' funds were created by Italian investment firms.

The majority of investments made through the examined funds are dedicated to government and bank bonds. Considering the very low returns granted today by government bonds and the diminished need and willingness of banks to issue debt instruments, these investments could be (at least partially) redirected to SME financing if the right vehicle were available in the market. However, for the moment, attempts to develop a specialized market for mini-bonds (i.e., bonds issued by SMEs) have produced meagre results. The total market for mini-bonds listed in the Extramot (a multilateral trading facility owned by the Italian Stock Exchange) is estimated to amount to only 5.5 billion euros.

With regards to investments in equity instruments, it is certainly necessary to increase the number of open-end mutual funds focused on domestic small-cap companies, and especially those engaged in innovative fields. This may allow retail investors to take advantage of a diversified portfolio invested in this type of firm while compensating for the sluggish private equity and venture capital market, which in 2014 was estimated to amount to roughly 30 billion euros (AIFI 2014).

11.5 Final Considerations

The Italian banking system has survived through a critical environment over the past few years; from the financial crisis of 2008 through to the government debt crisis of 2011, Italian banks have witnessed a tremendous increase in NPLs and a very strong decline in profitability. Many of these banks have been forced by authorities to recapitalize in order to respect minimum capital requirements imposed through CRD-IV regulations. Four banks (namely, Banca delle Marche, Banca Popolare Etruria-Lazio, Cassa Risparmio di Chieti and Cassa di Risparmio di Ferrara) were subjected to a sort of anticipated bail-in in November of 2015, only a few months before the introduction of the Bank Recovery and Resolution Directive (BRRD) on 1 January 2016.

In the meantime, some Italian academics have begun to develop a new way of thinking about the functioning of the domestic banking system and of different circuits of financial intermediation that could be implemented, especially to better finance SMEs. In 2014, for example, Forestieri (2014) proposed using more loan securitization and mini bonds as new channels for SMEs financing; subsequently, Aliano and Malavasi (2015) estimated the number of financial resources that could be freed up through the securitization of bank loans of between 50 and 100 billion euros.

The idea behind this reasoning is that banks could partially transform their business models by more intensively applying 'originate and distribute' approaches [i.e., by reducing the needs of regulation capital and earning more through commission-related activities (placement and advisory)].

The Italian legislature has taken steps in this direction by passing law 91/2014, which increases types of intermediaries that are permitted to grant loans. In fact, the law introduced the opportunity (under specific circumstances) for insurance companies, closed-end mutual funds established as AIFs, and special purpose vehicles normally used during the securitization process to extend credit to small companies. Even if this law has not yet produced important results, it can be recognized as a significant change in the structure of the banking sector. Nevertheless, it is correct to note that banks will likely remain as central players in the market, as they will act as servicing providers—that is, they will provide selection and monitoring services for third parties.

The analysis illustrated in the present chapter follows the same direction as previous studies, even if it is based on a different point of view. In fact, we tried to estimate how much of the financial resources currently invested by retail savers in open-end mutual funds (which are primarily distributed by banks) could be used to finance SMEs. We too anticipate that a change in traditional bank business models (which is actually under way) could allow the same banks to operate with fewer risk-weighted assets and then with less regulatory capital inasmuch as investor deposits could be directly invested in asset-managed products.

The starting point is the total AUM of open-end mutual funds that is equal to approximately 818 billion euros; this alone affirms that a reasonable source of SME funding could be obtained from this large sum of money if it were also partially used in this scope. Unfortunately, as we have demonstrated, only a relative percentage of the AUM of open-end mutual funds is controlled by investment firms domiciled in Italy, and an even smaller percentage is invested in domestic instruments (bonds and stocks). Moreover, the funds we studied are principally invested in government and bank bonds and in shares issued by large corporations.

In any case, by only considering funds domiciled in Italy that are managed by domestic investment houses, we estimated by defect that roughly 73 billion euros can in theory be dedicated to SME financing. It is reasonable to assume that half of these financial resources (roughly 35 billion euros) could be channelled toward the domestic micro-economy if adequate commercial 'propaganda' and the right investment instruments were used. In addition, the 50% assumption that we make here could even be considered conservative if one considers the fact that Italian savers (as noted in the introduction) maintain more than 500 billion euros parked in current accounts.

Two main investment vehicles can be used to increase SME financing through asset management products. On one hand, traditional open-end mutual funds specialized in Italian small cap companies, which could be rather appealing to retail investors, are practically absent among products offered by Italian investment firms. If more open-end mutual funds specialized in small cap instruments (bonds and stocks) were introduced by investment houses, we would likely witness an immediate increase in mini-bond issues and a subsequent increase in small companies listed in the domestic stock exchange.

On the other hand, high expectations could be placed on the future diffusion of ELTIFs: even if the creation and distribution of this new investment vehicle will take some time (as it may be considered somewhat unusual for the Italian market), a significant amount of money is currently available. Moreover, it is possible to assume that ELTIFs established in other European countries may be interested in investing in domestic SMEs.

Finally, it is correct to also consider the other side of the coin: the positions of SMEs. Indeed, it is easy to assume that SMEs could benefit if new instruments/intermediaries that can grant loans were introduced to the marketplace. However, SMEs are also called upon to change their modus operandi when they wish to be appealing to open-end mutual funds and ELTIFs. For example, they should become more inclined to issue mini-bonds, to present long-term projects to specialized investors, or to simply improve their image. In short, they are called upon to improve the efficiency of their financial management systems and to increase their relationship skills with regards to domestic and foreign institutional investors.

References

Accornero, M., Finaldi Russo, P., Guazzarotti, G., & Nigro, V. (2015). *First-time corporate bond issuers in Italy*(Occasional papers, n. 269). Bank of Italy.

AIFI. (2014). *Il mercato italiano del Private Equity e Venture capital nel 2014*. Available at http://www.aifi.it/category/dati-di-mercato/. Accessed 28 Feb 2016.

Aliano, M., & Malavasi, R. (2015). Bank loan securitization: An assessment of the possible effects for Italian banks. *Il Risparmio, 1*, 5–54.

Assogestioni. (2015a). *Mappa trimestrale del risparmio gestito, QIII 2015*. Available at http://www.assogestioni.it/index.cfm/1,243,0,49,html/mappa-trimestrale-del-risparmiogestito. Accessed 28 Feb 2016.

Assogestioni. (2015b). *The Italian asset management market. Key figures*. Available at http://www.assogestioni.it/index.cfm/3,839,10737/2015-02-18-the-italian-am-mkt-key-facts-dec-upd-def.pdf. Accessed 28 Feb 2016.

Bank of Italy. (2015a). *Statistic Bulletin, IV 2015*. Available at https://www.bancaditalia.it/pubblicazioni/bollettino-statistico. Accessed 28 Feb 2016.

Bank of Italy. (2015b). *La ricchezza delle famiglie Italiane*. Available at https://www.bancaditalia.it/pubblicazioni/ricchezza-famiglie-italiane. Accessed 28 Feb 2016.

European Central Bank. (2015). *The Euro area bank lending survey*. Available at https://www.ecb.europa.eu/stats/money/surveys/lend/html/index.en.html. Accessed 28 Feb 2016.

Forestieri, G. (2014). Loan securitization and mini-bonds, new channels for Smes financing. *Bancaria, 6*, 3–15.

Rapacciuolo, C. (2014). Italia: il credit crunch prosegue nel 2014. *Confindustria*. Available at http://www.confindustria.it/studiric.nsf/All/11C777A75E92D988C1257C5F0037EB83?openDocument&MenuID=42257EA28EF90910C1257547003B2F89. Accessed 28 Feb 2016.

Rota, A. (2014). *Breve storia dei fondi comuni in Italia*, Assogestioni. Available at http://www.assogestioni.it/index.cfm/3,820,10715/preview_libro30anni.pdf. Accessed 28 Feb 2016.

Index[1]

[1] Note: Page numbers with "n" denote endnotes.

S.P.S. Rossi (ed.), *Access to Bank Credit and SME Financing*,
Palgrave Macmillan Studies in Banking and Financial Institutions,
DOI 10.1007/978-3-319-41363-1

C

J

W

Y

The manufacturer's authorised representative in the EU is Springer Nature Customer Service Centre GmbH, Europaplatz 3, 69115 Heidelberg, Germany. If you have any concerns regarding our products, please contact ProductSafety@springernature.com

Printed and bound by CPI Group (UK) Ltd, Croydon, CR0 4YY

30/09/2026

02225195-0008